STRATEGIC INFORMATION SYSTEMS

STRATEGIC INFORMATION SYSTEMS

Charles Wiseman

Columbia University
Graduate School of Business
and Competitive Applications
New York City

1988

Homewood, Illinois 60430

© RICHARD D. IRWIN, INC., 1988

All rights reserved. No part of this publication may be
reproduced, stored in a retrieval system, or transmitted,
in any form or by any means, electronic, mechanical,
photocopying, recording, or otherwise, without the prior
written permission of the publisher.

Acquisitions editor: Lawrence E. Alexander
Project editor: Paula M. Buschman
Production manager: Carma W. Fazio
Designer: Maureen McCutcheon
Artist: Benoit Design
Compositor: TCSystems
Typeface: 11/13 Palatino
Printer: Arcata Graphics/Kingsport

ISBN 0-256-06030-4

Library of Congress Catalog Card No. 87–83239

Printed in the United States of America

1 2 3 4 5 6 7 8 9 0 K 5 4 3 2 1 0 9 8

Preface

Strategic Information Systems expands, updates, and revises *Strategy and Computers: Information Systems as Competitive Weapons*, published in 1985 by Dow Jones-Irwin. The expansion includes (1) over 50 new cases of strategic information systems (SIS) and a number of SIS failures (e.g., ZapMail by Federal Express, Gemco by Citibank and McGraw-Hill, Imnet by IBM and Merrill Lynch, and Sharetech by AT&T and United Technologies); (2) new chapters on competitive advantage, SIS planning and management, and SIS trends and challenges (e.g., competitive dynamics, legal risk) plus a new introduction; (3) new sections on global growth (documenting the transfer of information technology and the use of electronic networks to achieve advantage in the international sphere), the role of the chief information officer, and the GTE telephone operations division's implementation of the strategic framework proposed in the trade edition.

This implementation shows how a large, relatively slow-moving firm developed a planning process reflecting the strategic perspective propounded here and then, through a series of brainstorming sessions, identified a set of SIS opportunities linked to strategic thrusts designed to gain competitive advantage. Within a short period, GTE had for the first time moved systematically to discover and use its information technology resources and those of its allies for strategic purposes. My *MIS Quarterly* article (coauthored by Nick Rackoff and Al Ullrich of GTE), "Information Systems for Competitive Advantage: Implementation of a Planning Process," describes this work. Chapter 10 contains excerpts from the article, which won the $5,000 first prize in the 1985 paper competition sponsored by the Society for Information Management.

In addition to this new material, I have updated over 25 cases cited in the first edition and substantially expanded 10 of these. For jaded souls tired of the same old stories about American Air, American Hospital Supply, and the like, the rewritten cases here (based on information not available before 1985 or on new developments) reveal important SIS facets, trends, and challenges masked in the initial telling. There is more than bias packed into American Air's Sabre reservation system (see Chapters 1, 6, and 9).

Unlike the additions and updates, revisions have been relatively minor. Appendix A, "Conventional Perspective," and Appendix B, "Varieties of Information Systems," have been relocated to Chapter 2 and the appendix to Chapter 2, respectively, where logically they belong. Those familiar with earlier versions of the theory of strategic thrusts will find a few changes, intended primarily to clarify. While a handful of items have been deleted, over 90 percent of the trade edition remains.

Strategic Information Systems differs from the original in at least two fundamental ways. Before marking these differences, let me review the background and intent of the 1985 edition by quoting from its preface:

> I began collecting instances of information systems used for strategic purposes five years ago, dubbing them *strategic information systems* (SIS). But from the start, I was puzzled by their occurrence. At least theoretically, I was unprepared to admit the existence of a new variety of computer application. The conventional view at the time recognized only management

information systems and management support systems, the former used to automate basic business processes and the latter to satisfy the information needs of decision makers.

But as my file of cases grew, I realized that the conventional perspective on information systems was incomplete, unable to account for SIS. The examples belied the theory, and the theory in general blinded believers from seeing SIS. Indeed, some conventional information systems planning methodologies, which act like theories in guiding the systematic search for computer application opportunities, explicitly exclude certain SIS possibilities from what might be found.

This growing awareness of the inadequacy of the dominant dogma of the day led me to investigate the conceptual foundations, so to speak, of information systems. At first, I believed that the conventional gospel could be enlarged to accommodate SIS. But as my research progressed, I abandoned this position and concluded that to explain SIS and facilitate their discovery, one needed to view uses of computer [information] technology from a radically different perspective.

I call this the *strategic perspective* on information systems [technology]. The chapters to follow present my conception of it. Written for top executives and line managers, they show how computers [information technology] can be used to support or shape competitive strategy.

While this book may have its theoretical moments, it is intended primarily to be a practical guide. The best way to grasp the strategic perspective is by studying actual cases of SIS in an analytical framework that illuminates their significance. . . .

The use of information systems as competitive weapons and the relation between strategy and computers [information technology] are new subjects of inquiry. As far as I know, there are no books dealing specifically with these subjects. While I take a certain pleasure in being the first to publish, no one knows better than myself the limits of the present formulation. But whatever the shortcomings of my conception, *the book's purpose will be served if its readers can be persuaded to adopt a strategic perspective on information systems,* even if it differs from the one proposed here. [Italics added.]

The primary purpose of *Strategic Information Systems* is not to persuade top executives and line managers "to adopt a strategic perspective on information systems," although I wouldn't object if members of these two groups replaced their conventional beliefs on systems with the position advocated here. Rather, the objective is to explore a new, multi-disciplinary field of study—the strategic use of information technology—in all its dimensions. Second, the book is intended not just for practitioners (executives, managers, and users) but also for the wider audience that comprises, among others, academics (teachers, students, and researchers) and consultants.

Unlike the trade edition, written without the benefit of classroom discussion or extensive consulting with firms mobilizing to use information technology strategically, most of *Strategic Information Systems* has been exposed over the past three years to M.B.A. students at the Columbia University Graduate School of Business and to a large number of practitioners seeking to apply SIS concepts to disparate industry settings. I hope it reflects the salutary effects of that exposure.

Charles Wiseman

Acknowledgments

My obligations in this venture are numerous. I want first to thank my students at the Columbia University Graduate School of Business; their classroom responsiveness to the material and their research papers make the strategic use of information technology an intellectually exciting subject to teach. The following read drafts of the entire manuscript, and I want to express my gratitude for their comments: Professors Omar El Sawy (University of Southern California), Cynthia Beath (University of Minnesota), Jerry Kanter (Babson College), Martin Greenberger (University of California at Los Angeles), Ahmed Zaki (College of William and Mary), and Stan Soles (Fairleigh Dickinson University). I have, in addition, profited from discussions on topics covered in this book with Professors John O'Shaughnessy and Kirby Warren (Columbia University), Blake Ives and Gerald Learmonth (Amos Tuck School, Dartmouth), Eph McLean (Georgia State University), V. Venkatraman (Sloan School of Management, Massachusetts Institute of Technology), Brandt Allen (University of Virginia), Eric Clemmons (Wharton School, University of Pennsylvania), Michael Vitale (Graduate School of Business Administration, Harvard University), Donald Marchand (Syracuse University), Helmut Krcmar (University of Hohenheim, West Germany), Fabio Corno (who translated the trade edition into Italian;

Bocconi School of Business, Italy), Shinroku Tsuji (Kobe University, Japan), and Moriaki Tsuchiya (University of Tokyo, Japan). On the nonacademic side, for support, advice, and encouragement, I am gratefully indebted to David Mims, Bob Berland, Al Barnes, Jim Ransco, Bob Delaney, Del Smith, and Jack Scharf of IBM, Bertrand Kaulek of Bossard Consultants (who translated the trade edition into French), Gary Sanders of AT&T, Giulio Corno of the Center for Enterprise Studies (Milan), Ken Hawes of Blue Cross–Blue Shield (Maryland), and Nancy Wendt of Cigna.

Since this edition contains most of the material found in the trade book, I want again to express my thanks to Ian MacMillan, professor of management and director of the Center for Entrepreneurial Studies at the University of Pennsylvania's Wharton School. He encouraged me to write a paper for the *Journal of Business Strategy* on the strategic use of information systems. An early draft, which he sent to the publisher, led to the contract from Dow Jones-Irwin.

The following read the entire trade manuscript and greatly improved it by their comments: Nick Rackoff and Al Ullrich of GTE, Jerry Kanter and Frank Chen of Honeywell Information Systems, and Bill Heuser of Abex. Others read parts of it or discussed particular topics with me and made valuable suggestions: Mel Fleisher, John James, Mal Nechis, and Dick Rutledge of IBM, Randy Drummond of GE, Ralph Loftin of Loftin Associates, and Liam Fahey, professor of management at the Boston University School of Business Administration.

Contents

Introduction

Triggered by the growing use of information technology for strategic purposes, the conceptual revolution restructuring the information management field shows no sign of abating. Concepts imported from diverse fields (e.g., business strategy, law, economic history, marketing, philosophy, industrial organization economics, entrepreneurial studies, organizational development, and political science) are transforming what was originally a rather technical subject concerned with the development and management of computer-based systems into an interdisciplinary area of intellectual ferment.

Like all revolutions, this one brings venerable beliefs into question. In particular, it threatens the supremacy of an analytical framework (model, theory) that has guided exploration in information management for almost two decades. Unchallenged during this period, the model found itself incapable in the 80s of accounting for the rapidly spreading strategic uses of information technology.

The emergence of these uses, which I call *strategic information systems* (SIS), created a conceptual crisis within the area because they failed to fit the standard categories sanctioned by the theory, being neither management information systems (MIS) nor management support systems (MSS). In a word, SIS are anomalies, falling outside what has become the conventional line of sight.

When such crises occur in established disciplines such as physics, microbiology, or chemistry (domains acutely aware of their conceptual roots), researchers scramble to devise theories for explaining and exploring the new phenomena. Not so in the relatively young field of information management. Here, when something new emerges, the tendency has been to treat it as evolving naturally from that which immediately preceded it. Hence, we observe the almost ritualistic practice of invoking stages, periods, or eras to handle new data that cannot be pigeonholed into the current evolutionary unit, as if all conceptual progress follows a continuous, cumulative, orderly sequence, natural and inevitable.

In the chapters to follow, I depart from this practice, believing that the emergence of SIS marks a dramatic change in the field, a turning that calls for a new pattern of presentation. After introducing the SIS idea in Chapter 1, I move immediately in Chapter 2 to a critique of the conventional perspective on information systems and the planning and control model embedded within it. In the process, I show how this analytical framework blinded its believers to SIS opportunities and threats inherent in information technology.

The limits of the conventional exposed, its framework rejected as an SIS model, the remainder of Part I (Chapters 3 and 4) is devoted to the task of constructing a strategic perspective on information technology, a perspective designed to assist top executives, line managers, information management practitioners, consultants, and academics in their investigations of the new SIS world. In Chapter 4, I sketch the theory of strategic thrusts, a categorical matrix model (based on the strategic perspective described earlier in that chapter) to aid the systematic search for SIS possibilities.

Part II (Chapters 5 through 9) characterizes each strategic thrust—differentiation, cost, innovation, growth, and alliance—and details through actual cases how information technology has been used to support or shape it. Part III discusses SIS planning and management issues (Chapters 10 and 11), topics related to the implementation of the new strategic perspective and model within an enterprise. It concludes by noting some recent SIS trends and challenges (Chapter 12).

At least four reasons compel taking this route rather than the evolutionary path. First, it fosters the consideration of alternative views, be they complementary or conflicting. My positions on the meaning of the term *competitive advantage* or the role played by information technology in supporting or shaping an organization's competitive strategy, for instance, differ at certain points from those held by Michael Porter, a theorist of business strategy (see Chapters 3 and 4); other points of view also deserve examination. To see these positions in the context of alternative, perhaps rival perspectives and theories invites debate on their strengths and weaknesses. It also satisfies the pedagogical purpose of exposing students to a diversity of views.

Second, by casting the subject of the strategic use of information technology in terms of theories and phenomena to be explained, one can maintain a certain degree of neutrality with respect to the merits of the examples discussed. While winners appear by far to outnumber losers, there have certainly been a fair number of the latter. Some attempts to exploit the technology for strategic purposes have, to put it gently, resulted in failure. A complete account of SIS must encompass failures as well as successes.

Third, by emphasizing actual instances of SIS, gathered primarily from material found in the public domain (with a few exceptions culled, with permission, from my consulting practice or from research papers prepared by my students), I have sought to focus attention, again, on the phenomena to be explained. The examples illustrate important points *and* provide an historical record, which may include extensions and variations of an SIS or competitive responses to it. This not only anchors the discussion of conceptual frameworks in reality but also highlights the richness and variety of data to be comprehended by any theoretical account.

The use of real examples allows researchers to track the evolution of a particular SIS. They can investigate its unknown aspects and enrich its case description for others in the field. Actual instances tend to stick in one's mind, so that when references to an interesting SIS or to organizations associated with it appear in print, we are eager to read about the latest developments. Such cases serve yet another important function. They form an active, expandable database of SIS examples that is valuable as (1) a source of ideas for new applications, (2) possible counterexamples to resist the temptations of overly ambitious unified theories (claiming to account for all SIS instances), (3) an aid in assessing the risks and benefits of proposed systems, and (4) grist for theoretical mills.

Fourth and finally, taking the route outlined above ties my treatment of the strategic use of information technology directly to concepts employed by philosophers and historians of science to illuminate our understanding of conceptual change in other domains. With this linkage, we can address with dispatch a number of perplexing SIS-related issues. To see this, consider the following two questions often raised by practitioners.

1. The SIS discovery question.   Some organizations have for years used information technology to achieve strategic ends. Their applications were neither called SIS nor identified with the help of a so-called strategic perspective on systems or an analytical framework designed for the purpose. They just seemed to evolve, in some cases serendipitously, in others by strategic intuition. If so, how can the SIS discovery process be facilitated through the use of a "rational reconstruction" such as the one proposed in this book?

An analogy from the history of mathematics sheds light on this question. The Babylonians, adept at constructing buildings and planning towns, discovered (through trial and error, serendipity, necessity, or whatever) certain facts about numbers, measurements, and relations between physical objects. This knowledge, unearthed in the course of their work, later found its way into the branch of mathematics we now call Euclidean geometry, named after the third century B.C. Greek mathematician Euclid, the author of the classic mathematical text *The Elements*.

Euclid's *Elements* offered, for the first time, an axiomatic account of geometric truths. By mastering the Euclidean axioms and following some simple rules of inference, students of geometry could deduce as theorems all the facts discovered empirically by the Babylonians. Even more striking, they could prove propositions that never intruded into Babylonian consciousness. A rational reconstruction, whether in the shape of an axiom system or of a less formal conceptual structure designed to account for a certain set of objects or events, holds out the promise of a systematic exploration of an area, an exploration that might identify and explain all phenomena falling within its purview.

Today, knowledge of the strategic use of information technology is possessed in the main by *SIS Babylonians,* individuals and enterprises who have intuitively grasped connections between competitive strategy and computer-based systems, discovered SIS opportunities by serendipity or strategic intuition, and executed them successfully. But the situation is changing rapidly as others—we might call them *SIS Euclideans*—adopt more theoretical tools in the form of rational reconstructions to aid in their understanding and search for SIS.[1]

2. The SIS understanding question. SIS case descriptions, being relatively straightforward, generally do not tax the mind. A carefully constructed sampler would, it seems, suffice to teach the main points about the strategic use of information technology. But in practice, many prospective SIS Euclideans have found the SIS concept and related notions difficult to comprehend when first introduced to the subject. How can this apparent paradox be resolved? The philosophy of science suggests an answer.

Terms like *group* (in its mathematical sense), *DNA,* and *surplus value* (in Marxian economics) are "theory-laden." They become comprehensible only after one has mastered the theory in which they occur. When a mathematician says that a certain collection of objects forms an "additive group A," it is safe to conclude that if x, y, and z are members of A, then:

$$1.\ x + y = y + x$$
$$2.\ x + (y + z) = (x + y) + z$$
$$3.\ x + 0 = x$$

These inferences can be drawn with confidence because we know that A forms an additive group and statements 1–3 above are defining conditions for such mathematical objects.

Knowing that A is an additive group, mathematicians can appreciate a number of other truths about such objects, truths they "see" immediately whenever a group presents itself. When someone who understands group theory discovers that a set of entities (e.g., the natural numbers, the integers, or the myth symbols of a primitive tribe) forms a group, an intricate web of associations and implications comes to mind. Where the layman perceives but a mere collection of elements, the group theory practitioner sees a complex structure visible only to the informed eye.

The layman peering into an electron microscope in search of DNA molecules may see only tiny, thread-like entities. But when the microbiologist looks, the scientific mind perceives DNA strands and combinations in all their splendor. Similarly, the Marxist who recognizes instances of surplus value when analyzing certain activities in capitalist countries sees something undetected by those ignorant of Marxian economic theory.

Locutions such as "seeing (perceiving) x as y," "seeing (perceiving) that x is a y," or "identifying (discovering) that x is y" indicate that a conceptual structure—group theory, microbiology, Marxian economics, or the like—forms an integral part of the visual experience. Without the theoretical underpinning, neither groups, DNA molecules, nor surplus values could be discerned.

The term *SIS*, as we shall presently see in Chapter 1, also arrives theory laden. Unless one masters the conceptual apparatus behind it, systematic identification of SIS opportunities and threats will prove difficult at best. This goes a long way toward explaining the educational paradox mentioned at the beginning of this section. We should now appreciate why those exposed to examples of SIS without first receiving some theoretical guidance often find themselves, like the laymen in the examples just cited, blind to phenomena that others with an educated eye see clearly and distinctly.

NOTE

1. It should, of course, come as no great surprise that neither the reconstruction presented here nor alternatives advocated by F. Warren McFarlan, James Cash and Benn Konsynski, Michael Porter and Victor Millar, Michael Hammer and Glenn Mangurian, and others purport to provide an axiomatic account of phenomena in this area. See, for example, F. Warren McFarlan, "Information Technology Changes the Way You Compete," *Harvard Business Review*, May–June 1984, pp. 98–103; James Cash, Jr., and Benn Konsynski, "IS Redraws Competitive Boundaries," *Harvard Business Review*, March–April 1985, pp. 134–42; Michael Porter and Victor Millar, "How Information Gives You Competitive Advantage," *Harvard Business Review*, July–August 1985, pp. 149–60; Michael Hammer and Glenn Mangurian, "The Changing Value of Communications Technology," *Sloan Management Review*, Winter 1987, pp. 65–71.

I

Through Another Lens

1

The Strategic Use of Information Technology

PERSPECTIVES ON INFORMATION SYSTEMS

What we see is largely determined by what we believe. For centuries, Chinese astronomers identified stars, planets, and comets undetected by their Western counterparts. Neither the availability of powerful optical instruments nor the location, anatomy, or physiology of the scientists accounts for these instances of celestial vision and blindness. Rather, the explanation resides in the radically different conceptual perspectives from which these two groups viewed the universe.

When Western astronomers scanned the sky, they expected to see nothing new. They were religious men who believed the bodies in God's heaven to be fixed and immutable. The Chinese, on the other hand, adhered to cosmological ideas that did not preclude celestial change and novelty. Evidence that these different perspectives shaped the horizon of expectation, the mental set of those who adopted them, emerged in the late 16th century when the religious dogma was overthrown. Western observers then recorded for the first time what the Chinese had seen hundreds of years earlier. Fitted with a different pair of conceptual glasses, they saw objects previously invisible to them.

The ability to see requires more than eyes. Identifying information systems—like discovering stars, planets, and comets—depends on our conceptual perspective. From one vantage point, we see some information system varieties and miss others. Change that point, and we perceive a radically different system space. If a firm's destiny hinges on its use of information technology, it had better view systems from the proper perspective.

What is the proper perspective? As the pace of competition intensifies, this has become a critical question for many enterprises. Yet whatever the answer, one thing is clear. The reigning dogma on the organizational uses of information systems won't do. And the firm that fails to rethink these uses may find itself at risk.

This seems to be the position of a large number of firms today. Since the advent of data processing in the mid-50s, one viewpoint has exclusively dominated their thinking about information system opportunities. It holds that the organizational purpose served by computer applications is either (1) to automate a basic process (subprocess or task) or (2) to provide information for decision making. It is concerned primarily with information flows, data bases, and the production of reports related to the organization's planning and control operations. I call this the *conventional perspective* on information technology (systems) and present an evolutionary account of it in Chapter 2.

A data processing professional exemplified this viewpoint in the early 70s when he advocated a new approach for information systems planning, a top-down method "to focus on the critical tasks and decisions made within an organization and to provide the kind of information that the manager needs to perform those tasks and make those decisions."[1] The author of a recent book on the health care industry reflected it when he asserted that "the only computer services that a hospital really needs—the basic financial, billing, and accounting operations—could be purchased relatively inexpensively from any service company."[2]

When adherents of the conventional perspective search for information system opportunities, they look for two varieties: *management information systems* (MIS) and *management support systems* (MSS). (MSS includes as its two main species: *decision support systems* and *executive information systems*. See the appendix to Chapter 2 for a detailed description.) These varieties are intended to serve organizational purposes associated with the conventional perspective, that is, automating basic processes (the domain of MIS) and satisfying the information needs of managers and professionals, needs often closely connected with planning and control decisions (the domain of MSS).

The conventional perspective, important as it is for identifying and illuminating the significance of these two varieties, offers too limited a view of the world of information technology. Consider, for example, how Metpath Inc. uses systems to compete in the tough, fragmented clinical laboratory industry, where low differentiation of service has led to a lack of customer loyalty and frequent price discounting. Doctors send specimens to the lab for processing and in return expect timely, accurate analyses. Metpath enhanced its customer service by installing computer terminals in doctors' offices and linking them to its lab computers. For a small monthly fee, physicians receive test results as soon as they are determined.

From the conventional vantage point, the system might be seen as a transaction-processing, on-line database application providing critical diagnostic information to physicians. But this description captures neither its competitive import nor its innovative character. By changing conceptual lenses and viewing it from a *strategic perspective,* we see it as an attempt by Metpath to use its information system as a double-edged sword.

First, it builds barriers against new and existing rivals by raising the information systems ante. Second, it enables Metpath to gain an edge over other labs by differentiating an otherwise commodity service. Metpath keeps historical records of patient data on file and offers its customers computerized processing services for billing and accounts payable operations, as well as easy access to stock market quotations from the Dow Jones network. Finally, the system can expand the services it offers into such areas as diagnosis (when expert systems become available) and drug interaction testing. Referring to the latter, the vice president for scientific affairs of the American Pharmaceutical Association said: "If there is such a thing as the wave of the future, this is it."[3] Primed as it is to store patient profile data on such items as drug and food allergies, chronic illnesses, and medications taken, the Metpath system will permit physicians to conduct drug interaction tests prior to writing prescriptions. Each of these information system–based hooks serves to differentiate a commodity service (see Chapter 5) and thereby secures the loyalty of the estimated one in five doctors who annually switch from lab to lab in search of lower prices.

The application just described is an instance of a *strategic information system* (SIS), a use of information technology intended to support or shape the competitive strategy of the enterprise. SIS represent a new information system variety, radically different in organizational use from those countenanced by the conventional perspective (see Chapter 2).

The conventional perspective offers scant guidance to those who wish to discover SIS or explain their strategic impact. Nor is it of much help in accounting for the extended uses made by American and United Air Lines of their computerized reservation systems, Sabre and Apollo, respectively.

While the history of these systems goes back to the dawn of the computer age, when they were deployed internally as neutral scheduling mechanisms to automate the seat reservation process, it wasn't until the 70s and 80s that their competitive dimensions captured the strategist's imagination. During this period, Sabre and Apollo for the first time were leased to travel agents and used by their developers as weapons in the struggle for industry domination.

American and United programmed their systems with a bias—reflected on the primary and secondary screens seen by users—toward their own flights. An independent agent who subscribed to Sabre knew, when requesting a listing of flights from New York to Los Angeles with stops in between, that the first items to appear on the screen might show neither the most direct way nor the least expensive way, but for sure they would show the American way.

With Sabre and Apollo, American and United virtually preempted the major channel of ticket distribution. By the early 80s, they formed a powerful duopoly in the computerized travel agency market, with shares of 41 percent and 39 percent, respectively. The crumbs (the remaining 20 percent) were left to their rivals. While Delta, Eastern, and TWA developed smaller systems to limit their exposure, carriers without a system found themselves at risk. As one of the less fortunate put it, "We clearly didn't pay enough attention, and now it's a direct threat."[4] Within a few years, over 80 percent of the nation's 20,000 travel agencies, accounting for 90 percent of airline ticket sales, had been computerized. In regions where the airline with the reservation system had numerous flights, the built-in prioritization routines could lead to as much as 20 percent more revenue.

To appreciate from another angle the strategic role reservation systems now play in the airline industry, consider the following: Carriers pay travel agents an official commission of 10 percent for all flights they book with them. To attract business, "overrides" are often paid by the carriers to the agents, bringing the average commission to about 14 percent. If a large agency signs an "exclusive" contract with an airline (usually a long-term arrangement that forbids the agency, on pain of severe financial penalties, from contracting with another carrier offering a reservation system), it will probably receive a premium from the lucky line. "It's not uncommon for such premiums to reach $500,000 cash, plus extra commission payments, free use of the system for three years or more, free staff training, free trips, and the like."[5]

But Sabre and Apollo provide their developers with far more than increased ticket revenue due to bias. Both systems form the core of substantial profit centers. In 1985, for example, Sabre brought in $143 million in profit on revenues of $336 million. For the first quarter of that year, Sabre contributed more of American's $93.3 million profit before taxes than did its airline business. Fee-generated income flowed from:

- Other airlines that paid $1.75 for each of their flights booked on Sabre.
- Hotels, car rental companies, and others whose reservations were made via Sabre.
- Travel agents who leased Sabre terminals.
- Other airlines that bought data processing services (e.g., cargo tracking, reservations, accounting, weather analysis, passenger processing, flight planning, and inventory control) from American's service bureau spinoff, AMR Airline Automation Service.

During that year, Sabre accounted for "10 percent of all hotel reservations, 20 percent of all car rentals, and 45 percent of all airline reservations made through travel agents," according to a spokesman from American.[6] The carrier could cite statistics like these with confidence because they were derived from its massive Sabre database.

The Sabre database provides American with additional competitive advantages. Having exclusive access to sales data on passengers and travel agencies, American generates reports by agency, by airline, and by market on the number and percentage of passengers booked for a given period. American's sales representatives employ these reports in their dealings with Sabre-using travel agents, leaning on those who get out of line by writing too many tickets on other airlines, and rewarding others who prefer to fly the American way.

American's marketers use information gleaned from the Sabre database to respond rapidly to the strategic moves of rivals, employing such stratagems as bonus incentives, lower fares, or scheduling changes to counter their actions. Since a rival's move must be entered in advance on the Sabre system, American can react quickly to blunt the initiative or, at the very least, reduce the element of surprise as a strategic option.

Sabre also helps American manage its seat inventory. At headquarters in Dallas, 90 "yield managers" monitor, analyze, and adjust "fare mixes on 1,600 daily flights as well as 528,000 future flights involving nearly 50 million passengers."[7] Industry analysts consider American's Sabre-based yield management system to be the best in the industry and estimate it can increase revenues by 5 to 20 percent annually.

For its passengers, American offers a number of Sabre-linked amenities. For easy access to fare and schedule information, there is the automated voice response system. With a push-button, tone-generating phone, you can obtain this information for flights between any two American Air cities. For those who wish to do it all themselves, American offers "Eaasy" Sabre. If you have a personal computer (PC) and access to a data network (e.g., Dialcom or Geisco), you can book a flight, make a hotel reservation, and reserve a car. Eaasy is a scaled-down version of Sabre. A user can peruse flight schedules, identify the lowest fares with the help of a special bargain-finder feature, and select a hotel from the more than 12,000 listed. Eaasy Sabre poses an interesting strategic question for American as the number of PC users grows: How to ensure that its agency network doesn't erode as more and more reservations are made without the help of a travel agent. At the moment, American appears to be treading softly here. It seems to promote Eaasy only in its monthly in-flight magazine, *American Way*.

Sabre also supports American's "marketing idea of the decade," its American Advantage frequent-flyer program, which in 1987 claimed to have 5.3 million members. The Advantage program builds what was for a long time lacking in the airline industry: customer loyalty. If, say, you're an Advantage member and have flown 60,000 miles, you're entitled to two free round-trip economy-class tickets to American cities in Europe during the off-season. The prospect of such an award tends to encourage a certain kind of fidelity in many formerly fickle airline passengers. It has also encouraged other enterprises to form tie-in marketing deals with American in which customers of the enterprise receive Advantage credit when they make a purchase. Pan American, for example, used this incentive to help launch its shuttle service between New York, Boston, and Washington, D.C.

In addition, Sabre has become American's vehicle for diversification and growth, propelling it into new lines of business and expanding its traditional customer sets. According to Robert Crandall, American's chairman and CEO who championed Sabre's development in the 70s when he was the vice president of marketing, "This industry needs every cent it can generate. We've got to be creative about using our huge asset base to develop new revenues. We're looking at businesses that we can be in at low costs because some of the links are already in place."[8] These links form, in American's words, "the world's most powerful nonmilitary computer system." According to the vice president of marketing and automation systems at American, 65,000 devices hang off the network, which runs 23 hours a day, 365 days a year, and keeps track of 6.5 million domestic and international airfare combinations, more than 10,000 daily fare changes, and the flight schedules of about 650 airlines around the world.

To implement Crandall's vision, American reorganized in the mid-80s. It formed the AMR holding company (which includes the airline as a subsidiary) and created AMR Information Services, Inc. (AMR/IS) to capitalize on the wealth of diversification opportunities created by resources and knowhow associated with Sabre. AMR/IS now has close to 1,500 people engaged in eight different businesses. (The American Airlines unit of AMR continues to operate Sabre itself.) These businesses comprise three formerly internal groups:

- Airline Automation Services, which sells Sabre-related services to other airlines;
- Caribbean Data Services, a data-entry subsidiary;
- Direct Marketing Corp., a telemarketing operation that conducts marketing surveys, takes pledges from telethons, services American Air's catalog sales, and the like;

two acquisitions:

- Ticketnet Corp., a firm specializing in computerized ticketing services;
- Video Financial, an electronic facilitator firm formed by a group of eight banks to provide home banking, cash management, and other financial services to those with a personal computer, a modem, and access to a telephone;

and three startups:

- Travel Services, a unit that markets an array of techniques (developed by the airline in the course of managing its seat inventory) to hotels and car rental companies so that they can improve the management of their room and automobile inventories, respectively;

- Technical Training, a company that offers data processing courses;
- Freight Services, a group that uses a PC-based system to process information related to complex freight shipping operations involving different modes of transportation.

I have traced the evolution of American's use of the Sabre system from the conventional automation of the obvious, the seat reservation process of one airline, to its current role in shaping AMR's competitive strategy. (More details will be added in Chapter 8 to illustrate how American relies on Sabre to support its plan for penetrating the European market.) Indeed, the performance of AMR today depends heavily on the success of AMR/IS's ventures and the ability of Sabre to maintain its profit margins. Investment analysts have gone so far as to suggest that "every percentage-point drop in Sabre's margins costs AMR 4 cents in per-share earnings."[9] On this reckoning, Sabre impacts not only the bottom line but also share price.

For AMR, the connection between strategy, technology, and investment value reveals itself explicitly—perhaps too explicitly, some might say. For the connection has not gone unnoticed by AMR's rivals, who in response to the success of Sabre and its extensions have raised important legal, regulatory, and competitive issues associated with the strategic use of information technology. Consider, for example, the question of bias inherent in both the Sabre and the Apollo systems. After complaints from travel agents and disadvantaged airlines, the Civil Aeronautics Board issued a ruling (upheld by the U.S. Court of Appeals in 1985) prohibiting bias on screen displays.

But this decision just whetted the appetite of 13 airlines lacking computerized reservation systems. In 1985 and 1986, they initiated legal proceedings charging that "American and United, among other unfair practices, (1) violated . . . the Sherman [Anti-Trust] Act by conspiring to monopolize the computerized reservation system industry, (2) abused their monopoly power in violation of . . . the Sherman Act, and (3) denied access to their respective systems on fair, reasonable, and nondiscriminatory terms."[10] If found guilty of these and other charges, American and United might be forced to pay damages in excess of $2 billion.

Not to be outflanked, American filed a complaint with the Transportation Department in 1987 accusing Texas Air (TA) and three of its subsidiaries (Eastern Air, Continental Air, and the SystemOne Direct Access Corp., which is TA's computer reservation unit) of deception and unfair practices in the operation of SystemOne. A spokesman for TA called the complaint a "trumped up allegation" and a "harassment tactic" made in response to the suit Continental had pending against American's Sabre system.

While the proceedings move inexorably through the courts, AMR faces a far more direct and immediate challenge: shrinking profits from Sabre due to increased competition. In late 1985, Sabre enjoyed profit margins of 40 percent or more. But these dropped to 30 percent in 1986 and to 20 percent by mid-87, according to Max Hopper, American's vice president for information systems who helped design the system in the 70s. (Even at 20 percent, which is nothing to feel guilty about, Sabre's margin exceeds AMR's airline business profit, estimated at about 5 percent.) Both market share and cash flow are also declining. In 1987, market share (defined as the number of terminals installed) showed American with 52,397 (38 percent), United with 40,688 (30 percent), and Texas Air with 20,000 (15 percent); in the early 80s, American and United had accounted for 80 percent of the total.

It seems that the technological duopoly held for so many years by American and United is eroding in the face of fierce competition from systems developed by Texas Air's Eastern Air Lines unit, TWA, and Delta. In some cases, these carriers have offered to pay the legal fees of travel agents who subscribe to Sabre or Apollo if American or United act to enforce their "exclusive" contracts. A certain kind of pleasure is to be gained when a rival of the one that holds you in electronic bondage agrees to pay your switching costs.

To understand the import of Sabre, Apollo, and the system described in the Metpath case cited earlier, we need to go beyond the conventional perspective. Like the Western astronomers unprepared to see new celestial objects, believers in the conventional gospel on information systems are neither capable of discerning SIS opportunities and threats nor conceptually equipped to explain their strategic significance. Lying still further beyond the conventional range of vision, the entire spectrum of strategic alliances supported or shaped by information technology also goes undetected.

Citicorp, the largest U.S. bank-holding company, supports its global market expansion strategy through a series of carefully crafted alliances with an assorted group of partners, many of whom share a common attribute: operation of an automatic teller machine (ATM) network permitting its card-holding members to make, among other things, simple cash deposits and withdrawals. These agreements enable Citicorp to exploit information technology assets *developed by others* and thereby serve its own strategic objectives.

In the United States alone, Citicorp has access to over 6,500 ATMs in 42 states, which moves it closer to its goal of becoming a nationwide consumer bank despite federal laws prohibiting interstate banking. Citi's alliances form part of the distribution network supporting its Financial Account, a major element in its growth plan. Combining an interest-paying checking account, money market deposit account, CDs, a personal line of credit, and discount brokerage services, this product offers Citi's credit cardholders (over 12 million in the United States at the end of 1983) with one-stop financial services 24 hours a day.

To execute its strategy, Citi cut deals with Mpact, a bank-owned ATM net based in Texas; Publix and Safeway, supermarket chains in Florida and California, respectively, that have installed cash-dispensing machines in their stores; a Japanese bank operating an ATM net in Tokyo and other large cities in Japan; and Cirrus Systems, a network of U.S. banks giving each other access to their ATMs. This latter alliance permits Citi customers to gain access to ATMs operated by one of its rivals, Manufacturers Hanover Trust, in New York City and prohibits any bank from using Citi's extensive ATM net. But this isn't a total loss for Manufacturers. It collects a fee every time a Citi cardholder uses one of Manny Hanny's ATMs.

In 1986, Citi acquired Northeast Exchange Ltd., a network of 40 ATMs used by Pathmark customers in its New York and New Jersey supermarkets. It has now expanded the network to include other food chains in the metropolitan region. But even though customers of the 32 banks associated with Northeast are still able to use the system, Citi withholds their access to its main ATM network. In addition, the banking giant has made marketing arrangements with firms using point-of-sale terminals involving debit card transactions. A link with Mobil Oil, for example, allows Citi's ATM cardholders to use their cards at any of Mobil's 3,000 gas stations nationwide. Cardholders receive a record of transactions each month on their checking account statements.

Joint ventures illustrate another form of strategic alliance in which information technology may play a central role. IBM and Merrill Lynch announced in 1984 the creation of International MarketNet (Imnet), a new information service intended to provide users of IBM PCs with stock quotations, investment data, analytical processing, financial software, and so on. The service would enable end users to communicate via satellite links with Merrill's host computers. Monchik-Weber, a software house specializing in the securities industry (acquired by McGraw-Hill after Imnet opened its doors), won the contract to develop the systems that would run the service.

Imnet, a 50–50 joint venture alliance between IBM and Merrill Lynch, drew its customers from Merrill's 10,000 account representatives, other brokerage houses, commerical banks, money managers, and clients of these firms. The alliance supported IBM's strategy of market expansion and Merrill's plans to diversify into the information services industry and to reduce and eventually eliminate the fees it was paying to Quotron Systems, Inc. for the use of its stock-quotation system. (At the time, 25 percent of Quotron's customers were employees of Merrill.)

Unfortunately for the partners, this venture failed. What had initially seemed like an irresistible combination evaporated at the end of 24 months upon contact with a far more potent duo: rising costs and shrinking market. At the time of its demise, Imnet had reached less than 1 percent of projected sales, with only 50 buyers emerging from the ranks of Merrill's account reps and about the same number from other financial institutions.

According to some Wall Street sources but denied by a Merrill spokesperson, the project cost over $70 million. Analysts cited a variety of reasons for failure: poor management of the venture, with no clear lines of responsibility established between the partners; inadequate systems design of the user interface, which forced brokers to become technological jugglers of floppy disks, modems, function keys, and the like instead of playing their more familiar telephone-sales role; inappropriate pricing that asked potential customers to pay between 5 and 10 times the going rate for services of unproven value; customer resistance to signing on to a service offered by a competitor. Why should we (Hutton and Shearson brokers presumably asked themselves) support our arch rival, Merrill?

This example establishes from the start that failures like Imnet are just as much a part of the SIS landscape as successes like American Air. Recognition of losers as well as winners helps us to understand better the possible risks and rewards associated with the strategic use of information technology.

Both the Citicorp and the Imnet examples, as well as AMR/IS's acquisitions described previously, illustrate instances of *strategic information system alliances* (see Chapter 9), intra- or interorganizational combinations that make use of information technology to support or shape competitive strategy. Since, by definition, such technology uses are strategic information systems, remarks that follow about SIS (unless otherwise noted) should be taken to apply to SIS alliances as well.

The SIS cases detailed above mark a conceptual discontinuity in the brief evolutionary history of information systems. But to appreciate more deeply this break with the past, this movement from the conventional to the strategic, requires something more than the trotting out of SIS cases. What we need to show are examples of firms that have developed a vision of information systems to guide their strategic course.

STRATEGIC INFORMATION SYSTEM VISION

To see that an information system application *is* a SIS, we need to understand how information technology is used to support or shape the firm's competitive strategy. This ability to see and understand I call *strategic information system vision*.

A firm with a powerful SIS vision zealously encourages the search for opportunities to use information technology to gain or maintain a competitive advantage or to reduce a rival's edge. And when they are discovered, it marshalls the proper resources to support them. In some cases, SIS vision develops into an *image* of the future that top management uses to navigate the firm's strategic voyage.

How can we determine whether a firm possesses SIS vision? The best test, I believe, is to examine what the firm says and does. If it purports to appreciate the strategic significance of information technology and if it launches thrusts supported or shaped by systems, we are justified in believing that SIS vision is operating. Admittedly, this is only a rough guide. It would be preferable, to be sure, to explore from within, to observe in detail the strategic decision-making process and how information systems are woven into the fabric of strategic programs, before making a judgment.

But until interdisciplinary studies (involving business strategists, academics, line managers, information systems professionals, and leading-edge firms) are conducted on the strategic use of information technology, we must content ourselves with establishing indirectly, through whatever evidence can be mustered, whether an enterprise possesses SIS vision.

This is the approach I have followed in assembling the facts on Dun & Bradstreet, McKesson, and Banc One—the three firms discussed below—to support my contention that each possesses its own highly developed SIS vision, a vision that lights its strategic path.

Dun & Bradstreet

Dun & Bradstreet (D&B) traces its origin back to 1841 when Louis Tappan, a New York dry-goods jobber, founded the Mercantile Agency, the first credit-reporting firm in the United States. Within a decade, the Bradstreet Agency became the second company to enter the field. By 1890, Mercantile (now run by R. G. Dun) had established 69 branch offices in major business centers. Being the first two firms to create nationwide networks, Bradstreet and Dun dominated the credit-reporting business. In the 1870s, Dun employed over 10,000 reporters or investigators and received some 5,000 requests a day for information. In 1930, the two firms merged to form Dun & Bradstreet.

By 1978, D&B had become a $763 million diversified information services company with four major divisions:

- Business Information Services (D&B Credit, D&B Commercial Collection, D&B International, D&B Group Life and Health Insurance Administration).
- Publishing (Reuben H. Donnelley, Official Airline Guides, Moody's Investors Service, Technical Publishing, Funk & Wagnalls).
- Marketing Services (Donnelley Marketing, Dun's Marketing, International Marketing).
- Broadcasting (Corinthian Broadcasting's Television Stations, TVS Television Network).

Business Information Services contributed 38 percent of the revenues and 27 percent of the operating income.

In 1979, D&B recorded its best year ever and made two significant strategic moves. It purchased for $164 million National CSS (NCSS), a leading computer services company with a nationwide, 80,000-mile time-sharing network, and agreed to acquire its sixth television station together with half a dozen small cable systems, giving D&B its first hands-on experience in the growing cable industry. The NCSS acquisition became part of D&B's Business Information Service Division while the television station and cable systems were to become part of the Broadcasting group. D&B saw these moves as consistent with its strategic vision:

> There are three principal resources that are central to the continued success of the Dun & Bradstreet Corporation: our ability to collect timely and relevant *information* for the decision-making use of our various customer groups; our capacity for applying *technology* effectively to maximize information delivery and utility; and the *management* to anticipate the needs of our customers and, in partnership with our highly skilled people, to provide quality products and services worldwide.[11]

At the close of 1983, D&B had become a $1.5 billion information services giant. The contribution of the Business Information Services Division had risen in four years to 45 percent of total revenue and 34 percent of operating income. During the year, D&B made two significant strategic moves. It acquired McCormack & Dodge, a major software company specializing in financial and human resources packages, and departed from the broadcasting industry by selling its stations and systems. In 1984, D&B underlined its focus on business services and information by acquiring, through merger (a $1.08 billion stock transaction), A. C. Nielsen Company, the nation's leading consumer research concern.

D&B's recent evolutionary history, I claim, reflects SIS vision. D&B's management has executed strategic moves supported or shaped by information technology, moves that serve to support or shape D&B's long-term objective of concentrating its efforts and resources in the business services and information industry.

In 1979, Robert Weissman (NCSS's president when it was acquired by D&B and, since 1980, D&B's executive vice president and now its president and chief operating officer) proclaimed:

> NCSS and the Dun & Bradstreet Corporation are the best fit in the information industry—data from D&B operating companies plus NCSS leadership in computer services. We're going to rewrite the book on combining information and technology to develop new products for our customers.[12]

The battle cry voiced by Weissman is reflected in the following thrusts made during the 1979–87 period (including the NCSS acquisition).

Acquisition of NCSS.   This major diversification move enabled D&B to enter the time-sharing business, a new market pioneered by NCSS, and to exploit NCSS's information system resources (its hardware, software, and highly skilled work force) synergistically. Within a few months after the acquisition, 12 joint projects were initiated, among them Duns Vue, a new credit product, and Moody's Municipal Credit Report Service, both designed for electronic delivery over NCSS's network. But NCSS's time-sharing business has been a disappointment. As demand declined over the past few years, due primarily to the rapid spread of microcomputer processing, D&B has had to find new uses for its valuable NCSS resources. In 1984, it decided to phase out the NCSS operation, taking a $47 million write-off.

Acquisition of McCormack & Dodge.   Like the NCSS purchase, this SIS alliance illustrates a major diversification move with a dual purpose. D&B expects to exploit M&D's software, systems knowhow, and 3,000-customer base synergistically across its various product lines. And it expects M&D, an established leader in its market niche, to continue its impressive growth. Already, joint projects have emerged between M&D and D&B's other units. M&D introduced PC–Link, a product that allows users of IBM's PC to retrieve and transfer mainframe data. PC–Link ties directly to another D&B offering, DunsPlus, which is itself the result of efforts by an NCSS division (D&B Computing Services) and an SIS alliance struck between D&B and IBM (see below).

Acquisition of Nielsen. In the case of the NCSS and M&D acquisitions, D&B exploited the information systems assets of others. With the Nielsen merger, on the other hand, D&B saw opportunities to capitalize on its own information technology and related business assets. Steps have already been taken to adapt DunsPlus (see below) software so that it can deliver Nielsen data via DunsNet (see below) "on the sales volume, market share, pricing, distribution patterns, and inventory levels of consumer goods."[13]

D&B's Donnelly Marketing unit, which possesses one of the world's most extensive demographic databases, offers another opportunity area for information technology synergies, fitting perfectly into the SIS vision of Nielsen's chairman and CEO, who is also a D&B vice president: "Our future will lie in customizing single source systems that integrate TV and product databases for consumer packaged goods companies."[14] To round out its data-gathering abilities so that it can provide single-source reports, Nielsen in 1987 acquired the Majers Corp., which collects data on print advertising, and formed a joint venture with the NPD Group, which collects data on consumer purchases.

Development of Official Airline Guide/Electronic Edition and acquisition of Thomas Cook USA. D&B's Official Airline Guides (OAGs) provide printed information on North American, Worldwide, and Air Cargo flights. In 1983, D&B announced an electronic version of these guides. With a computer terminal, modem, and telephone, a user of the

OAG/Electronic Edition can query the flight database for comparative fare information within specified arrival or departure periods and determine the lowest fare between two points. D&B distributes the Electronic Edition directly or through such information network channels as CompuServe, Dialcom, Dow Jones News/Retrieval, Bell Canada, and Viewdata.

Prior to 1985, the Electronic Edition merely mimicked the printed guides. In March of that year, D&B entered a new ball game. It purchased for an undisclosed amount the Thomas Cook USA travel agency network. With Cook's ticket-selling capability, D&B now offers an unbiased version of the airline reservation systems currently operated by such carriers as American and United. A user of the Electronic Edition can get objective data, favoring only the airlines with the lowest prices, *and* book a flight, hotel room, and car. For this enhanced service, D&B marketers target corporate travel departments and airlines that are at a competitive disadvantage because of their lack of a general-purpose system.

Creation of DunsPlus. By forming SIS alliances with IBM, Lotus Corp., and Softword Systems, D&B created a unique product complementing its other offerings as well as providing a stand-alone, integrated professional workstation. DunsPlus consists of an IBM PC (D&B forged an agreement with IBM to act as a value-added remarketer), spreadsheet (Lotus 1-2-3) and word-processing (MultiMate) programs, and specifically developed D&B software (from NCSS) outfitting end users with electronic mail, file maintenance, data integration, and other capabilities. As incentives to purchase DunsPlus, D&B included as standard features one year's sign-up charges for Western Union's electronic mail service and its own OAG/EE. Use of DunsPlus, need it be said, also made access to D&B's extensive collection of electronic data bases, and others as well, a relatively straightforward procedure.

Built into the offering, in addition, is a micro-to-mainframe utility program called PC–Link, developed by McCormack & Dodge, which allows PC users to transmit and receive data from corporate data bases. Within the first six months after its introduction in January 1984, DunsPlus had attracted over 50 major corporate customers. One of these, the vice president and treasurer of Olin Corp., testified to the usefulness of D&B's new integrated product by saying, "I don't see why anyone would order anything else."[15]

Development of DunsNet. This D&B offering is a packet-switched telecommunications network, similar in function to General Telephone & Electronics Corporation's Telenet and Tymshare's Tymnet. With DunsNet, D&B offers its customers value-added networking services and distributed processing through the use of such microcomputer systems as DunsPlus. Other D&B units can also make use of the net.

DunsNet enables all D&B users to access its data bases using one standard procedure. It reduces D&B-generated revenues for Telenet and Tymnet. DunsNet represents a strategic growth move for D&B, a kind of forward integration that takes the company a step further toward its goal of being a full-service provider of information services and data to its clients.

Global expansion. In 1984, D&B opened a $40 million processing center in England. This move in the direction of global electronic growth, constituting a form of information technology transfer (see Chapter 8), offers to the European market many of the products and services now provided to the firm's American customers.

From this short selection of strategic actions taken over an eight-year period, it seems evident that D&B possesses SIS vision. If it didn't, how else can we account for such efforts to use information technology to support strategy. The reader may object that since D&B is an information services company, each of the moves cited is natural and has nothing to do with SIS vision.

But this objection is not persuasive. D&B had choices. It wasn't forced to acquire M&D or Nielsen. It wasn't bullied into forming an alliance with IBM to market the PC and build a product around it. DunsNet was not inevitable. Different data-rich firms have made different strategic choices, some emphasizing information systems, others not. D&B itself did not have such a clear vision of its future in 1979, as indicated by its broadcasting acquisitions. After the acquisition of NCSS, however, the die seems to have been cast, with Weissman probably sounding the clarion call.

The current evolution of D&B, inspired by SIS vision, is far from complete. By the end of this decade, in all likelihood, it should emerge as one of the leading information services firms in the world, providing a full line of products supported or shaped by information technology. The examples cited above are just the tip of the iceberg; economy-of-scale and economy-of-scope (see Chapter 6) opportunities, among others, have yet to be exploited to the fullest.

McKesson

McKesson Corp., formerly Foremost-McKesson and originally McKesson-Robbins (M–R), provides another example of a firm with a powerful SIS vision. As one of the nation's largest wholesalers of nondurable consumer goods, McKesson distributes:

- *Ethical and proprietary drugs, toiletries, fragrances, and sundries.* These are sold to chain and independent drugstores and hospitals. The company operates over 50 distribution centers, receives more than 50,000 goods from 2,500 suppliers, and serves 14,000 drugstores and 2,000 hospitals in 35 states.
- *Wine and spirits.* These are sold through the company's 36 distribution centers to liquor stores, restaurants, bars, and other establishments. It holds distribution rights from most U.S. distillers, importers, and wineries in one or more markets.
- *Industrial and specialty chemicals.* These are sold through the

company's over 60 distribution centers to customers in the pharmaceutical, cosmetic, food, and automobile industries.

McKesson, like D&B, traces its history back to the first half of the 19th century. Indeed, the growth of independent wholesale jobbers like McKesson-Robbins (M–R), Marshall Field, and others was one of the principal reasons for the new type of credit service offered by the Tappans, Duns, and Bradstreets of the day. M–R imported and wholesaled drugs, chemicals, and related lines. By 1926, however, little remained of the original M–R but its name, as competitive pressures and import tariffs forced it to close its distribution business and maintain only a small manufacturing facility in Brooklyn, New York.

Resurrected in the late 20s, M–R at first continued in its traditional lines and then diversified over the next 50 years into such businesses as alcoholic beverage distribution, dairy products (through merger with Foremost Dairies), and pasta and dehydrated vegetable manufacture (through the acquisition of C. F. Mueller Co.). In 1984, the new McKesson announced that it was leaving the food business (having sold Foremost and Muellers in 1983) to concentrate its resources on the value-added distribution of a variety of products.

Between 1980 and 1987, McKesson transformed itself from a diversified conglomerate into a highly automated distributor. It sold about half of its 1980 assets ($720 million) and in 1986–87 derived "about 80 percent of its profit from its retail-distribution businesses."[16]

What shapes McKesson's new strategic direction is what shapes D&B's: SIS vision. Top management believes that the name "McKesson Corporation" now "reflects our history, the present structure of our business, and the *path* we are traveling." According to Thomas Drohan, McKesson's former president (now deceased):

> Perhaps the single greatest *advantage* that the McKesson distribution companies enjoy has been—and will continue to be—in *computer technology,* where our size and diversity have enabled us to achieve the necessary critical mass. Our data processing

resources now involve 550 people and an annual budget of over $65 million. We intend to continue the proliferation of this technology among our current distribution businesses and to seek out opportunities to apply it to other distribution-related businesses. This shift in emphasis—making *Value-Added Distribution* our *primary thrust* with a secondary thrust in certain proprietary product areas—reflects the facts as they are today.[17][Italics added.]

McKesson sees a direct connection between its ability to gain competitive advantage and its use of information technology to support and shape strategies aimed at this objective. According to a senior vice president in its drug group (the company's biggest business), "Everything we've been able to do has been driven by getting the customer on computers."[18] Over the past decade, the company has introduced computer-based goods and services to help it gain an edge with both its suppliers and its customers, an edge that has translated into a distinct advantage over other distributors. These strategic moves run the gamut from those designed to exploit scale and scope economies to growth and alliance maneuvers to expand into new markets. Among the SIS and SIS alliances implemented by McKesson, the following are particularly noteworthy:

CosMcK/Econoscan. CosMcK, a computer-based merchandising program created in 1981 for druggists, supermarkets, and mass merchandisers, helps retailers stock, price-label, rotate, and display merchandise according to marketing reports generated by CosMcK. Covering 20 departments in 1982, it now extends to 28 categories such as over-the-counter drugs, pet care, and school supplies.

Econoscan, a computerized order-entry system, enables a retailer holding an Econoscan scanning device to record data from shelf labels and then to transmit the captured data in the form of an order over telephone lines to a McKesson distribution center, at the rate of 600 items per minute. McKesson fills the order overnight and delivers it the next day in tote boxes arranged to correspond to the various shelf divisions of the retailer's store.

What pharmacist Dick Ramsey from Everett, Washington, says about these services indicates their strategic importance to McKesson:

> The people at McKesson have always gone out of their way to encourage success in business, from the CosMcK service merchandisers who manage my various departments—pet supplies, hair and foot care products, and cosmetics—to their advertising circular program for independent druggists. McKesson has genuinely worked to help me, as an independent businessman, *survive* in an economic climate where a lot of people don't. . . . We probably save a minimum of eight man-hours a week that were once spent ordering and putting away merchandise. Now it's as simple as a quick scan of the shelves with a computerized device that fits right into the palm of my hand. Time is money, and when I can save time, I know I'm increasing my profits.[19]

The value of McKesson's drugstore SIS—developed initially in 1969 at a company warehouse in San Francisco, expanded nationally in the mid-70s, and now grouped together under the name Economost—is equally evident to the firm. According to its vice president for sales, when a pharmacy signed on to the Economost system, "our share of its business immediately doubled or tripled."[20] Sales reps often observed that Economost had such a powerful effect on some druggists that they began to deal exclusively with McKesson. In addition, the firm has been able to reduce the number of its distribution centers from 92 to 52 and shrink its sales force of 601 in the early 70s to 340 in 1987, with sales per rep increasing from $1.4 million to $7 million a year. Other applications (for warehouse management, delinquency payments, and electronic order entry with its suppliers) support Economost systems and give McKesson an integrated, automated distribution operation.

McKesson Chemical. This division, the nation's leading full-line distributor of industrial chemicals, implemented a computer-based service for its customers that saves them costly inspection time and enhances McKesson's image of a high-quality, reliable distributor. At selected chemical distribution centers, McKesson installed highly sensitive instruments to analyze the chemical composition of substances. This ensures, for example, that chemical solvents meet stringent customer standards. The instruments are tied via telephone lines to a McKesson computer at its research center in Dublin, California, so that the data can be interpreted and checked for compliance.

This is another of the many differentiation-based strategic thrusts supported by McKesson's information systems. McKesson Chemical, like the drug and alcoholic beverage division, also offers its customers an on-line order-entry system designed to streamline ordering, inventory control, purchasing, accounts receivable, delivery, and invoicing procedures. For the chemical division, it provides instantaneous information on inventory, customer needs, and the safe handling of the more than 1,000 chemical products it sells. Most likely, economies of scope based on order-entry systems knowhow are at work here.

Pharmaceutical Card System. PCS, a prescription drug claims processing system, led McKesson to spin off a special business unit to exploit its potentialities. Introduced a few years ago, PCS now processes more than 27 million claims from 2.3 million cardholders covering 6.5 million people. Employers issue PCS cards as an employee benefit. More than 45,000 pharmacies, representing more than 80 percent of the nation's retail druggists, fill prescriptions for PCS cardholders. Coverage is offered by 155 insurance companies in the United States and Canada. Data from pharmacists is transmitted to a central McKesson computer for processing. Claims are completed automatically, and tapes are forwarded to third-party reimbursers.

In itself, PCS represents a strategic diversification maneuver. Perhaps even more interesting is the continued expansion of McKesson's PCS operation, symbolizing the power of the company's SIS vision. As claim data is collected by PCS, a special unit, Pharmaceutical Data Services (PDS), uses its software to analyze the data and produce a series of marketing reports targeted at major drug manufacturers, financial institutions, and government agencies. The reports include analyses of prescription drug use, by hospital, nursing care facility, and the like. It is capable of analyzing the flow of pharmaceutical products through the health care system.

In 1983, PCS acquired Dresden/Davis Organization, a medical research company that collects data on drugs prescribed by physicians. This, of course, is now part of PCS's growing database and moves the unit closer to its goal of "becoming a full-service market research company and the nation's leading supplier of health care data."[21]

Acquisition of SKU.   In 1983, McKesson joined Action Industries Inc., a Pittsburgh maker of household and hardware items, in a 50–50 venture in which they acquired SKU Inc., a microcomputer software distributor. The leader in the embryonic micro software industry at the time was Softsel Computer Products (1983 sales estimate, $75 million), followed by Micro D (1983 sales estimate, $28 million), and SKU (1983 sales estimate, $25 million). The market for personal computer software, then at $2.1 billion, was projected to reach $11.7 billion by 1988, with 25 percent handled by independent distributors. It is "the nation's fastest growing distribution business,"[22] the president and chief executive officer of McKesson Corporation claimed in 1983.

Whatever Action's motives, McKesson's aim was clear: to expand the scope of its distribution business and transform the cottage industry of software distribution (with aftertax margins of 4 percent at most) into a larger, more profitable game. McKesson planned to use previously developed information systems as the synergistic fuel for its entry vehicle. The computerized order-entry systems and other proprietary products it provided to over 14,000 mass merchandisers, supermarkets, and other outlets, would be tailored to this new marketplace. These information systems would be used not merely as aids to improve efficiency but as weapons to shape competitive strategy.

"The name of the game," McKesson's CEO said at the time, "has become adding value to distribution. Our primary goal is to set ourselves apart from the competition in dramatic enough ways that we become the first distributor a supplier thinks of. At the other end, by tying your customers to you as tightly as possible, you get more and more of his business as he grows."[23]

With the past as prologue to the future, current and new participants in the software distribution industry could expect McKesson to use its information systems to gain competitive advantage by:

- Establishing on-line links with software suppliers and retailers.
- Providing information to suppliers and retailers to help them better manage inventories, collect and analyze market data, and plan sales campaigns.
- Providing retailers with shelf management plans, price labels, inventory systems, and so on.
- Conducting computer-related technical seminars for suppliers and retailers.
- Joining with software suppliers to develop new products.
- Marketing associated services through its network.

Unfortunately for McKesson and Action, however, this strategic alliance failed. In August 1984, the partners announced they were writing off their combined investment of $8 million and discontinuing the operations of SKU. A spokesman for McKesson said that "the market for computer software hasn't developed as we had anticipated."[24] The parties were unable to stem accelerating losses at SKU.

This second instance of a failed strategic thrust, included to emphasize the point that strategic moves entail considerable risks, shows again that neither information systems support nor shaping nor anything else can guarantee success with certainty. What looked like a promising move failed because market demand was misread.

While this venture failed, another headed for success. In 1983, McKesson purchased 3 P.M., a software developer and marketer of packages for pharmacies and florists. In 1984, McKesson negotiated a pact with the Florists' Transworld Delivery Association. Under the terms of the agreement, McKesson delivers, installs, and maintains personal computers and systems intended to handle a florist's business management functions like payroll and accounts receivable and payable.

Banc One

The final example of a successfully evolving SIS vision involves one of the most innovative and entrepreneurial firms in the financial services industry, Banc One of Columbus, Ohio. John G. McCoy, chief executive officer of this multibank-holding company formed in 1967, retired in 1984 at age 71 after 25 years in that position. When he took the reins at City National Bank (Banc One's forerunner) from his father in 1959, the bank had under $150 million in assets and primarily business customers. Under his leadership, the bank flourished.

With assets of over $7 billion and customers drawn primarily from the consumer sector, Banc One ranked in 1984 in the top 10 among the 100 largest banks in the United States on three commonly acknowledged measures of superior performance. Through an ongoing series of mergers, it controlled 22 affiliate banks in Ohio. For the 16th consecutive year, net income and earnings per share had increased. In the 1980–83 period, net income skyrocketed from $32.8 million to $83.3 million, employees from 3,145 to 6,939, and branch offices from 127 to 314.

These figures represent an extraordinary record of profitability and growth. How can it be explained? Why has Banc One, a relatively small, local bank in 1967, been able to succeed so well in the increasingly competitive financial services industry, where the competition consists not only of banking colossi like Citibank, Chase, and Chemical but also of retail giants like Sears and financial supermarkets like American Express?

While a number of explanations running from luck to charisma have been suggested, I believe that the most convincing account of Banc One's success can be given in terms of its powerful SIS vision—a vision embodied, to be sure, in McCoy, but a vision nevertheless of the integral role to be played by information technology in the bank's strategic evolution.

McCoy, like some of his colleagues, long believed that banks competed at a disadvantage vis-à-vis such omnibus rivals as Sears or American Express. While the latter were free to develop an almost unlimited product portfolio or expand without geographical limit, banks were handcuffed in these two strategic areas by federal and state regulations. Unless banks could find ways around the regulations or get them changed in their favor, they faced the growing prospect of erosion in some of their major business lines.

McCoy's strategic response to these threats was twofold. First, to overcome the geographical expansion constraint, he formed the Banc One holding company, which permitted the acquisition of other banks but not across state lines. Second, to overcome the product development restriction, he encouraged his managers to search for new products that would yield new sources of income and would protect the bank's cash flow stream from exposure to interest-rate fluctuations. Thus, expansions through acquisition and product innovation were two strategic thrusts that Banc One would follow in its strategic journey. Both, it turned out, were precisely the kinds of thrusts that could be supported or shaped by information systems (see Chapters 7 and 9).

McCoy developed his SIS vision early. When he assumed the presidency, one of his first moves was to seek board approval for an annual R&D budget, not to exceed 3 percent of annual profits. He won approval, and every year, Banc One has been able to experiment, primarily in the area of information systems. In 1966, for example, it introduced the first Bank Americard credit card service outside California. In 1967, it initiated a major on-line credit card processing network that today spans over 30 states. In 1971, it joined with IBM in making the first significant test of point-of-sale systems using magnetically encoded cards. In 1980, with others, it conducted the first test of in-home banking through the use of customer TVs and the telephone system.

From the 60s, McCoy realized the importance of information systems in the financial services industry. In a recent interview, he was asked why Banc One was so eager to become the first Bank of America licensee and what made him think it was such a good idea.

> Well, there was some luck involved but you have to remember that was the time when the computer was first beginning to produce important changes in banking. We thought the credit card was an idea whose time had come because of the new computer capability. The first on-line computer systems in banking were designed for credit card authorization. We had one of the first ones here in Columbus. *We committed major efforts to computer development in those early years and we still do today*, I might add. By 1970, to tell you how this *innovation* happens, we began to install the first automatic teller machine equipment in our Upper Arlington branch because we saw it as a way to link the customer, with a plastic card, directly to the computer.[25][Italics added.]

As Banc One's reputation for information system innovation grew, other firms approached it for processing services. In the late 70s, Merrill Lynch contracted with Banc One for data processing and Visa debit card issuance services associated with its new cash management account (CMA) (see Chapter 7). As a result of this SIS alliance, now also negotiated with other brokerage houses, Banc One is one of the nation's three largest Visa processors.

The primary vehicle to expand Banc One's processing services—related chiefly to credit and debit card processing outside Ohio banking markets, and producing more than 30 percent of the corporation's net income—is the Financial Card Services Division. This spinoff has had an impressive growth record.

> In 1983 the cardholder account base processed by Financial Card Services grew by 41.3 percent to over 3.9 million. Of these accounts, 14 percent were Banc One affiliate banks' customers and 7 percent were Banc One customers originating from outside our market area, while 79 percent were derived from third-party processing for other banks, thrifts, credit unions, finance companies, and brokers. Financial Card Services revenue grew 26 percent in 1983. This resulted from growth in Banc One customer accounts and in third-party processing contracts originated within the last several years. The relatively more mature Merrill Lynch processing program generated a 4 percent revenue increase in 1983.
>
> Late in 1983 a new four-year contract was negotiated with Merrill Lynch relating to Banc One's processing of its "CMA" brokerage accounts. This was the third contract Banc One . . . had with Merrill Lynch since 1977 when Banc One was selected to be the processor for this revolutionary financial product. Although this contract permitted Merrill Lynch the option of converting to internal processing of the CMA debit cards, Banc One would receive consulting fees from Merrill Lynch for assisting in this conversion.[26]

When Merrill announced soon after the signing that it would act on the option to do its own processing, Banc One's stock price dropped 15 percent. But the bank responded swiftly to the loss of this business (1.3 million accounts) by cutting a deal with Comp–U–Card International (CUC), a consumer purchasing service (see below), whereby it gained 1.2 million new credit card accounts.

While credit and debit card processing is important to Banc One's overall strategic scheme, it is the centralization of bank processing activities that has enabled the holding company to make its acquisition program work.

A small bank sees in the Banc One affiliation (read: acquisition) proposition an opportunity to cope with the accelerating changes in financial services that would otherwise engulf it—new regulations, the prospect of interstate banking, interest-rate deregulation, and perhaps the most critical, new technology demands induced by the convergence of information processing and telecommunications.

For Banc One, its acquisition program—called the "Uncommon Partnership" because it allows the acquired bank a reasonable degree of independence—enables it to reap large economies of scale. Listen to McCoy on this partnership:

> More recently the "Uncommon Partnership" represents our chosen way of managing the holding company even though we could merge everything into a single bank. Instead, each bank is run by bankers from that area; each trying to be sensitive to community needs. As a result, a lot of our management strength and certainly the growth and earnings potential, lies with our affiliates. *We have limited the concentration of management to those areas that are most sensitive to economies of scale such as data processing* or the handling of investments. I expect this philosophy will remain for some time into the future.[27] [Italics added.]

Thus, Banc One uses the strategic cost thrust (see Chapter 6) to shape its competitive strategy of growth via acquisition. In the case of a recent affiliation, according to another officer at Banc One, "We were able to save almost a million dollars a year in combined operating expenses by converting the affiliates' data processing systems into our single system. There are some real *economies of scale* at work here."[28] [Italics added.]

Banc One also forged an innovative strategic alliance with Comp–U–Card, a computerized shopping and below-retail buying service (see Chapter 7). The two partners created Super Visa, a credit card issued by Banc One that CUC offered as bait to lure new customers. The card carries a $1,000 line of credit and can be used to buy consumer goods (watches, washing machines, and the like) through CUC. Under the terms of the agreement between Banc One and CUC, customers pay an annual fee of $25 for the card and the shopping service package. This is split 50–50 between the two partners. On purchases that roll over, Banc One assessed (in 1984) a 21.6 percent annual rate.

This SIS alliance served CUC's purpose of enhancing its offering to customers and forgoing the risk and expense associated with starting its own credit card system. For Banc One, the alliance increased the bank's credit card account base by 100 percent. This proved to be particularly profitable, as CUC's customers tended to let their accounts roll over to a greater extent than Banc One's other cardholders.

When John G. McCoy retired at the end of 1984, Banc One's strategic course was set. As a senior vice president put it, "We're interested in building our bank into a mega-regional organization, and we think others will want to do likewise. . . . In the 1990s we'll see some mega-regionals getting together to form banks that will be competitive with Citibank and Chase Manhattan."[29] By 1987 Banc One reached $17 billion in assets.

Under the new leadership of John B. McCoy, who succeeded his father and represents the third generation of McCoys to head the bank, it has continued to pioneer in banking automation. In its newly remodeled Kingsdale, Ohio, branch, customers enter an actual financial supermarket where they can "deposit money, sell their homes, buy insurance, make travel plans, buy or sell stocks, and open trusts."[30] Information technology supports each of these activities. In its Columbus, Ohio, branch, the bank experiments with interactive video and advanced ATMs developed by a leading vendor, Diebold Inc. "We're pushing to see just how much the customer is willing to take in automation," a Diebold spokesman said.[31]

A Banc One customer planning to open a Keogh retirement account sits before a computer terminal at the bank. When the new account menu appears on the screen, the customer touches the square marked "Keogh." This triggers replacement of the menu by a short video program explaining the account. It includes a series of questions that can be answered by touching the appropriate square on the screen or by typing the information at the keyboard. When completed, the computer directs the customer to another banking area to receive the printed application form and confer with an account representative poised to answer any further questions and obtain a signature.

Leslie Wexner, a member of the board of directors and CEO of The Limited, an innovative clothing chain known for its strategic use of information technology (see Chapter 8), suggested even further changes for Banc One's main Columbus branch. His proposal would turn it "into a glittering, two story showcase [with] whirring machines that count coins and sort checks in the front window."[32]

The results of these experiments are not all in. But some look promising. At the Upper Arlington branch, which has adopted the financial boutique look, deposits are up 15 percent since the "strategic" renovation.

For Banc One, McKesson, and Dun & Bradstreet, SIS vision functions as a creative force transforming the organization through strategic moves supported or shaped by information technology. Other enterprises—AMR, Citicorp, Federal Express, and General Electric's Information System Company (Geisco), to list a few discussed in this book—also possess successful SIS visions. Each comprehends, in its fashion, the strategic importance of information technology.

But neither the possession of an SIS vision nor the operation of a profitable SIS guarantees strategic success. To appreciate this point, consider the case of Allegis Corp., known prior to 1987 as United Air Lines or UAL Inc. In 1985, UAL acquired Hertz Corp. from RCA. This acquisition produced a $9 billion conglomerate comprising United Air, Hertz rental cars, and the Westin hotel chain. To explain this move, United's CEO Richard Ferris "began touting his vision of a three-part travel empire linked by his expansive Apollo computer network,"[33] intended to exploit synergies among the divisions.

Shortly after the purchase of Hertz, Ferris said that "he might spend up to $1 billion on Apollo over the next five years."[34] He contemplated "a future in which thousands of travel agents around the world perch in front of computer screens coordinating reservations for his airline, hotel, and rental car operations, [a world in which] his greatest advantage could come later, if the economics of the business persuade him to bypass travel agents and go directly to corporations with discounted, full-service packages that no one else can match."[35]

Ferris's strategic dream turned into a nightmare in 1987 when, after four quarters of earnings totaling less than 1 percent of revenues, Allegis found itself a takeover target. An impatient and strategically skeptical group of investors wouldn't wait for the promised travel empire synergies to arrive. Ferris resigned, and Allegis's board fought off the invaders only by agreeing to sell both Hertz and Westin. The daring SIS vision that seemed to make so much sense (at least to Ferris) in 1985, a vision shaped by a highly successful SIS application (Apollo), was no match for the far stronger forces allied against it.

SIS visions, like SIS, may succeed or fail. But whatever the final assessment in a particular case, the existence of such visions or systems should, after the evidence presented in this chapter, no longer be in doubt. Yet, if one views information systems from a conventional planning and control point of view, only two varieties are visible: MIS and MSS. Like Western astronomers blinded by their religious beliefs to the existence of a vast array of planetary phenomena, those in the thrall of the conventional perspective lack the vision to see the SIS opportunities and threats that fall forever beyond their line of sight.

We need to examine the conventional perspective in some detail to appreciate its power and see how it prevented researchers, practitioners, and others from focusing their attention on SIS. Once this conceptual ground has been covered in Chapter 2, we shall be in a position to build an alternative, complementary view: the strategic. This perspective, and the analytical framework supporting it (see Chapter 4), can help enterprises identify SIS and guide—with sensitivity to potential risks and rewards—their SIS planning and management efforts (see Chapters 10 and 11). By adopting a strategic perspective, by viewing information technology through another lens, one discovers the new SIS world and can explore it systematically for opportunities and threats.

NOTES

1. Richard Nolan, "The Plight of the EDP Manager," *Harvard Business Review*, May–June 1973.
2. Stanley Wohl, *The Medical Industrial Complex* (New York: Crown Publishers, 1984).
3. Lisa Belkin, "Computers Cross-Checking Use of Medicines," *New York Times*, July 21, 1984.
4. "American Rediscovers Itself," *New York Times*, August 23, 1982.
5. Howard Banks, "The Start of a Revolt," *Forbes*, October 7, 1985.
6. "Information Users Own the Future, Keynote Says," *Conference Call, National Computer Conference*, Summer 1986.
7. Eric Schmitt, "The Art of Devising Air Fares," *New York Times*, March 4, 1987.
8. "Now Airlines Are Diversifying by Sticking to What They Know Best," *Business Week*, May 7, 1984.
9. Paulette Thomas, "Airlines Launch New Bid to Lure Frequent Flyers," *The Wall Street Journal*, May 28, 1987.
10. Peter Marx, "The Legal Risks of Using Information as a Competitive Weapon," *Information Management Review* 2, no. 4 (Spring, 1987).
11. Dun & Bradstreet, Annual Report, 1979.
12. Ibid.
13. Stuart Gannes, "Dun & Bradstreet Redeploys the Riches," *Fortune*, August 19, 1985.
14. Claudia Deutsch, "The Battle to Wire the Consumer," *New York Times*, July 26, 1987.
15. Anne W. Studabaker, "Why Companies Are Crazy about DunsPlus," *Management Technology*, July 1984.
16. "McKesson Officers Named to New Jobs in a Restructuring," *The Wall Street Journal*, November 20, 1986.
17. McKesson, 1983 Annual Report, pp. 2–3.
18. David Wessel, "Computer Finds a Role in Buying and Selling, Reshaping Businesses," *The Wall Street Journal*, March 18, 1987.
19. McKesson, 1983 Annual Report, p. 7.
20. Joan O'C. Hamilton and Catherine Harris, "For Drug Distributors, Information Is the Rx for Survival," *Business Week*, October, 14, 1985.
21. Foremost-McKesson, 1983 Annual Report.
22. Thomas Hayes, "Parceling Out the Software," *New York Times*, December 14, 1983.

23. McKesson, 1983 Annual Report.

24. "Action Industries Inc., McKesson Write Off SKU Inc. Investment," *The Wall Street Journal*, July 23, 1984.

25. Banc One, Annual Report, 1983, p. 21.

26. Ibid., pp. 3–4.

27. Ibid., p. 23.

28. Steven Greenhouse, "Midwest Bank Focus: Growth," *New York Times*, February 17, 1986.

29. Eric Berg, "Banc One Stretches Borders," *New York Times*, July 7, 1986.

30. Ibid.

31. Steve Weiner, "Banks Hire Retailing Consultants for Help in Becoming Financial-Products 'Stores'," *The Wall Street Journal*, May 20, 1986.

32. Kenneth Labich, "How Dick Ferris Blew It," *Fortune*, July 6, 1987.

33. Ibid.

34. Kenneth Labich, "United Is Changing Its Flight Plan," *Fortune*, September 30, 1985.

35. Ibid.

CASE REFERENCES

Metpath

"Has Metpath Diagnosed a Winner?" *Business Week,* January 25, 1982.

Lisa Belkin. "Computers Cross-Checking Use of Medicines." *New York Times,* July 21, 1984.

American Air

"American Rediscovers Itself." *Business Week,* August 23, 1982.

"Do Airlines Play Fair with Their Computers?" *Business Week,* August 23, 1982.

Agis Salpukas. "Changing American's Rules." *New York Times,* April 29, 1984.

"Now Airlines Are Diversifying by Sticking to What They Know Best." *Business Week,* May 7, 1984.

Si Dunn. "Super Sabre." *American Way,* September 1984.

Irwin Molotsky. "Airlines Dispute Computer Systems' Fairness." *New York Times,* March 21, 1985.

Christopher Conte. "Three Airlines to Drop Feature on Flight Listings." *The Wall Street Journal,* March 28, 1985.

John Paul Newport, Jr. "Frequent-Flyer Clones." *Fortune,* April 29, 1985.

Mitch Betts. "Justice Monitoring Bias in Airline Reservation Systems." *Computerworld,* May 1, 1985.

"Airlines Propose Creating 'Neutral' Booking System." *The Wall Street Journal,* June 24, 1985.

Peter Petre. "How to Keep Customers Happy Captives." *Fortune,* September 2, 1985.

Howard Banks. "The Start of a Revolt." *Forbes,* October 7, 1985.

Catherine Harris. "Information Power." *Business Week,* October 14, 1985.

Thomas Hayes. "American Joins the Low-Cost Ranks." *New York Times,* December 8, 1985.

"Information Users Own the Future, Keynote Says." *Conference Call, National Computer Conference,* Summer 1986.

"Pan Am Will Become User of American's Computerized System." *New York Times,* April 23, 1986.

David Ludlum. "Pan Am Exploring DP Sharing with American Airlines Group." *Computerworld,* May 5, 1986.

Robert Buday. "Sabre Gives the Edge to American Airlines." *InformationWeek,* May 26, 1986.

Agis Salpukas. "Delta Air Accuses American." *New York Times,* June 17, 1986.

"Delta Charges American Air with Bias." *The Wall Street Journal,* June 17, 1986.

Eaasy Sabre advertisement. *American Way,* September 16, 1986.

"AMR Airline Automation Names Grossman President." *Computerworld,* September 22, 1986.

Kenneth Labich. "Bob Crandall Soars by Flying Solo." *Fortune,* September 29, 1986.

Paulette Thomas. "Computers Permit Airlines to Use Scalpel to Cut Fares." *The Wall Street Journal,* February 2, 1987.

Laurie McGinley. "U.S. Probes Airline Reservation Systems over Complaints They Curb Competition." *The Wall Street Journal,* February 3, 1987.

Eric Schmitt. "The Art of Devising Air Fares." *New York Times,* March 4, 1987.

"AMR's American Air Accuses Texas Air of Unfair Practices." *The Wall Street Journal, May 27, 1987.*

Paulette Thomas. "Airlines Launch New Bid to Lure Frequent Flyers." *The Wall Street Journal*, May 28, 1987.

Randall Smith. "AMR's Outlook Is Clouded as Competition Erodes Profit of Airline Unit's Sabre System." *The Wall Street Journal*, May 28, 1987.

Catherine Harris, Jo Ellen Davis, and James Ellis. "A Shoving Match in the Travel Agency." *Business Week*, June 22, 1987.

Paul Schindler, Jr. "AA Leverages Its Expertise with Expanded DP Subsidiary." *InformationWeek*, June 22, 1987.

Peter Marx. "The Legal Risks of Using Information as a Competitive Weapon." *Information Management Review* 2, no. 4 (1987).

Citicorp

Julie Salamon. "Citicorp's Big Push into Automatic Tellers and Higher Charges Finally Turns a Profit." *The Wall Street Journal*, April 30, 1982.

Daniel Hertzberg. "Some Bankers Would Like to Open a Branch in Your Home or Office." *The Wall Street Journal*, December 2, 1983.

"Now Merchants Can Learn More about Charge Customers." *Business Week*, March 19, 1984.

"Citicorp Plans to Move into Texas Market for Financial Services." *The Wall Street Journal*, May 4, 1984.

Monci Jo Williams. "The Great Plastic Card Fight Begins." *Fortune*, February 4, 1985.

Daniel Hertzberg. "Citicorp Is Testing 'a Small, Portable' Banking Terminal." *The Wall Street Journal*, April 11, 1985.

Phillip Zweig. "Citicorp Chairman Avoids Wholesale Change." *The Wall Street Journal*, July 3, 1985.

Michael Sesit. "Citibank Interested in Expanding Role in Japan." *The Wall Street Journal*, December 27, 1985.

Robert Bennett. "John Reed's Calming of Citicorp." *New York Times,* February 2, 1986.

"Citicorp Makes Move to Purchase Quotron." *New York Times,* March, 19, 1986.

Charmaine Harris. "Citi's Interest in ATMs Paid Off." *InformationWeek,* May 26, 1986.

Eric Berg. "Supermarket Machines to Take Citicorp Cards." *New York Times,* June 28, 1986.

Sarah Bartlett. "How Citi Is Playing It Cool with Quotron." *Business Week,* December 8, 1986.

IBM/Merrill Lynch (Imnet)

Dennis Kneale and Scott McMurray. "Merrill Lynch and IBM Unveil Venture to Deliver Stock-Quote Data to IBM PCs." *The Wall Street Journal,* March 22, 1984.

"IBM, Merrill Lynch Set Financial Service." *Computerworld,* March 26, 1984.

"A Souped-Up Ticker Tape from IBM and Merrill Lynch." *Business Week,* April 2, 1984.

"IBM and Merrill Lynch Pick a Name, President for Stock-Data Service." *The Wall Street Journal,* May 17, 1984.

"McGraw-Hill to Widen Financial Service with Monchik-Weber Buy." *Information Systems News,* September 10, 1984.

John Marcom, Jr. "Automatic Data Says Its Statistical Service Is Off and Running." *The Wall Street Journal,* September 19, 1984.

Tom Lawton. "Imnet Takes the Field." *Datamation,* May 1, 1985.

John Marcom, Jr. "Electronic Market-Data Delivery Expands beyond Simple Stock-Quote Terminals." *The Wall Street Journal,* June 19, 1985.

John Marcom, Jr. "IBM, Merrill Lynch Stock-Quote Service

Cuts Sales Effort." *The Wall Street Journal,* September 4, 1985.

Michelle Louzoun. "IBM and Merrill Lynch Dissolve Plans for Stock-Quote Service." *InformationWeek,* January 12, 1987.

Alan Alper. "IBM, Merrill Lynch to Close Imnet Financial Services Venture." *InformationWeek,* January 12, 1987.

Dun & Bradstreet

Johanna Ambrosia. "Fortune 1000 Are Target of D&B PC Push." *Computerworld,* September 5, 1983.

Johanna Ambrosia. "D&B PC Merges Public DBs, OA." *Computerworld,* November 21, 1983.

"Unprejudiced Electronic Edition Helps Consumers." *Software News,* November 1983.

"Dun & Bradstreet Agrees to Buy A. C. Nielsen Co." *The Wall Street Journal,* May 18, 1984.

Sandra Salmans. "Dun and Nielsen: Compatible Goals." *New York Times,* May 21, 1984.

"D&B Widens Its Data Net in Europe." *Business Week,* May 28, 1984.

Anne Studabaker. "Why Companies Are Crazy about Duns-Plus." *Management Technology,* July 1984.

John Marcom, Jr. "Dun & Bradstreet Picks C. W. Moritz to Succeed Drake." *The Wall Street Journal,* September 20, 1984.

"Dun & Bradstreet Fills 2 Top Posts." *New York Times,* September 20, 1984.

Eric Arnum. "DunsPlus Adds Micro-to-Mainframe Links for IBM PC XT Line." *CommunicationWeek,* October 8, 1984.

Michael Blumstein, "Dun & Bradstreet's New Boss: Charles Moritz." *New York Times,* October 14, 1984.

"Dun in Deal for Cook Unit." *The Wall Street Journal,* November 7, 1984.

Mel Mandell. "M&D Adds to D&B's Muscle in DP." *Computer Decisions,* 1985.

Donna Raimondi. "M&D Acquires RSSP, Aims to Expand Product Offerings." *Computerworld,* April 15, 1985.

"Dun & Bradstreet Buys Tulsa Directory Publisher." *CommunicationWeek,* May 6, 1985.

"DunsPlus Tool Kit Debuts, Aids Software Customization." *Computerworld,* May 27, 1985.

Stuart Gannes. "Dun & Bradstreet Redeploys the Riches." *Fortune,* August 19, 1985.

William Martorelli. "Can D&B Computing Get Back in the 4th-Generation Race?" *InformationWeek,* October 18, 1985.

William Martorelli. "M&D Is Still Dodging the Industry Slump." *InformationWeek,* January 27, 1986.

Richard Layne. "Credit D&B's Systems for Strategic Success." *InformationWeek,* May 26, 1986.

Peter Contino. Research paper on A. C. Nielsen prepared for a course on the strategic use of information technology. Columbia University Graduate School of Business, 1987.

Claudia Deutsch. "The Battle to Wire the Consumer." *New York Times,* July 26, 1987.

McKesson

"Foremost-McKesson: The Computer Moves Distribution to Center Stage." *Business Week,* December 7, 1981.

McKesson, annual reports, 1982, 1983.

Judy Chi. "McKesson at Turning Point." *Drug Topics,* June 20, 1983.

Anthony Bianco. "McKesson's New Freedom Spurs a Shopping Spree." *Business Week,* October 24, 1983.

Victor Zonana. "McKesson's to Buy Software Distributor, Marking Debut in Fast-Growing Business." *The Wall Street Journal,* October 24, 1983.

Thomas Hayes. "Parceling Out the Software." *New York Times,* December 14, 1983.

Eric Larson. "Many Firms Seek Entry into Software." *The Wall Street Journal,* January 6, 1984.

"McKesson Corp. Buys Rawson Drug & Sundry for Undisclosed Sum." *The Wall Street Journal,* January 24, 1984.

"McKesson Disbands Foods Group, Will Sell Two Remaining Units." *The Wall Street Journal,* January 26, 1984.

"McKesson Plans to Buy Division of Champion International Corp." *The Wall Street Journal,* April 6, 1984.

Juli Cortino and Ellen Peck. "For McKesson, Computers Are the Magic in Profit Margins." *Management Technology,* July 1984.

"Action Industries Inc., McKesson Write Off SKU Inc. Investment." *The Wall Street Journal,* July 23, 1984.

N. R. Kleinfield. "For Wholesalers, a New Look." *New York Times,* August 26, 1984.

"McKesson Corp. Acquires American Legal Systems Inc." *The Wall Street Journal,* October 17, 1984.

Joan O'C. Hamilton and Catherine Harris. "For Drug Distributors, Information Is the Rx for Survival." *Business Week,* October 14, 1985.

Paul Schindler, Jr. "McKesson Is Thriving, Thanks to Economost." *InformationWeek,* May 26, 1986.

"McKesson Officers Named to New Jobs in a Restructuring." *The Wall Street Journal,* November 20, 1986.

David Wessel. "Computer Finds a Role in Buying and Selling, Reshaping Businesses." *The Wall Street Journal,* March 18, 1987.

Banc One

Banc One, annual reports, 1981, 1982, and 1983.

John Helyar. "Regional Banks Search for a Niche in Face of

New Rules, Competition." *The Wall Street Journal*, February 4, 1982.

Damon Darlin. "Home-Banking Network Due in Florida in September, but Costs May Limit Appeal." *The Wall Street Journal*, February 23, 1983.

"ATM Sharing: How Much Is Too Much?" *ABA Banking Journal*, December 1983.

Steve Cocheo. "Joint Marketing Builds Card Volume." *ABA Banking Journal*, December 1983.

Jolie Solomon. "Banc One to Stop Some Processing for Merrill Lynch." *The Wall Street Journal*, December 21, 1983.

"Banc One Doesn't Need Merrill Lynch." *Business Week*, January 16, 1984.

Paul Ingrassia. "Under Its New Chief, Banc One Is Seeking Other Innovative Ways to Sell Its Products." *The Wall Street Journal*, April 24, 1984.

Bernard Wysocki. "The Chief's Personality Can Have a Big Impact—For Better or Worse." *The Wall Street Journal*, September 11, 1984.

Claire Ansberry. "Bank of Future: More Services and Less Service." *The Wall Street Journal*, June 11, 1985.

Steven Greenhouse. "Midwest Bank Focus: Growth." *New York Times*, February 17, 1986.

Claire Ansberry and Jeff Bailey. "Banc One Sets Pact to Acquire Banking Firm." *The Wall Street Journal*, May 8, 1986.

Steve Weiner. "Banks Hire Retailing Consultants for Help in Becoming Financial-Products 'Stores.' " *The Wall Street Journal*, May 20, 1986.

Jerome Colonna. "Holding Firm Banks on Several Systems." *InformationWeek*, May 26, 1986.

Claire Ansberry. "Banc One's McCoy Lauded for Keeping Profit Strong during Acquisition Drive." *The Wall Street Journal*, May 27, 1986.

Eric Berg. "Banc One Stretches Borders." *New York Times,* July 7, 1986.

Constance Mitchell and Jeff Bailey. "Marine Corp. Board Agrees to Purchase by Banc One Despite Rival's Higher Bid." *The Wall Street Journal,* July 27, 1987.

United Air (Allegis)

Judith Valente, Laurie Cohen, and Scott Kilman. "Canceled Flight: Allegis Shakeup Came as Shareholder Ire Put Board Tenure in Doubt." *The Wall Street Journal,* June 11, 1984.

Kenneth Labich. "United Is Changing Its Flight Plan." *Fortune,* September 30, 1985.

Diana ben-Aaron. "United Gets a Lift from Apollo System." *InformationWeek,* May 26, 1986.

David Ludlum. "Merger Skies Unfriendly." *Computerworld,* June 15, 1987.

Judith Dobrznski. "Allegis Will Live On—In the Nightmares of CEOs." *Business Week,* June 29, 1987.

Kenneth Labich. "How Dick Ferris Blew It." *Fortune,* July 6, 1987.

2

The Conventional Perspective

To understand the conventional perspective on information technology and to appreciate the hold it has had for almost two decades, one needs to examine its roots and the conceptual landmarks that have sustained it. These sources of growth reflect intellectual efforts made by a tightly knit community dedicated to explicating the fundamental concepts of information systems.

From this examination, a coherent pattern emerges. The conventional perspective, I shall show, is based on Robert Anthony's paradigm (conceptual framework) for planning and control systems, developed in 1965 and applied in the information management field by William Zani in 1970. Zani's work spotlighted areas in need of more penetrating analysis. In the 70s and 80s, academics and others working on the conceptual foundation of information systems explored in greater depth topics merely mentioned in passing by Zani. Anthony Gorry, Michael Scott Morton, and Peter Keen focused on systems designed especially for managerial decision making; Richard Nolan, IBM planners, William King, and John Rockart concentrated on information systems planning topics; Rockart and Michael Treacy specialized in systems targeted for top managers.

In each of these explorations and in countless others undertaken by members of the rapidly expanding band of information management professionals, Anthony's paradigm looms large. For these are the efforts of community members to articulate the planning and control model.

After describing Anthony's paradigm, I shall trace its application in the information management field from 1970 to 1984 and its articulation in three of the most important information systems areas: decision support systems, executive information systems, and information systems planning. These are critical areas because they guide the methodical search for information system investment opportunities and determine the allocation of an organization's scarce system development resources.

ANTHONY'S PARADIGM

Professor Anthony's *Planning and Control Systems: A Framework for Analysis* has gone through a dozen printings since its publication in 1965. Its success confirms the prescient opinion of Bertrand Fox, the former director of research at the Harvard Business School, who wrote in the foreword to the first edition:

> This statement of a *conceptual framework* for the study of planning and control systems can be expected to have an important effect on later analytical studies undertaken at the school. The basic purpose of this volume is not to report research findings themselves but to set forth *a framework which will influence the conduct of research* in the broad area of planning and control systems.[1] [Italics added.]

When the book appeared, at least two of Anthony's colleagues were using the framework in research projects, and several graduate students had incorporated it into their dissertations. Anthony himself hoped that his conceptual grid would aid not only researchers and students but also those who designed and used such systems.

During the past 20 years, Anthony's schema achieved paradigm status, taking root first in the soil of management planning and control and spreading later to adjacent fields as well. Before tracing its application and articulation in the information management area, I shall highlight its salient features.

Prior to proposing the framework, it appears that Anthony viewed the realm of planning and control systems in much the same ways as a thoroughbred handicapper with an analytical bent might see his chosen domain—as one in which there are "scarcely any generally accepted principles, and everyone in the field, therefore, works by intuition and folklore."[2] But unlike the handicapper, Anthony addressed a field amenable to analytical persuasion. To reduce its intellectual chaos, he proposed a framework that has become, for some, the "holy trinity" of planning and control:

- *Strategic planning:* The process of deciding on objectives of the organization, on changes in those objectives, on the resources used to attain those objectives, and on the policies that are to govern the acquisition, use, and disposition of those resources.
- *Management control:* The process by which managers assure that resources are obtained and used effectively and efficiently in the accomplishment of the organization's objectives.
- *Operational control:* The process of assuring that specific tasks are carried out effectively and efficiently.

According to Anthony these three processes tend to form a hierarchy, with strategic planning at the top and operational control at the bottom, along a variety of dimensions: *time* (long-range, medium-range, day-to-day), *organizational level* (top management, top and operating management, supervisory management), *degree of judgment* (great, some, none), *importance of decisions* (major, medium, minor), and so on.

Planning and control systems facilitate the processes with which they are associated; they are the means by which the processes occur. Such systems are intended to help managers make, implement, and control decisions. A strategic planning system designer, for example, might organize the process through which line managers work to resolve strategic issues. This should not be confused with a computer-based system (incorporating a model of the firm) used by strategic planners to explore alternative scenarios.

Strategic planning is the process of determining organizational objectives and policies. It is concerned with major decisions (e.g., diversification, acquisition, "resizing") having long-term consequences. Management control has to do with the ongoing operations of the enterprise, adhering as best it can to guidelines established through the strategic planning process. In operational control, the emphasis switches from more general issues to individual tasks and transactions: scheduling or controlling jobs through a shop, procuring certain items of inventory, and so on. Many of the activities subject to operational control are programmable—that is, capable of being formulated in terms of well-defined rules that could, in theory, be represented by a computer program.

The control aspects of strategic planning include top management's need to monitor staff progress on issues outstanding, to appraise the performance of those involved in the process, and to determine whether agreed-upon strategies are being implemented. This kind of control is usually neither systematic nor objective, since standards of comparison are difficult to formulate.

In the process of management control, line managers take center stage. Their judgments

> are incorporated in the approved operating plans, and they are the persons who must influence others and whose performance is measured. Staff people collect, summarize, and present information that is useful in this process, and they make calculations that translate management judgments into the numbers that appear on the budget. . . . The decisions, which are the important part of the whole process, are made by the line, not the staff.[3]

The focus of operational control differs substantially from the other two processes in the trinity. For one thing, "the system itself is a much more important part of the process."[4] stating, as it often does, the action to be taken and sometimes even making the decision. "With a properly designed system, operational control will require a minimum of management intervention."[5] But operational control systems are not necessarily simple or restricted activities. Production-scheduling systems for General Motors, for example, would involve worldwide networks of plants, parts, suppliers, and so on.

APPLYING ANTHONY'S PARADIGM

In "Blueprint for MIS," a six-page article perhaps best known for its broad scope, William Zani addresses the question, How should top management think about management information systems (MIS)? Appearing in the November–December 1970 issue of the *Harvard Business Review* (five years after Anthony's *Planning and Control Systems*), this brief piece represents the first widely circulated application of Anthony's paradigm in the information management field.

Zani, an assistant professor of business administration at the Harvard Business School, where he specialized in computer systems, was concerned about the failure of traditional MIS to meet the information needs of managers. As he saw it, most MIS were not designed according to a well-conceived plan but rather emerged, ad hoc, from the bowels of the business. They were spinoffs, by-products, that formed a "crazy quilt of residues from automated clerical procedures"[6] and generated far more paper and frustration than valuable managerial information. If the long-heralded promise of MIS was to be realized, a new approach to information systems design was needed, a top-down method "to focus on the critical tasks and decisions made within an organization and to provide the kind of information that the manager needs to perform those tasks and make those decisions."[7]

Zani's blueprint for improved MIS design centers on managerial decision making, on the problem of how to identify the information needs of managers. The only way to solve this problem, Zani suggests, is to isolate the organization's major decisions and the information they require. What are these decisions? Precisely the ones that fall within Anthony's holy trinity of planning and control processes.

Guided by an awareness of organizational objectives, strategy, and critical success factors, the Zanian information system designer analyzes the "company's decision-making patterns in strategic planning, management control, and organizational control." Through this process, the designer will uncover the organization's critical information needs and identify MIS opportunities to satisfy them.

Consider, for instance, the planning area. Zani claims:

> The implications of corporate strategy for MIS design have largely escaped attention. Strategy should exercise a critical influence on information systems design. . . . If a company changes its strategy so that its MIS focuses on factors no longer relevant—if now it urgently needs cash flow data, say, when it formerly needed sales data, then the system is no longer valuable. Strategy dictates firm, explicit objectives for systems design.[8]

Zani's views here are typical of conventionalists like King (see below) who believe that corporate strategy should determine system design objectives and that the organization's information systems plan should be aligned with its strategy. But with their vision channeled by the boundaries of Anthony's paradigm, they look only for system opportunities to support managerial decision making, opportunities falling exclusively within the holy trinity of planning and control processes. What they discern on the information system horizon is what they expect to find: conventional management support systems.

Zani recognizes the existence of two types of information system: (1) those automating clerical operations and (2) those supplying decision-making information to managers. He calls Type 2 "management information systems" and leaves Type 1 unnamed. In terms of my taxonomy (see the appendix to this chapter), Type 2 should be understood as instances of management support systems and Type 1 as management information systems. This terminological discrepancy is a bit confusing because Zani wrote in 1970, before information systems varieties had been more clearly differentiated. (In 1971, Gorry and Scott Morton (see below) introduced a new framework in which Zani's MIS, following what was quickly becoming common usage, would be classed as decision support systems.)

DECISION SUPPORT SYSTEMS

In 1971, the Massachusetts Institute of Technology's *Sloan Management Review* published "A Framework for Management Information Systems," written by Gorry and Scott Morton. Both were faculty members at MIT and part of the growing information management community, the latter a recent graduate of the Harvard Business School whose dissertation dealt with the subject of management decision systems. Aware as they must have been of Anthony's paradigm and Zani's application of it in the information management field, Gorry and Scott Morton, unlike their predecessors, were concerned explicitly with *how* information systems could have a greater impact on managerial decision making.

To address this problem, they focused first on describing organizational activities in terms of the type of decision involved. This done, they then proposed a new conceptual grid for screening computer application opportunities. Whereas Zani had been content to suggest a better design approach to cope with the failure of MIS to fulfill their promise, Gorry and Scott Morton advocated a far more radical alternative, dividing information system opportunities into two distinct kinds: *structured decision systems*—which they claimed encompassed "almost all of what has been called management information systems (MIS) in the literature—an area that has had almost nothing to do with real managers or information but has been largely routine data processing"[9] (e.g., accounts receivable, inventory control, and order entry)—and *decision support systems* (DSS).

How, then, did Gorry and Scott Morton define DSS? At this point, the reader should not be surprised to learn that they appealed to Anthony's holy trinity for support. But they did more than this. They combined Anthony's paradigm with concepts introduced by Herbert Simon when he investigated the decision-making process. For Simon, "decisions are *programmed* to the extent that they are repetitive and routine, to the extent that a definite procedure has been worked out for handling them so that they don't have to be treated de novo each time they occur. . . . Decisions are *nonprogrammed* to the extent that they are novel, unstructured, and consequential."[10] Gorry and Scott Morton use "structured" and "unstructured" in place of "programmed" and "nonprogrammed" to avoid associations with computers and to encourage links to problem-solving activities.

By combining Anthony's holy trinity of management activities and their own variations of Simon's decision types, Gorry and Scott Morton define DSS as information systems that support either semi- or unstructured decisions made in the areas of strategic planning, management control, and operational control. For them, "information systems should exist only to support decisions," and therefore, understanding managerial decision making "is a prerequisite for effective systems design and implementation."[11]

Although Gorry and Scott Morton were the first to define this new species of information system, the promise of DSS wasn't realized until the late 70s and early 80s. Advances in information processing technology, coupled with the further expansion and dissemination of the DSS concept by Keen and Scott Morton in their 1978 book *Decision Support Systems: An Organizational Perspective,* paved the way.

Keen and Scott Morton modified the original definition of DSS somewhat by restricting the decisions to be supported to the semistructured. But they continued to use Anthony's paradigm in their information system framework. They also made their characterization of DSS more concrete by pointing out four levels of support. DSS could provide (1) access to data, (2) filters for data selection and sorting, (3) simple calculations, comparisons, and projections, and (4) decision-making models. At each level, the system used is assumed to be, unlike the typical MIS, under the control of the manager.

Gorry and Scott Morton recognize the existence of two kinds of information systems: structured decision systems (roughly coextensive, they claim, with MIS) and decision support systems. They note that other kinds of computer applications including "straightforward data handling with no decisions"[12] are possible, citing payroll as an example. Keen and Scott Morton, writing in 1978, observe that the term *MIS* "means different things to different people, and there is no generally accepted definition recognized by those working in the field."[13] Data processing professionals, for instance (according to the authors), count "payroll and accounts receivable programs and other clerical data processing activities"[14] as MIS.

In terms of the taxonomy introduced in Chapter 1 and described more fully in the appendix to this chapter, decision support systems are a species of management support systems; structured decision systems and data handling applications are instances of management information systems.

EXECUTIVE INFORMATION SYSTEMS

In "The CEO Goes On-Line," published in the January–February 1982 issue of the *Harvard Business Review,* Rockart and Treacy announced "the emergence in a number of companies of a new kind of executive information support (or 'EIS') system." In a 1981 paper on this topic, "Executive Information Systems," they (like their intellectual progenitors, Zani and Gorry and Scott Morton) had voiced concern about the failure of existing systems to satisfy the information needs of managers. But by 1981, the reason for concern had switched from the inadequacies of MIS to the incompleteness of DSS.

Rockart and Treacy contend that the conceptual framework developed for DSS by Gorry and Scott Morton in 1971 and refined by Keen and Scott Morton in 1978 cannot be used to identify and explain the new, top executive uses of EIS. DSS, they argue, are for middle- and lower-level managers, those who make well-defined, repetitive decisions. For these corporate cogs, building a model that generates information to support such decisions is the goal. Top managers, on the other hand, are paid to deal with uncertainty, to make decisions today and tomorrow unlike decisions they made yesterday. For these executives, flexibility is the key. A capability to access data and manipulate it to their own ends with an easy-to-use computer language is essential.

Citing Ben Heineman, president and chief executive officer (CEO) of Northwest Industries (he spends a few hours a day at a computer terminal in his office retrieving reports on Northwest's business units and analyzing data with the help of an effective computer language), John Schonenman, chairman of the board and CEO of Wausau Insurance Companies (he sits at a terminal tapping into on-line databases containing information about Wausau's operations and those of its competitors), and others as exemplary users of the new EIS, Rockart and Treacy propose "a simple model of EIS structure and development into which fit all individual systems" they have observed.[15]

Within their framework, an information system is an EIS if it possesses the following four features:

1. Central purpose: "The top executives who personally use computers do so as part of the *planning and control processes in their organization*. The provision of information to senior management for such purposes is certainly nothing new; the reason for EIS is to support a more effective use of this information."[16] [Italics added.]
2. Information repositories: These are tailored, often idiosyncratic databases containing detailed past, present, and future data—by business unit—on important business variables drawn, for example, from the general ledger, sales reports, and industry statistics.
3. Methods of use: "(a) For *access* to the current status and projected trends of the business and (b) for personalized *analyses* of the available data."[17] [Italics added.]
4. Support organization: A group of consultants, or "EIS coaches," who provide ongoing assistance to the top executive user team.

Rockart and Treacy see the emergence of EIS as signaling a new era in the organizational use of computers. What they mean, evidently, is that more and more top managers and their staffs will use computers to access and analyze data contained in information repositories. But does this expanded use of computers constitute an organizational use radically different from former uses? The answer here, it seems, is no.

In the preceding paragraph, the word *use* is employed equivocally. What Rockart and Treacy mean by it is indicated by Item 3 above: that is, *use* of computers to access and analyze data. When I use the term *use*, I mean organizational role or purpose. In the jargon of the appendix to this chapter, Rockart and Treacy's "use" is equivalent to our "technical function." Their "central purpose" (see Item 1 above) is our "organizational use."

With the semantic fog lifted, EIS can be seen as instances of management support systems. What Rockart and Treacy tout as signs of a new era appear on inspection to be repackaged versions of systems reflecting Anthony's planning and control paradigm. If they differ from DSS (and here Keen and Scott Morton could offer good reasons for taking EIS as subspecies of DSS), they must be distinguished in terms of their targets and thrusts.

EIS are targeted at top managers and their staffs who engage in planning and control activities at the corporate office, business unit, or functional level of the organization. This emphasis on executive management is intended to differentiate EIS from DSS.

The conventional thrust of EIS is to supply top managers and their staffs with information to support the full range of their activities. On this description, EIS satisfy more than the decision-making needs of top managers. Using EIS, for example, may simply put an executive in a better position to understand the operations falling under his or her aegis.

The conventional perspective on information systems, as the above discussion indicates, offers six generic opportunity areas for the development of computer applications (see Figure 2–1). This perspective focuses attention on three targets (people or processes associated with strategic planning, management control, and operational control) and two thrusts (auto-

Figure 2–1   Opportunities for Conventional Information Systems

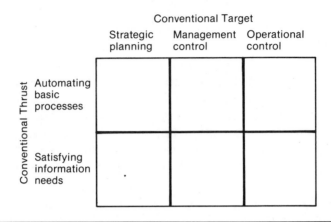

mating basic processes and providing information for decision making or other managerial or professional purposes). In Chapter 4, these conventional targets and thrusts will be contrasted with those linked to SIS (see Figure 4–3).

INFORMATION SYSTEMS PLANNING

Narrowly defined, the term *information systems planning* signifies the planning required to develop a single computer application. This might involve such activities as defining the requirements of the application, designing the program, and allocating the proper resources for development. More commonly, however, the term is understood in a wider sense as meaning the planning undertaken by an organization when it seeks to determine its information systems requirements *globally* and *systematically,* so that it can prepare to meet its short- and long-term needs. I shall use the term in this latter sense.

An information systems planning *methodology* is a valuable tool that an organization can use when conducting its study. A general-purpose planning methodology aims to identify all the information system application opportunities that would satisfy its needs; a special-purpose methodology focuses on a particular kind of information system, such as DSS or EIS, and aims to identify all such application opportunities that would satisfy the organization's needs.

One test of the adequacy of a methodology is its completeness. By this I mean: Are the steps in the process such that a planner trained in following them can identify and explain all and only the information system application opportunities the methodology intends to account for? A methodology is *complete* if the answer is yes. Otherwise, it is *incomplete*. Incompleteness is cause for concern, as it indicates that there are applications the methodology cannot account for. This is a crippling defect in a general-purpose methodology; in a special-purpose approach, it is noteworthy only when the methodology fails to identify and explain instances of the kind of systems it purports to identify and explain. Certainly, we wouldn't want to hold a DSS methodology in contempt if it didn't identify MIS opportunities, and vice versa.

The above definitions prepare the ground for my analysis of the primary information systems planning approaches developed over the past 20 years. I have selected the most representative and best-known methodologies while recognizing that many have found other approaches to be of use in planning for information systems. In general, the core of these alternatives is reducible to or an extension of one or more of the representative methodologies. My aim here is not, however, to examine in detail the extant approaches to information systems planning. Rather, it is to show that Anthony's paradigm is central to each.

Nolan's Stage Methodology

Nolan's stage methodology, one of the best-known approaches to information systems planning, was formulated in the early 70s and enhanced during the next decade, when Nolan left his teaching post at the Harvard Business School and formed the consulting firm of Nolan & Norton, Inc. This is not the place to rehearse the specifics of the stage hypothesis. Roughly speaking, Nolan claims that organizations pass through various stages in their use of information processing technology. In the original hypothesis, he postulated four growth stages: initiation (computer acquisition), contagion (intense systems development), control (proliferation of controls), and integration (user/service orientation).[18] In "Managing the Crises in Data Processing,"[19] he added two others—data administration and maturity—to account for organization behavior indicating a transition from the task of managing the computer to that of managing the data resource.

The stage hypothesis provides the basis for Nolan's information systems planning methodology, as each stage is characterized by certain benchmarks relating to information processing technology, data processing organization, user awareness, data processing planning and control, and the organization's portfolio of applications. By determining where an organization fits on the various benchmark scales and knowing when it ought to be at the next stage, a planner can use Nolan's approach to formulate programs that facilitate the transition from stage to stage.

To get the feel for this routine, consider the assessment of the application portfolio. Nolan proposes, first, that one "define the set of business functions for the organizational unit that represent cost-effective opportunities (e.g., manufacturing, marketing, distribution, finance, accounting, personnel, administration) to apply DP technology."[20] He calls this the "normative applications portfolio." It represents "the business functions that would be receiving DP support if the company had achieved Stage 6 maturity." Second, take each function, and "indicate for each set of systems the support that data processing gives to the function in the organization." Third, he suggests using a 10-point scale to determine the support currently provided relative to what should be provided for the function. These assessments are then compared to Nolan's investment benchmarks for data processing applications: strategic planning, management control, and operational systems.

Strategic planning systems include those designed for economic forecasting, management planning, strategic and operating plans, and sales and profit planning. Management control systems include those designed for purchasing, inventory control and valuation, and market research. Operational systems include those designed for cash management, machine control, credit, payroll, general ledger, and stockholder relations.

Nolan's universe of information systems application opportunities seems to have been set in concrete back in the early 70s, at the time Anthony's paradigm was beginning to be articulated in the information management field. In "Plight of the EDP Manager,"[21] Nolan draws a "basic map of opportunities for EDP applications" in the form of a triangle, horizontally trisected. In the top third are the application opportunities for senior management, in the middle third those for middle management, and in the bottom third those for operations. Recall from the earlier description of Anthony's paradigm that these levels correspond exactly to the holy trinity of planning and control processes: strategic planning, management control, and operational control. Nolan has modified Anthony's lowest level, from operational control to operations. This permits him to accommodate the operational systems such as payroll that Anthony excluded from his taxonomy.

But the effect on an information systems planner's vision is essentially unchanged. The focus is still on internal operations, on automating basic processes or satisfying the decision maker's needs for information. Within each level, according to Nolan, there are areas where it is neither feasible nor economical to apply computers, and there are areas where computers can be used for operations processing and for generating reports for decision making. While recognizing that an organization's opportunities may be a bit more complex than his models, he claims that this "basic layout is generally valid."[22]

From 1973 to 1978, Nolan's published views about the range of system opportunities remained unchanged. In his spring 1983 letter to management, "Building the Company's Computer Architecture Tactical Plan,"[23] he extends the analysis of the application portfolio by adding a technological dimension. He continues to look at the planning, control, and operations functions but now with respect to such information processing technologies as CAD/CAM, robotics, data processing, office automation, and personal computers. In terms of a planner's mental set of application opportunities, it's business as usual. Up to 1983 at least, Nolan's general-purpose approach to information systems is clearly incomplete, for it offers no guidelines for identifying or explaining SIS opportunities.

Critical Success Factors (CSF)

In "Chief Executives Define Their Own Data Needs,"[24] Rockart reported on a new approach to defining the information needs of top executives—CEOs and general managers. Developed by a research team at MIT's Sloan School of Management, the CSF method addresses the still-common complaint of managers about their information systems support: "too much and in general irrelevant."

The CSF approach homes in on individual managers and their information needs. Critical success factors for any business are defined as "the limited number of areas in which results, if they are satisfactory, will ensure successful competitive performance for the organization. They are the few key areas [three to eight] where things must go right for the business to flourish." In the supermarket industry, for example, they might include product mix, inventory, sales promotion, and pricing. "If results in these areas are not adequate, the organization's efforts for the period will be less than desired. . . . [CSFs] should receive constant and careful attention from management. The current status of performance in each area should be continually measured, and that information should be made available."[25]

Rockart notes that the CSF concept, introduced by Daniel and picked up by Anthony and his colleagues, fits nicely into the planning and control framework. "That is, the control system must report on those success factors that are perceived by the managers as appropriate to a particular job in a particular company."[26] For Rockart, "the CSF approach does not attempt to deal with information needs for strategic planning. Data needs for this management role are almost impossible to pre-plan. The CSF method centers, rather, on information needs for *management control* where data needed to monitor and improve existing areas of business can be more readily defined."[27]

When the CSF concept was introduced by Rockart in 1979, its primary use was to help individual managers determine their information needs. It is now thought to be another tool, like IBM's business systems planning (BSP) or Gibson and Nolan's stages, to guide organizations in the information systems planning process. In "A Primer on Critical Success Factors," Rockart and Bullen discuss how the CSF method can be used to identify the CSFs of individual managers; these "will indicate one or more key 'information data bases' or 'data processing systems' which should receive priority treatment in the information systems development process."[28] Such key data bases are precisely the information repositories that support the development of executive information systems, systems designed to make information available to top executives for query and analysis.

We have come full circle. The CSF method, now used primarily as a special-purpose information systems planning approach, aims at identifying executive information systems opportunities. There is an admirable consistency here. Just as EIS are defined within the context of Anthony's paradigm, the CSF method also is rooted in the holy trinity of planning and control processes. It is a methodology dedicated to identifying and developing conventional information systems, at satisfying the information needs of an organization's top managers.

IBM's Business Systems Planning

IBM's BSP, like Nolan's stage routine, is a general-purpose methodology for information systems planning. Its first and most important objective "is to provide an information systems plan that supports the business's short- and long-term information needs and is integral with the business plan."[29] The importance of BSP in the information management field is due largely to IBM's supremacy in the computer industry. Thousands of customers have been introduced to the concepts of BSP through reading the various editions of IBM's *The Information Systems Planning Guide* (the Blue Book, 1975; the Pumpkin Book, 1978; the Green Book, 1981), attending executive presentations conducted at IBM education centers in Poughkeepsie, New York, and San Jose, California, and studying in formal training classes held at IBM locations around the world. Most of the other general-purpose approaches to information systems planning (e.g., Honeywell's *planning methodology*, James Martin's information engineering, and those offered by large accounting firms) are lineal descendants of BSP.

From IBM's viewpoint, BSP serves two purposes. First, it provides the marketing group with an opportunity to project what they believe to be the full range of systems a customer account could use. This helps marketing set sales goals for IBM hardware, software, and services. Second, it offers customers a chance to view their information management function globally, from the top down, and to determine the set of information and databases required to support its operations.

My interest in BSP is pragmatic. Being the dominant methodology for identifying information systems application opportunities, its influence is widespread and deeply rooted. It reflects, perhaps more than any other process, the conventional perspective on information systems. Moreover, as BSP has evolved, it has incorporated elements of other planning approaches in an effort to adapt to changing needs.

IBM pictures BSP as a mechanism for translating an organization's business strategy into its information systems plan.

This is an idea developed by King in "Strategic Planning for MIS"[30] and extended in his "Achieving the Potential of Decision Support Systems."[31] As King has it, MIS strategic planning is the process of mapping an organizational strategy set—consisting of the organization's objectives (e.g., increase earnings by 10 percent per year), strategies (e.g., diversify into new businesses), and strategic attributes (e.g., sophisticated management)—into its MIS strategy set—consisting of MIS objectives (e.g., provide information on new business opportunities), constraints (e.g., system must provide reports involving various levels of aggregation), and design strategies (e.g., design on a modular basis).

Each element of the MIS strategy set is "derived" or "inferred" by an information analyst from the organizational strategy set. Thus, the MIS objective of "providing information on new business opportunities" is derived from the organizational strategy of "diversifying into new businesses," which in turn is related to such organizational objectives as "increasing earnings by 10 percent per year."

This process of strategy set transformation purportedly enables the organization to identify information systems that are closely related to its strategy. King believes that what he is proposing is a methodology for linking an organization's decision-supporting MIS (he still adheres to the term *MIS* rather than adopting the more fashionable *DSS*) and its goals and strategies. He sees his approach as

> valid for the support of middle-level organizational decisions, a management level which Anthony has classified as the *management control* level. Moreover, the approach is even valid for an MIS which is designed to support strategic choice, since there must be some starting point at which a system is developed to feed back information on the validity and degree of attainment of strategies already chosen.[32] [Italics added.]

King's work is of interest to us on two counts: first, because IBM has stamped its seal of approval on it; second, because it is symptomatic of the conceptual blindness induced by an almost religious belief in Anthony's holy trinity.

When King proposes to link information systems support directly to corporate strategy (a noble intention, to say the least), he sees only the support offered by applications that ply managers with decision-making information. Indeed, all the MIS objectives that he derives from the sample organizational strategy set and that identify information system application opportunities relate exclusively to supplying timely, accurate, speedy *information* to managers.

Take the example given above concerning the organization's diversification strategy. King views this as implying a system that will "provide information on new business opportunities."[33] This may be just what the CEO desired, but it reveals a narrow mental set that is incapable of conceiving another kind of organizational use for information systems. When Toys "Я" Us, for example (see Chapter 8), diversified into children's apparel, it used information systems developed for its toy business to propel its growth thrust. It saw opportunities to use information systems assets to shape its strategy. This kind of move would never occur to an information analyst using King's strategy-set transformation approach for identifying information system opportunities. If you're set on thinking about reports to management, you're probably blind to strategic opportunities like those that could transform your business.

Returning now to BSP, let us review how it defines the range of application opportunities open to an organization. Like Zani, Gorry and Scott Morton, Keen and Scott Morton, and Rockart and Treacy, IBM perceives the need for some reasonable framework in terms of which it can define information system opportunities. IBM proposes that "first, the emphasis in information systems should be in support of management decision making. This is in contrast to more traditional bookkeeping or record-keeping functions. Business decisions are made for various purposes, but most can be associated with either *planning* or *control*."[34]

The stage has been set. Anthony's paradigm enters IBM's

framework at this point in full force, with definitions of the holy trinity quoted.

Yet BSP doesn't stop here. It needs more than Anthony's paradigm to capture all the information system opportunities it seeks. The vehicle for accomplishing this represents one of the most significant contributions made by BSP. To get at the myriad application opportunities lying outside Anthony's paradigm, BSP introduces the notions of *resource management* and *business process*. Every organization must manage such universal resources as people, facilities, materials, money, and information. The requirements dictated by these resources are in turn determined by the organization's product. This latter, having all the life-cycle attributes of the other resources, is known as the *key* resource.

> Each resource is managed through planning and control decisions of the three levels previously discussed. Resource management has the desired characteristic of cutting across organizational boundaries—vertically across management levels and horizontally across functional lines. Thus a framework based on resources as well as planning and control levels can be established, and an information system architecture can be applied within this framework.[35]

Business processes are the basic activities and decision areas of the organization, independent of reporting relationships or management responsibilities. BSP claims that a logical set of such processes can be defined for any business. Examples of business processes include market planning (marketing research, forecasting, pricing, etc.), accounting (payroll, fixed asset, cost, cash management, etc.), financial planning and control (budgeting, managerial accounting, funds acquisition, etc.), production planning, distribution, and manufacturing. "Business processes can be identified to describe the major activities performed and decisions made by the business in the course of managing its resources throughout their life cycles."[36] Since each process uses or creates data, it is possible to construct an *information architecture* matrix that depicts the organization's basic processes, the data used or created by each, and the information systems needed to support or automate them.

BSP, the general-purpose information system planning methodology, aims at covering the waterfront of application opportunities. It has no reason to exclude a priori any information system variety. Why then is the following injunction issued to those who participate in BSP studies as interviewers of top executives?

> [Define] environment as [being] those things outside the scope of the study and over which the business has little or no control.[37]

And what does BSP see when it looks at the environment?

> [the] economy, *government regulations, labor,* consumerism, *competition,* industry position and *industry trends, suppliers,* and *technology.*[38] [Italics added.]

The italicized items represent possible targets and opportunity areas for SIS and SIS alliances. Why has BSP stipulated that they are "outside the scope of the study"? The only explanation I find satisfying is that those who formulated the BSP methodology were captives, in the thrall of Anthony's paradigm. They believed, and were supported by some of the most influential thinkers in the information management field (Zani, Gorry, Scott-Morton, Keen, Nolan, King, and Rockart), that there were basically only two kinds of information systems application opportunities, MIS and MSS. Why? Because Anthony's paradigm had narrowed their vision, had blinded them to the new world of strategic information systems (SIS) opportunities lying over the horizon. To see the objects in this world, a new perspective is needed.

CONCLUSION

I have attempted to show that beneath the conventional gospel on information systems lies an analytical framework that has (1) captured the allegiance of a community dedicated to its articulation and (2) governed the design of tools (instruments) to explore the world from the perspective it supports. Analytical frameworks with these properties have come to be known as *paradigms,* after the work of Thomas Kuhn in the philosophy of science.[39]

The adoption of Anthony's paradigm contributed significantly to the development of the information management discipline. Researchers, consultants, and practitioners refined and expanded the paradigm to cover new cases. This process of *paradigm articulation* is reflected in the landmark works summarized above.

But the further development of the information management discipline requires a new conceptual foundation, as the conventional perspective (based as it is on the planning and control model) can't account for SIS. By concentrating its efforts on the narrow range of objects sanctioned by the paradigm, it necessarily precludes other entities, the anomalies that fail to meet its stringent entrance requirements, its criteria for existence. The excluded, the deviant, the novel that the paradigm refuses to admit, are the sorts of things that (if perceived by members of the community) cause sleepless nights. These are the objects the paradigm can't handle, the objects that prove its incompleteness, its inability to account for the reality it is supposed to explain.

Ever since the advent of computer processing some 30 years ago, the overwhelming majority of those responsible for thinking about applications has embraced some form of the conventional perspective on systems. While under its sway, the members of this diverse group—ranging from top managers and end users to computer specialists, consultants, and academics in the information management field—never focused their attention on SIS.

Puzzling as this may appear at first sight, it can be explained, I believe, quite simply. With these practitioners, SIS had no ontological status. Not existing as objects to be identified, SIS formed no part of their horizon of expectation, their mental set, when they searched for opportunities to apply information technology. Is this surprising? Not to one who understands the ontological commitments of the conventional perspective. For this viewpoint countenances only two information system varieties: management information systems (MIS) and management support systems (MSS). (See the appendix to this chapter for more on each and a discussion of their relationship to SIS.)

The strategic perspective presented in Chapter 4, on the other hand, grants the existence of SIS and accounts for their occurrence. It is a perspective closely coupled with the notion of competitive advantage, the subject of the next chapter and a prerequisite for understanding the strategic viewpoint.

NOTES

1. Robert N. Anthony, *Planning and Control Systems: A Framework for Analysis* (Cambridge, Mass.: Harvard University Press, 1965), p. v.

2. Ibid., p. vii.

3. Ibid., p. 49.

4. Ibid., p. 80.

5. Ibid.

6. William Zani, "Blueprint for MIS," *Harvard Business Review*, November–December 1970, p. 96.

7. Ibid., p. 95.

8. Ibid., p. 98.

9. Anthony Gorry and Michael Scott Morton, "A Framework for Management Information Systems," *Sloan Management Review*, 1971, p. 61.

10. Ibid., p. 60.

11. Ibid.

12. Ibid.

13. Peter Keen and Michael Scott Morton, *Decision Support Systems: An Organizational Perspective* (Reading, Mass.: Addison-Wesley Publishing, 1978), p. 33.

14. Ibid.

15. John Rockart and Michael Treacy, "The CEO Goes On-Line," *Harvard Business Review*, January–February 1982, p. 83.

16. Ibid., p. 83.

17. Ibid., p. 84

18. Richard Nolan and Charles Gibson, "Managing the Four Stages of EDP Growth," *Harvard Business Review*, 1974.

19. Richard Nolan, "Managing the Crises in Data Processing," *Harvard Business Review*, March–April 1979.

20. Ibid., p. 122.

21. Richard Nolan, "Plight of the EDP Manager," *Harvard Business Review*, May–June 1973.

22. Ibid.

23. Richard Nolan, "Building the Company's Computer Architecture Tactical Plan," *Stage by Stage*, (Lexington, Mass.: Nolan & Norton, 1983).

24. John Rockart, "Chief Executives Define Their Own Data Needs," *Harvard Business Review*, March–April 1979.

25. Ibid., p. 85.

26. Ibid., p. 86.

27. Ibid., p. 88.

28. John Rockart and Christine Bullin, "A Primer on Critical Success Factors," *CISR Working Paper*, Sloan School of Management, MIT, 1981, p. 39.

29. IBM, *Information Systems Planning Guide: Business Systems Planning*, 3rd ed. (1981), p. 6.

30. William King, "Strategic Planning for MIS," *MIS Quarterly*, March 1978.

31. William King, "Achieving the Potential of Decision Support Systems," *Journal of Business Strategy*, Winter 1983.

32. Ibid., *MIS Quarterly*, March 1978, p. 37.

33. Ibid., p. 35.

34. IBM, *Information Systems Planning Guide: Business Systems Planning*, 3rd ed. (1981), p. 6.

35. Ibid.

36. Ibid.

37. Ibid., p. 20.

38. Ibid., p. 20.

39. Thomas Kuhn, *The Structure of Scientific Revolutions*, 2nd ed. (Chicago: University of Chicago Press, 1970).

Appendix: Varieties of Information Systems

INFORMATION SYSTEMS: FUNCTION AND USE

This appendix characterizes the major varieties of information systems and points out the environmental conditions contributing to their emergence and growth. Let us agree at the outset to understand the term *information system* broadly as a computer-based system capable of serving organizational purposes. This definition allows us to distinguish varieties of information systems in terms of their technical functions and organizational uses.

The distinction between an object's *use* and its *function* applies not only to information systems but to other complex and diverse entities as well. Take airplanes, for example. Like many technological wonders, they have multiple uses: Prior to World War I, they were used exclusively as recreational and sporting vehicles. During the war, they were used primarily for scouting purposes behind enemy lines. After the war, the first commercial use of aircraft was established. The Post Office Department created airmail routes, first between New York and Washington and then across the country. The next major use of aircraft was as transportation vehicles, which led to the formation of the commercial carrier fleets that we are accustomed to today. In the military sphere, the use of aircraft evolved from scouting to systematic aerial reconnaissance, routine bombing, transport, etc. The military counts these uses of aircraft as *conventional* to distinguish them from their various *strategic* missions.

When talking of the functional features of an airplane, I have in mind such elements as speed, capacity, maneuverability, and distance. Combining the categories of use and function allows us to distinguish various classes of aircraft (for example, fighter planes from transports) in terms of their respective technical functions and intended uses.

The distinction between use and function on the one hand and conventional and strategic on the other may be applied in the information management field as well. It is my contention that information systems have multiple uses and that some of these are conventional and some are strategic. Just as it took the military awhile to appreciate the strategic significance of some weapon systems, it has taken users of computers and telecommunication networks a long time to appreciate the strategic significance of information technology. To see this, one must first be clear about the conventional varieties of information systems, MIS and MSS.

MANAGEMENT INFORMATION SYSTEMS (MIS)

The term *management information systems* has never been defined to everyone's satisfaction. At one point in its early history, it meant for some what most today would call "decision support" or "executive information systems." But it has also had other definitions. In the late 60s and early 70s, MIS were frequently considered to be those systems that did not provide the information needed or wanted by management. After the framework proposed by Anthony Gorry and Michael Scott Morton for decision support systems (see Chapter 2), MIS began to be viewed as those applications not counted as decision support systems. This is roughly the sense I am trying to capture here.

Management information systems (see Figure A–1) may be defined as information systems that have as their primary function the processing of predefined transactions to produce fixed-format reports on schedule. Their principal use is to automate the basic business processes of the organization. Typical transactions handled by MIS are payroll records, customer orders, purchase requests, and the like. MIS were the first information system variety to blossom, taking root easily in the fertile financial and accounting soil of large firms. It took no great conceptual leap on the part of MIS pioneers to conclude, after observing a room full of payroll clerks performing calculations, that here was a good opportunity to use the new technology.

In this initial period of explosive growth, the objective was to replace the manual with the automated. Information system

Figure A–1   Varieties of Information Systems

Use \ Function	Automating basic processes	Satisfying information needs	Supporting or shaping competitive strategy
Transaction processing	MIS	/////	SIS
Query and analysis	/////	MSS	SIS

application opportunities were identified by inspection, by observing the performance of routine tasks and concluding that computers could be programmed to perform them. As time went on, MIS were developed in other areas: manufacturing, purchasing, marketing, and so on.

MIS sufficed when the environmental challenge was to employ the new computer technology to automate manual operations, to develop efficient applications that could reduce or avoid organizational costs. But from the viewpoint of managers or professionals, such systems were frequently judged to be irrelevant, failing to satisfy their information needs. They looked at the explosive growth of MIS and found many systems wanting, unable to support purchasing or scheduling decisions, incapable of producing ad hoc reports, and so on. This rising managerial and professional demand for information systems–based support in decision making, coupled with advances in information processing technology, led to the emergence of management support systems, a variety that includes decision support systems and executive information systems as its two main species.

MANAGEMENT SUPPORT SYSTEMS (MSS)

The primary function of management support systems (see Figure A–1), by definition, is to provide end users with query and analysis capabilities. The principal use of MSS is to satisfy the information needs of managers and professionals, needs often closely connected with decision making. Typical query and analysis functions include searching a data base for an item of information, generating what-if scenarios to test implications of planning models, and so on.

Within the past decade, the use of information systems by managers and professionals has grown exponentially, stimulated by the increasing supply of software tools for end-user computing available on mainframes, micros, and through outside time-sharing services. MSS development and demand show no signs of abating.

The tasks supported by MSS are often ill-defined. While some MSS do automate tasks previously performed manually, others reflect creative applications often developed by end users who, for the first time, have been given the computer power to experiment. Also contributing to the avalanche of MSS applications has been the availability of microcomputer software like VisiCalc and Lotus 1-2-3, fourth-generation time-sharing languages like Focus and Ramis, and financial planning packages like IFPS and Express.

The emergence of MSS signals the diversification of the information management business into a new product line, with new technology, new customer groups, and new customer needs to be attended to. Unlike MIS, MSS depend primarily on time-sharing and, more recently, on microcomputer technology. The MSS target groups are managers and professionals rather than the clerical and operational markets served by MIS. MSS satisfy the needs of decision makers and professionals for information. With MSS, the definition of the information management business changes as it expands its scope along the dimensions just mentioned.

It is interesting to note that many MIS veterans resisted the emergence of MSS, refusing to admit their existence. Some claimed that MSS were merely extensions of well-conceived MIS. Others argued that MSS were the cream and MSS developers just skimmers. But none of these objections could stem the tide bringing waves of new MSS applications. By the early 80s, demand for MSS far outstripped the demand for MIS applications.

The emergence of this new information system variety brought with it a different group of information system developers, developers not only trained in the intricacies of information technology but also skilled in business disciplines like logistics, inventory control, and strategic planning. Many MSS developers had backgrounds in management science/operations research. They differed culturally from their MIS colleagues, having different career goals, different views about the role of computers in the organization, and different degrees of interest in information technology.

To be an MSS developer, one must be willing and able to empathize with business managers and professionals who cannot always specify their requirements with the degree of precision expected by MIS designers. Unlike the MIS pioneers, who relied on observation, the MSS vanguard, those who aid end users (and not all MSS are built by developers trained in this line of work), often must draw upon their conceptual understanding of the decision-making process, frequently unobservable.

Just as the unmet information needs of managers and professionals present MSS opportunities, the savage competitive forces of the 80s—unleashed by deregulation, foreign competition, and accelerated product change, for example—open up SIS opportunities. Just as MSS extend the use of information systems beyond the automation of basic business processes, the recent emergence of SIS (the newest information system variety) extends the use of information systems still further.

STRATEGIC INFORMATION SYSTEMS (SIS)

Strategic information systems (see Figure A–1) are information systems in which the primary function of the system is either to process predefined transactions and produce fixed-format reports on schedule or to provide query and analysis capabilities. The primary use of SIS is to support or shape the competitive strategy of the enterprise, its plan for gaining or maintaining competitive advantage or reducing the advantage of its rivals.

As the vast majority of SIS cases today come from the business sector, where use for competitive purpose dominates, I have defined SIS narrowly by closely coupling it with competitive strategy and competitive advantage. This coupling dictates the strategic perspective on information technology advanced in Chapter 4 and, indeed, the whole content of this book.

But it is also possible to sever the linkage with competitive strategy, competitive advantage, and associated concepts and to speak more generally about SIS as the use of information technology to support or shape strategy. With this generalization, most of the SIS presented in this book would form a special class of strategic systems: those used by an enterprise for competitive purposes. This opens the possibility of other SIS classes within the organization (e.g., SIS used to support or shape restructuring efforts, human resources policy, or manufacturing strategy) or in different sectors (e.g., SIS used to support or shape military strategy, political strategy, or educational policy). In time, I believe, these will become active areas for research and application. While new strategic perspectives and frameworks will most likely be needed for each, many of the ideas proposed here would, with appropriate modifications to suit the context, be applicable to these other fields, especially the material on SIS planning and management introduced in Chapters 10 and 11.

SIS represent a new information management product line, targeting new user groups, satisfying new user needs—needs unsatisfied by MIS or MSS and sometimes requiring new technologies. Like the emergence of MIS, the emergence of SIS forces the information management group within an enterprise to redefine its business and its goals. The scope of information management activities is again extended.

With extended scope and a clearer sense of the tasks imposed by the existence of SIS, organizations must turn their attention to implementation issues such as personnel, organization, and culture. Adjustments must be made to accommodate the new SIS product line. The sorts of actions taken to further the growth of MSS must be repeated for SIS.

With the emergence of SIS, emphasis switches from function to use. What is critical is the use of information technology to support or shape strategy rather than the capability to process transactions or do query and analysis. SIS planners must discover application opportunities through reflection, by thinking about how the use of information technology can enable the organization to satisfy its competitive goals.

HYBRID INFORMATION SYSTEMS

To avoid possible confusion about applying the taxonomy just introduced, note that the two dimensions of an information system, technical function and organizational use, each comprise overlapping categories: hence the possibility of *hybrid* information systems—MIS/MSS, MIS/SIS, and MIS/MSS/SIS—appearing at the MIS, MSS, and SIS intersections in Figure A–2.

For example, American Air's Sabre reservation system is an MIS/SIS hybrid. RCA's human resource management system, IRIS, is an MIS/MSS hybrid. In its MIS use, IRIS records significant events in the history of each RCA employee and generates standard, usually mandatory reports periodically. In its MSS use, IRIS permits RCA executives to query and analyze its data base when information is needed to support decisions concerning project team composition, training budgets, and so on.

When applying this taxonomy, keep in mind also that an

Figure A–2   Information Systems: Varieties and Hybrids

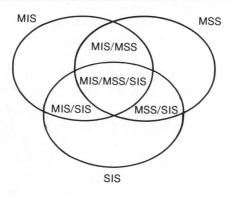

information system may, from the point of view of its organizational developer, be classed as an SIS but, from the perspective of an external user, it may be taken as an MSS, MIS, or MIS/MSS hybrid. The Metpath information system mentioned in Chapter 1 illustrates this situation. For Metpath, it is an SIS; for the physicians using it, it is an MIS or perhaps even an MIS/MSS hybrid.

3

Competitive Advantage

THINKING ABOUT COMPETITIVE ADVANTAGE

The three-toed sloth inhabits the lowland forests of South America. Tiny moths of the species Cryptoses choloepi live in their fur. When a sloth makes its weekly descent from its tree abode to defecate on the forest floor, female moths leap from the comfort of their furry homes to deposit eggs on the fresh dung. This, according to sociobiologist E. O. Wilson, "assures their offspring first crack at the nutrient rich excrement and a *competitive advantage* over the myriad of other coprophages."[1] [Italics added.]

Cryptoses are niche players. They exist nowhere else on earth. What is their competitive advantage? For sure, it's not that they're the "low-cost producers" or the "differentiators" of the lowland forests. Rather, to coin an expression, Cryptoses are endowed with "first-feeder advantages." This preemptive edge is based on timing and proximity. The caterpillars emerging from their eggs feed immediately on the dung and then build their silky nests. Twenty-one days later, transformed into moths, they complete their cycle by flying into the trees in search of sloths. These tiny moths possess what appears to be an unassailable competitive edge over their less fortunate rivals, a sustainable advantage evolved eons ago.

In what ways, if any, does the competitive advantage enjoyed by the Cryptoses differ from the advantages possessed by certain firms over their less fortunate rivals? Are there different kinds of competitive advantage, depending on the arena in which the competition occurs? What are the sources of advantage? What is the duration of the advantage? Is it possible to possess a competitive advantage that is unsustainable, or is the expression "unsustainable competitive advantage" a contradiction in terms, as some business strategists seem to suggest? How vulnerable is the advantage? What is the value of the advantage? What is the relation between competitive *advantage* and competitive *strategy*?

To understand the strategic perspective on information technology proposed in the next chapter, we first need to address such questions by clarifying the meaning of the terms *competitive advantage, competitive strategy,* and related terms introduced below. For on them depends the meaning of pivotal concepts such as *strategic information systems,* defined as uses of information technology to support or shape an organization's competitive strategy, its plan for gaining or maintaining a competitive advantage or reducing a rival's advantage (i.e., decreasing its own disadvantage).

The concept of competitive advantage finds application in a variety of contexts: sports, law, sociobiology, and business, to list a few. In this section, I shall present a sample of these contexts (such as the one just described) to help explicate a sense of the concept that will, in turn, serve as the basis for our study of the strategic use of information technology.

In the next section, I shall discuss Michael Porter's position on competitive advantage and competitive strategy. It is my contention that Porter's view, while powerful and illuminating in many contexts, fails to capture a large class of cases in which it is natural to say, "Firm X has a competitive advantage over Firm Y" while knowing, for example, that X and Y are not rivals in their industry or that the advantage is not sustainable. In other words, the narrow, *economist's* view best exemplified by Porter's work needs to be widened to accommodate the broader, *practitioner's* sense of competitive advantage and competitive strategy.

Widening Porter's model should not be taken as a rejection of it. On the contrary, understanding his position is an indispensable prerequisite for appreciating the strategic perspective on information technology that I shall advance in this text, a perspective that incorporates Porter's position as a special case.

In the last section of this chapter, I shall discuss the relation between competitive advantage and information technology and show how the practitioner's sense of competitive advantage expands the range of possibilities in which information technology can be used to support or shape competitive strategy far beyond the restrictive line drawn by those subscribing to the economist's doctrine.

Let us begin by observing that competition, while ubiquitous, always occurs within certain boundaries called *competitive arenas*. These include, for example, the baseball field, the courtroom, the tropical rain forest, and the retail store, arenas that may be identified by their physical attributes; they also comprise those more loosely specified by the nature of the adversaries and the stakes involved: soft-drink manufacturers battling to win the business of fast-food restaurant chains, local politicians competing for the limited funds available from national political action committees, labor struggling with management over contract terms. Opponents battle, compete, and struggle for "arena-relative prizes":[2] winning the baseball game, persuading the jury of your client's innocence, outselling the other retailers in your area, or acquiring food to survive.

Individuals as well as organizations compete in a variety of arenas, usually confronting different competitive casts as they move from one to another. To achieve success in one arena may even call for cooperation with natural rivals in another. I call the set of arenas in which an individual or an organization competes its *competitive space*.

Within a competitive space, some arenas may be *independent* while others are *linked*, forming chains in which advantage in one is determined by actions in one or more of the others. Success on the tennis court or in business usually entails nothing about performance at the gambling table or in the courtroom. But Jack Nicklaus, the golfing great, parlayed his fame and skill on the links into a lucrative new real estate venture. Instead of putting around the course, Nicklaus now, with the stroke of his pen, scores over $1 million each time he signs a contract for designing and promoting a golf community, a high-priced housing complex with adjacent golf course(s).

Within its competitive space and within the same arena, a competitor may win one competitive battle (e.g., a World Series baseball game or a new customer account) and lose another. Victorious over 90 percent of the time at one location (e.g., the Celtics basketball team at Boston Garden or AT&T competing for contracts against Nippon Telegraph and Telephone in the United States), the winner may be defeated more frequently elsewhere. Or a rival may enjoy supremacy for an extended period of time but suffer losses thereafter. Recall Xerox in copiers before its patent protection expired; American firms in world markets prior to competition from the Pacific Basin; or the small, privately owned air transport operations that prospered while the CIA assigned missions to them, but crashed when the Company (as it is affectionately known by some of its ex-agents) decided to fly with Southern Air Transport for the bulk of its clandestine operations.

To explain the *victory* of one adversary over another or others in a competitive battle, we need to know those factors responsible for its win at the time. The New York Mets, for instance, lost the first game of the 1986 World Series to the Boston Red Sox. An error by the Mets second baseman that allowed the Red Sox to score the only run of the contest was, according to baseball pundits, the factor responsible for Boston's victory and New York's defeat.

To explain, on the other hand, the *dominance* of one competitor over another or others in an arena, we need to know those factors conducive to its success over a period of time. We are not primarily attempting here to explain the outcome of a particular battle. Rather, we seek to understand those powers, consisting of certain abilities or combination of abilities, that the superior performer possesses uniquely or to a greater degree than any of its competitors. I call such powers *competitive advantages*.

K mart, the large discount chain, operates in linked arenas. It obtains goods from suppliers at lower cost than its smaller rivals. And it offers these goods to customers at prices competitors can't match. The chain thus enjoys advantages in two arenas: it is able to negotiate price concessions from suppliers because the volume of its purchases yields substantial bargaining power, and it is able to set lower retail prices vis-à-vis its rivals because of its reduced purchasing costs. This latter advantage enables it to win customers whose only purchase criterion is price.

We need to draw a distinction here. K mart wins battles in the supplier arena by virtue of its negotiating power, which is based on the volume of its purchases. Its competitive advantage lies in its ability to negotiate the lowest possible prices. This enables it to dominate battles fought in the supplier arena (not all battles, by the way; some manufacturers may refuse to be bludgeoned into reducing their margins). The ability to make large purchases is the *source* of its competitive advantage, the reason it is able to negotiate for the lowest prices. But a source of advantage is only an *instrumental* advantage, which does not in itself win battles in the arena but rather serves as a means to this end. The *essential (intrinsic)* advantage remains K mart's power to bargain for rock-bottom wholesale prices.

In the computer business, IBM assigns a team of technical and marketing personnel to its major accounts. In many cases, the team resides in an office at the customer's premises. This intimate relationship gives IBM a number of instrumental advantages over its rivals. It enables the computer giant to learn about the needs of a customer's business and to craft an effective marketing program to meet them. It encourages a close working relationship with top data processing managers, the ones most likely to be involved in purchasing decisions. And it gives the account a sense of security about its computer operations: if something goes wrong, Big Blue will be there immediately (or so the story goes) to fix it. These instrumental advantages all contribute to IBM's essential competitive advantage: its ability to prevent rivals from penetrating deeply into its major accounts.

Superior competitors in an arena dominate by virtue of their competitive advantage(s). But while the exercise of an enterprise's advantage generally leads to victory or to the prevention of key battles that might erode its dominance, it doesn't (to underline the point again) guarantee victory in particular encounters. And it may be possessed independently of any plan for attaining it—that is, independently of any competitive strategy.

Consider the success of Japanese enterprises in selling to the Chinese. Japanese merchants lead, in part, because of their talents as foreign traders. But only in part. According to *The Wall Street Journal,* a number of factors contribute to Japanese dominance over their Western counterparts. "Among them are Japan's location and cultural affinity with China. Although their spoken languages are different, the pictographic writing systems of the two countries are similar enough to give Japanese business people a big *advantage.*"[3] [Italics added.] In addition, trading firms have often been able to reestablish old ties with Chinese firms in places that the Japanese once occupied, such as Manchuria.

The instrumental competitive advantages just cited—the ability of the Japanese to reach their Chinese customers readily, share cultural values, understand the ideographic Chinese language, and reestablish business relations formed decades ago—did not result from any explicit competitive strategy. No Japanese firm planned to gain these advantages. They are based on certain givens: geographical proximity, the evolution of Japanese culture and language from the Chinese, and the Japanese occupation of Manchuria. These advantages are just as "hard-wired" as those enjoyed by certain animal species.

Leafcutter ants—unlike the Cryptoses (mentioned at the start of this chapter), who thrive in a limited region—do business over a much larger territory. Leafcutters convert fresh vegetation, usually leaves, into mushrooms. Since they evolved this process millions of years ago, no other creature has found a way to duplicate it. According to Wilson, "it gave the ants an enormous *advantage:* they could now send out specialized workers to collect the vegetation while keeping the bulk of the population safe in subterranean retreats."[4] [Italics added.]

The leafcutter advantage, the source of which is an innovative conversion process, enables this species to dominate large parts of the American tropics, consuming as it does vast quantities of vegetation, indeed more than any other animal group. If ever there was a sustainable competitive advantage independent of competitive strategy, this is it. Leafcutters don't earn their edge, they are born with it.

Yet, in many instances, advantage results directly from an explicit strategy—that is, the conscious choice or action designed to achieve an edge. When a gambling casino sets the odds for the various games of chance it offers to its patrons, the house guarantees its long-run success. Customers—in this case, competitors of the casino—always play at a disadvantage. In arenas in which a firm contends with its patrons for certain prizes, casinos represent a competitive ideal often sought but seldom realized.

From the above discussion, it follows that competitive advantage is a relation holding between two or more competitors (opponents, adversaries) and that it applies relative to a competitive arena. The expression "X has a competitive advantage over Y in A," where A is a competitive arena and X and Y are competitors, means that X possesses some ability or combination of abilities that Y lacks and that this ability or combination enables X to dominate competitive battles fought in A. The Japanese possess the ability to reach their Chinese customers readily; Cryptoses possess the ability to "assure their offspring first crack at the nutrient rich excrement"; leafcutters possess the ability to send specialized workers to collect food while keeping the rest of the nest safe underground; gambling casinos possess the ability to set the odds; K mart possesses the ability to negotiate price concessions from its vendors and the ability to win the business of price-conscious consumers; IBM possesses a combination of abilities enabling it to learn about its customer's needs, develop better relations with managers involved in purchase decisions, and so on.

Since an organization's competitive space generally comprises many different arenas (e.g., those in which it may encounter as competitors its suppliers, channels, or customers, as well as direct rivals), it logically may possess multiple competitive advantages or disadvantages *within or among its independent or linked arenas.*

Since what is a competitive advantage in one arena may not be in another, an organization may have multiple competitive strategies because it competes in multiple arenas. And the purpose of any competitive strategy is to gain or maintain one's own advantage or to reduce the edge of adversaries *in an arena,* either independent or linked.

Let us consider now a few additional attributes of competitive advantages and strategies: their duration, vulnerability, and value. The *duration* of an advantage/strategy refers to the length of time it is expected to obtain (be followed). It is convenient in many arenas to calibrate the duration scale at three places: short term (e.g., less than one year), medium term (e.g., from one to three years), and long term (e.g., more than three years). In some arenas, though, short-term advantage may be measured in minutes, hours, days, months, or seasons; in others, long-term advantage may be counted in decades. For different arenas and terms, different advantages/strategies may be required.

The *vulnerability* of an advantage/strategy refers to the degree to which it is susceptible to attack. Any advantage/strategy may find itself vulnerable (1) when the environment in which it operates, including the rules of the game, changes radically or (2) due to a direct challenge or to one that attempts to overcome it indirectly by reducing its importance (shifting the terms of combat, so to speak) in struggles for arena domination. Therefore, any advantage/strategy is, to some degree, vulnerable to attack.

But some are more vulnerable than others. To capture these differences in degree, we need some terminology. Let us agree that a *sustainable* advantage/strategy is one that makes its possessor immune from attack by competitors attempting to duplicate, emulate, or copy it; it is *strongly sustainable* if it enables its possessor to resist indirect attacks as well. If an advantage/strategy is open to attack by competitors attempting to duplicate, emulate, or copy it, let us call it *contestable.*

In principle, one might say that any competitive strategy worthy of its name should concern itself with only those arenas in which it is possible to achieve a long-term, sustainable—or better, strongly sustainable—competitive advantage. Yet we know that sustainability, like other virtues, tends to be sought more often than achieved, because long-term sustainability depends in large part on who's playing the game and what rules are being followed. Change either, and the competitive balance in an industry may be upset, an occurrence more frequent than some strategists care to admit. What counts as a sustainable edge today may erode or evaporate tomorrow as new entrants appear, demand disintegrates, or key personnel depart. It therefore seems prudent to expand the class of advantages worthy of pursuit to include the contestable as well as the sustainable. A firm with a contestable advantage possesses an edge capable of being matched or overthrown, but for some reason—lack of will, politics, vision, or the like—it endures for a reasonable period, long enough for the firm to recoup its investments, reap a profit, and move on to other things.

While these definitions help focus attention on the vulnerability issue, they leave open key questions related to practical application. Under what conditions would we be justified in saying that an advantage/strategy is sustainable, strongly sustainable, or contestable over the short, medium, or long term? It is these conditions that interest managers responsible for formulating competitive strategy, because strategic moves must be designed to satisfy them. The conditions also concern other practitioners responsible for investing large sums in information technology projects promising to yield substantial advantages. In the last section of this chapter, I shall return to this question with reference to the sustainability or contestability of advantages dependent on information technology.

The *value* of an advantage/strategy refers to how much it is worth to possess the advantage or follow the strategy. Such value may be determined by a variety of measures: revenue, cost saving or cost avoidance, profit, return on investment, quality improvement, market share, units sold, stock price, and the like. American Air and Banc One, for example, might measure the value of their information technology-based advantages in terms of their stock prices, since investors assess the performance of American's Sabre and Banc One's processing activity when making buy or sell decisions on these stocks (as indicated in Chapter 1).

The analysis of competitive advantage just sketched provides the foundation for understanding the strategic perspective on information technology presented in the next chapter. This perspective relies on the *theory of strategic thrusts,* a theory that concerns itself with the major moves an enterprise may make in its quest for advantage in its main competitive arenas. It admits any kind of edge that makes sense, and recognizes both contestable and sustainable advantages over the short, medium, or long term. But before moving to Chapter 4, we need first to contrast our analysis with the position of Michael Porter, an exponent of a conception of competitive advantage and competitive strategy narrower than the one I am advancing.

PORTER'S POSITION

Michael Porter's seminal works *Competitive Strategy*[5] and *Competitive Advantage*[6] represent the best statement of the narrow, economic view of competitive advantage and competitive strategy. The position he advocates derives from his theory of industry competition. In every industry, he hypothesizes, the state of competition depends on five basic forces: the threat of new entrants, the intensity of rivalry among direct rivals, the pressure of substitute products, the bargaining power of buyers, and the bargaining power of suppliers. "The collective strength of these forces determines the ultimate profit potential in an industry, where profit potential is measured in terms of long run return on invested capital."[7]

Threat of new entrants.   The strength of this competitive force depends primarily on the height of barriers that must be scaled by new entrants seeking the potential rewards of industry participation; it also depends upon reactions anticipated from existing competitors. The entry threat is high if barriers are low or severe retaliation is not expected. In general, barriers will be low if an entrant need not invest to match cost savings due to economies of scale, economies of scope (i.e., cost savings attributable to the use of shared resources), economies of experience, and so on (see Chapter 6).

Entry barriers will also be low if there is no need for the entrant to differentiate the product sold, no cost involved when customers switch from an incumbent's product to an entrant's offering, and no difficulty for the entrant in securing access to distribution channels. Finally, barriers will be low if there are no absolute cost disadvantages that the entrant must overcome, such as proprietary technology due to patent protection or favored access of existing competitors to raw materials. In effect, without barriers to entry, existing firms enjoy no competitive advantages. By raising barriers, existing firms acquire either cost or differentiation advantages.

Intensity of rivalry among direct rivals.   The strength of this competitive force depends on factors often beyond the control of industry participants, such as:

1. *Degree of concentration.* In highly concentrated industries, leader(s) may impose some form of price leadership and therefore avoid intense, no-win competition based solely on price.
2. *Rate of industry growth.* In fast-growth industries, the focal point of strategy is expansion to meet demand, not to outrun other competitors.
3. *Lack of switching costs.* In industries where product differentiation is low and buyers consequently feel no compunction about changing vendors, severe price competition is the norm.

Rivalry is reflected in price competition, advertising battles, new product introduction, and increased customer services.

Pressure of substitute products.   The strength of this competitive force depends on the existence in other industries of products that customers view as having features similar to those of the industry's product(s). In the packaging industry, steel and aluminum manufacturers competed for the business of, for instance, American Can and Continental Can on the basis of price and performance features of tin plate and aluminum. In the financial services industry today, the products of brokers, banks, and insurance companies (previously seen as noncompetitive) now vie vigorously for the same investment dollars. Substitute products put limits on industry profitability, as price depends in part on the availability of alternative products offering similar features. To increase this pressure, firms outside the industry must develop product or process innovations. To decrease it, firms in the industry must distinguish their offerings by either price or performance.

Bargaining power of buyers.   "Buyers compete with the industry by forcing down prices, bargaining for higher quality or more services, and playing competitors against each other, all at the expense of industry profitability."[8] The power of this competitive force depends on such factors as whether buyers possess enough information about the supplier's products and operations to prevent it from acting opportunistically with respect to them, whether they pose a credible threat of backward integration, or whether they may purchase a commodity product (if the product is differentiated, switching costs may reduce the bargaining power of buyers). Affirmative responses indicate that buyers hold the bargaining power in their negotiations with suppliers. Strategic moves, however, could alter the strength of this force.

Bargaining power of suppliers.   Suppliers compete with buyers over price and product features, each party negotiating or acting to win the best deal, to gain advantage. The strength of this competitive force depends on such factors as whether suppliers possess an information edge that permits them to act opportunistically with respect to buyers, pose a credible threat of forward integration, or sell a differentiated product. Affirmative responses indicate that suppliers possess the bargaining powers in their negotiations with buyers.

The collective strength of the above forces, determined by underlying economic and technological factors such as economies of scale and access to raw materials, varies from industry to industry. In the face of such powerful environmental forces, each representing a potential threat to "ultimate" profitability, how can a firm achieve above-average profitability over the long term and, in the process, outperform its rivals?

Porter suggests an answer to this question. The firm should "establish a profitable and sustainable position against these forces."[9] This might sound a bit like the "Buy low and sell high" advice uttered in response to the question "How can I earn high returns on my investments over the long run?" But Porter wishes us to see it in another light, as part of a far more powerful argument. He believes that "the fundamental basis of above-average performance in the long run is *sustainable competitive advantage*."[10] That is, a firm must possess a sustainable competitive advantage if it is to achieve above-average profitability over the long haul and outperform its rivals. Porter appears to be stipulating, as an analytical truth akin to a definition, that without a sustainable advantage any hope for long-term profitability is doomed.

Before explaining what he means by "sustainable competitive advantage," we need to grasp how he uses the term *competitive advantage*. In his view, "Competitive advantage grows fundamentally out of value a firm is able to create for its buyers that exceeds the firm's cost of creating it,"[11] where value is identified with what buyers are willing to pay for a firm's goods and services.

With this move, Porter takes us to the core of his argument. The firm aspiring to achieve competitive advantage must create for its customers superior value, meaning value superior to that offered by its rivals. Superior value, Porter informs us, "stems from offering lower prices than competitors for equivalent benefits or providing unique benefits that more than offset a higher price."[12] *Thus Porter construes competitive advantage as a relation between rivals competing for the business of customers (buyers).*

From the above, we perceive two kinds of competitive advantage. A firm can gain an edge over a rival by offering products at lower prices (i.e., price advantage) or by offering products with unique features valued by customers (i.e., feature advantage). Porter doesn't use these terms, but what he says comes to the same thing. "Though a firm can have a myriad of strengths and weaknesses vis à vis its competitors, there are two basic types of competitive advantage a firm can possess: low cost or differentiation."[13] It possesses a cost advantage "if its *cumulative* cost of performing all value activities is lower than competitor's costs."[14] [Italics added.] It possesses a differentiation advantage if it is "uniquely able to create competitive advantage for its buyers in ways besides selling to them at a lower price."[15]

Merely possessing a low-cost or differentiation advantage, however, is not enough unless this edge is endowed with the ultimate virtue: sustainability. "The strategic value of a cost advantage," Porter asserts, "hinges on its sustainability. Sustainability will be present if the sources of a firm's cost advantage are difficult for competitors to replicate or imitate."[16] The same applies to the strategic value of a differentiation advantage: it must be sustainable.

We may conclude from the above that a firm possessing a sustainable competitive advantage, be it either low cost or differentiation, will achieve its goal of long-run, above-average profitability and performance superior to its rivals. It will also be in a position to defend itself against the five competitive forces. This conclusion takes us to the subject of competitive strategy, which, in Porter's view, "is the search for a favorable position in an industry,"[17] a position in which the firm can defend itself against the five forces. *For Porter, the purpose of competitive strategy is to achieve sustainable competitive advantage.*

Associating the two kinds of advantage (low cost and differentiation) with two categories for the competitive scope of a firm's activities—*broad* (participating in a range of industry segments) or *narrow* (participating in a single or limited number of industry segments)—he defines "three *generic strategies* for achieving above-average performance in an industry: *cost leadership* [i.e., low-cost advantage and broad scope], *differentiation* [i.e., differentiation advantage and broad scope], and *focus* [i.e., differentiation advantage or low-cost advantage and narrow scope]. The focus strategy has two variants: *cost focus* and *differentiation focus.*"[18]

But just following a generic strategy, like merely possessing a competitive advantage, is not enough. The strategy will "not lead to above average performance," Porter cautions, "unless it is *sustainable vis-à-vis competitors.*"[19] [Italics added.] Thus, in Porter's theory, both strategies and advantages must be endowed with the virtue of sustainability.

Generic competitive strategies are "the logical routes to competitive advantage that must be probed in any industry."[20] Every firm possesses a generic strategy, Porter claims, either explicitly, as a result of developing it via a strategic planning process, or implicitly, as a result of evolution from the actions of various functional departments. At the heart of any strategy, he maintains, is competitive advantage. And "achieving competitive advantage requires a firm to make a choice—if a firm is to attain a competitive advantage, it must make a choice about the type of competitive advantage it seeks to attain [i.e., low cost or differentiation] and the scope within which it will attain it [i.e., broad or narrow]."[21]

Porter is quite emphatic about the importance of strategic choice. He argues that "a firm must choose the type of competitive advantage it intends to pursue in the long run."[22] Why is this choice important? Because, Porter believes, at bottom the two generic strategies are mutually exclusive. Cost leadership and differentiation ultimately are inconsistent because differentiation is costly. "To be unique and command a price premium requires that the differentiator deliberately elevate costs. Conversely, cost leadership often requires a firm to forgo some differentiation."[23] A firm that pursues more than one but fails to achieve any is "stuck in the middle," a position that Porter claims is "usually a recipe for below average performance" because the firm will be at a competitive disadvantage vis-à-vis "the cost leaders, differentiators, or focusers [who] will be better positioned to compete in any segment."[24]

Choice of a generic strategy is also important because of its organizational implications. According to Porter, each "strategy implies different skills and requirements for success, which commonly translate into differences in organizational structure and culture."[25] The cost leader with tight controls, large scale, and standardized procedures for all activities might have trouble if forced by market conditions "to differentiate itself through a constant stream of creative new products."[26]

Porter's position described, let us now examine it with a critical eye. To start, note that it rests on two unstated assumptions:

1. The only arena worth considering to achieve competitive advantage is the one in which rivals strive to dominate each other.
2. The only kind of competitive advantage/strategy worth talking about is the one that promises to be sustainable.

No one disputes the fact that competition among rivals (where rivals do not include suppliers or customers) and sustainability provide important focal points for business strategists to concentrate their attention. But is there nothing more to say on the subject?

First, do only two kinds of sustainable competitive advantage exist in the arena in which rivals compete for customers? There seems to be no agreement on this question. Pankas Ghemawat, one of Porter's colleagues at the Harvard Business School, for instance, believes that "sustainable advantages fall into three categories: size in the targeted market, superior access to resources or customers, and restriction on competitor's options."[27] Moreover, Ghemawat claims that these advantages are not mutually exclusive. "They can, and often do, interact. The more of them the better."[28] This position appears to contradict Porter's view that simultaneous pursuit of more than one kind of sustainable advantage ultimately leads to strategic inconsistency.

Second, what if you're in an industry in which, for all intents and purposes, there are no sustainable competitive advantages, yet a number of firms have maintained an enviable record of profitability over the long term? For example, as Amar Bhide points out, "Some leaders in financial service have not subscribed to the competitive religion because they are secure in their profits and understand the reality of their business. Major sustainable competitive advantages, as Warren Buffett puts it, 'are almost nonexistent in the field of financial services,' "[29] If true, this proposition poses a serious threat to Porter's theory, for he maintains that it applies to any industry context.

Third, Porter's suggestion for fitting generic strategies into the firm's strategic planning process, while perhaps appropriate for the ideal, logically consistent universe he constructs, bears little relation to the competitive realities faced by most firms in today's world. Porter proposes that "the centerpiece of a firm's strategic plan should be its generic strategy, [which] specifies the fundamental approach to competitive advantage a firm is pursuing, and provides the context for the actions to be taken in each functional area."[30]

But we know that some forms of competitive advantage do not result from competitive strategy, either implicit or explicit, but are, so to speak, genetically encoded (like the Cryptoses), determined by geographic or cultural proximity, or ordained by others—as some of the examples given in the first section of this chapter show. Moreover, some competitive strategies aim at competitive advantage but not at sustainable advantage. Ghemawat's conclusions support this last point. He notes that "managers cannot afford to ignore *contestable advantages*. For one thing, even moves that offer ephemeral advantages may be worth making, if only to avoid a competitive disadvantage. For another, *some contestable advantage may survive uncontested.*"[31] [Italics added.]

The distinction between contestable and sustainable advantages, which Ghemawat notes is a matter of degree, opens a universe of possibilities that Porter has closed by, in effect, equating competitive advantage with sustainable competitive advantage. As Ghemawat correctly observes, "To create a sustainable advantage, you must either be blessed with competitors that have a restricted menu of options or be able to preempt them."[32] This also leaves a rather meager plate for those who seek advantage and assume, as Porter does, that it must be equated with sustainability.

Even in an industry in which the seeking of a sustainable edge made some sense, a firm might be facing substantial risk if it pursued the advantage. If it decided to invest and point the ship of state in one direction or another, it would (according to Porter) be committing the organization, culture, and the like to one course, incompatible in the main with any other. Is the loss of strategic flexibility in the competitive environments that confront most firms worth the possible rewards that might flow if the advantage is secured?

Finally, there is the issue of other competitive arenas within the firm's competitive space. Porter's theory defines competitive advantage and competitive strategy relative to one linked arena: the industry battlefield in which rivals (defined as direct rivals, those offering substitute products, or possible new entrants) compete for the business of customers, each rival striving to gain a sustainable competitive advantage by being the low-cost producer, a differentiator, or a focuser.

But we know that firms encounter other competitors (e.g., suppliers as competitors, customers as competitors) in the same linked arena, or other arenas as well, and that competitive advantages (not necessarily the three hypothesized by Porter) may be achieved in these. IBM competes against Schlumberger, the oil exploration company, for the best computer science graduates with advanced degrees. But the two firms are not industry rivals, and the advantage, if one exists, would not be low cost or differentiation. General Motors competes against its suppliers for the best deal on components. Because of its size, it dominates in this competitive arena, and most suppliers do not find themselves in an enviable position when they do battle with GM. GM's advantage here is vis-à-vis its suppliers. It is not a competitive advantage vis-à-vis Ford or Chrysler, its *direct rivals* who also dominate in their respective supplier arenas because of their size.

Clearly, a firm following a single generic, across-the board strategy in all arenas in which it competes courts disaster. The arenas and the advantages to be gained are too diverse to be managed by means of the simple options suggested by Porter's theory.

In a word, Porter's position on competitive advantage and competitive strategy, the *economist's* view, is too narrow. We need a wider, *practitioner's* conception to capture the variety of advantages, strategies, and arenas found within the firm's competitive space. Hamlet's words, "There are more things in heaven and earth, Horatio, than are dreamt of in your philosophy," apply with even greater force to Porter than they do to Horatio.

COMPETITIVE ADVANTAGE AND INFORMATION TECHNOLOGY

How shall we understand the connection between competitive advantage and information technology? The answer to this question, like many others, depends on one's point of view. Practitioners, we can be sure, will see it differently from economists, because the positions taken by these two groups diverge on at least six key points with respect to competitive advantage and competitive strategy (see Table 3–1): the (1) duration, (2) vulnerability, (3) value, and (4) kind of advantage sought; (5) the competitive arenas in which advantage/strategy operates;

**Table 3–1   Economist versus Practitioner Positions on
Competitive Advantage and Competitive Strategy**

Key points	Economist	Practitioner
Duration of advantage	Long term.	Short, medium, and long term.
Vulnerability of advantage	Sustainable.	Sustainable and contestable.
Value of advantage	Return on investment (ROI) greater than industry average.	Variety of measures, including ROI greater than industry average.
Kind of advantage	Price or feature advantages.	Price or feature advantages and others.
Competitive arena	Rivals only.	Rivals, suppliers, channels, customers.
Strategic moves to achieve advantage	Generic strategies: low cost, focus, differentiation.	Strategic thrusts: cost, growth, differentiation, innovation, alliance.

and (6) the strategic moves that should be followed to gain or maintain one's advantage or reduce an opponent's edge.

Where the economist seeks long-term, sustainable price or feature advantages measured by return on investment greater than the industry average, the practitioner pursues a far wider range of opportunities: short, medium, or long term; sustainable or contestable; price; feature; or other advantages measured by return on investment greater than the industry average or by a variety of other measures such as market share and number of new customers. The economist sees competition in only one arena, among industry rivals, and fashions a single generic strategy aimed at establishing a defensible position against industry forces working to drive down profitability, while the practitioner perceives a multitude of arenas for which strategic thrusts may be designed to support or shape an enterprise's competitive strategies.

These divergencies translate into fundamental differences with respect to possible uses of information technology to gain or maintain advantage or to reduce a competitor's edge. The economist envisions a generic strategy (low cost, differentiation, or focus) that will employ information technology to achieve long-term, sustainable competitive price or feature advantages. But binding uses of information technology in this manner drastically limits admission into the class of strategic information systems (SIS). Many SIS cases cited in the trade press, academic literature, and this book would not pass muster. Yet such cases clearly convey some kind of advantage; and they are not, generally speaking, planning and control applications falling into the conventional management information systems and management support systems categories. If adopted, the economist's position would exclude this rather large set of SIS instances on the grounds that the members do not satisfy its stringent sustainability standards. It would, to say the least, have a chilling effect on the search for SIS opportunities and the future development of this promising interdisciplinary area.

To appreciate the threat posed, consider the position of Eric Clemons and Steven Kimbrough, professors at the Wharton School who adhere (following Porter) to the economist's view.[33] When discussing competitive advantage, they observe that emulatable projects might "reduce costs and thereby permit realization of better than normal returns on investments" and provide temporary advantage. But, they argue, "[i]t is misleading to speak of them as being strategically important. Our practice will be to speak of information systems investment as yielding competitive advantage *only if the advantage is sufficiently long-lived to be considered as altering industry structure.*"[34] [Italics added.] The authors hypothesize that applications such as "interorganizational information systems that convey sustainable competitive advantage [must] reduce costs or add value for customers and users, . . . entail substantial switching costs . . . on the part of the customer or user . . . [and fit through a] small window of opportunity . . . [i.e.,] the ratio of customer adoption time to competitor copy time [must be] quite small."[35] In other words, "real" competitive advantage implies long-term, sustainable price or feature advantages as measured by returns on investment (ROI) "(in a given industry) that are better than normal."[36] Note that the first condition (reduce costs or add value) harks back to Porter's two kinds of sustainable competitive advantage: low cost or differentiation, which I translate into price or feature advantages.

Clemons and Kimbrough's practice leads them, not unexpectedly, to "suspect that the difficulty in locating opportunities for strategic and competitive uses of information systems may in large part be because such opportunities are rare."[37] Granted, such SIS opportunities might be rare, perhaps even rarer than Clemons and Kimbrough suspect. Electronic bondage, their second necessary condition, tends to get short-circuited when, say, a customer's costs as a user of an SIS become onerous or the system is found wanting in desired features, as illustrated in the first-hand report of a pharmacist who switched rather easily from McKesson's Economost system (see Chapter 1) to a rival's SIS.[38] When a rival vendor's offer of assistance includes training, installation, and the tab for any other costs the user may incur in converting from one system to another, the ties that appeared to bind so strongly tend to loosen and then fall. If this is not sufficient, additional enticements may be tendered, as the dynamics of evolving competition in the computerized airline reservation system business show (see Chapter 1). Indeed, it's not clear that the instances of sustainable SIS cited by Clemons and Kimbrough—American Air (see Chapter 1); McKesson (Chapter 1); Merrill Lynch, with its cash management account (Chapter 8); and American Hospital Supply, with its order-entry system (Chapter 8)—satisfy the above three conditions, since the authors have not operationalized what they mean by "substantial switching costs."

Yet I am not so much concerned with their conditions for sustainability as I am with the dampening implications that the economist's position they represent may have for those investigating the strategic use of information technology. For if it is only the economist's understanding of competitive advantage and competitive strategy that guides the search for SIS opportunities and threats, the results are bound to be disappointing. Why? Because opportunities are rare for achieving sustainable competitive advantage independent of any possible contribution by information technology; still rarer are such opportunities supported or shaped by information technology.

Is there no escape from the economist's cul-de-sac? By now, there should be no doubt about the answer to this question. Adoption of the practitioner's position, which includes the economist's as a special case, encourages us to consider SIS opportunities and threats that are short, medium, and long term; sustainable or contestable; found in any competitive arena; and so on. It can, as we shall see in the next chapter, lead us to more fertile fields of SIS possibilities. Recall that SIS are defined as uses of information technology that support or shape the enterprise's competitive strategy, its plan for gaining or maintaining competitive advantage or reducing the edge of adversaries. By understanding competitive advantage and competitive strategy in the practitioner's sense, we can open acres of SIS possibilities that would go forever uncultivated if the economist's view held exclusive sway.

NOTES

1. Edward O. Wilson, *Biophilia* (Cambridge, Mass.: Harvard University Press, 1984).
2. Alfred Oxenfeldt and Jonathan Schwartz, *Techniques for Analyzing Industries and Competitors* (New York: American Management Association, 1981).
3. Barry Kramer, "Japanese Dominate the Chinese Market with Savvy Trading," *The Wall Street Journal*, October 19, 1985.
4. Wilson, *Biophilia*, p. 33.
5. Michael Porter, *Competitive Strategy: Techniques for Analyzing Industries and Competitors* (New York: Free Press, 1980).
6. Michael Porter, *Competitive Advantage: Creating and Sustaining Superior Performance* (New York: Free Press, 1985).
7. Porter, *Competitive Strategy*, p. 3.
8. Ibid., p. 24.
9. Porter, *Competitive Advantage*, p. 1.
10. Ibid., p. 11.
11. Ibid., p. 3.
12. Ibid.
13. Ibid., p. 11.
14. Ibid., p. 57.
15. Ibid., p. 131.
16. Ibid., p. 97.
17. Ibid., p. 1.
18. Ibid., p. 11.
19. Ibid., p. 20.
20. Ibid., p. 11.
21. Ibid., p. 12.
22. Ibid., p. 19.
23. Ibid., p. 18.
24. Ibid., p. 16.
25. Ibid., p. 23.
26. Ibid., p. 123.
27. Pankas Ghemawat, "Sustainable Advantage," *Harvard Business Review*, September–October 1986, p. 54.
28. Ibid.

29. Amar Bhide, "Hustle as Strategy," *Harvard Business Review,* September–October 1986, p. 60. Warren Buffett heads Berkshire Hathaway, a financial services firm.

30. Porter, *Competitive Advantage,* p. 25.

31. Ghemawat, "Sustainable Advantage," p. 58.

32. Ibid.

33. Eric Clemons and Steven Kimbrough, "Information Systems, Telecommunications, and Their Effect on Industrial Organization," *Proceedings of the 1986 International Conference on Information Systems,* San Diego, California, pp. 99–108.

34. Ibid., p. 101–2.

35. Ibid., p. 104.

36. Ibid., p. 101.

37. Ibid., p. 107.

38. Curtis Andrews, "Experiences with McKesson's Economost Order-Entry System," Research paper prepared for a course on the strategic use of information technology, Columbia University Graduate School of Business, 1987.

4

Strategic Perspective

The strategic perspective on information technology proposed here relies on an analytical framework built to capture the major moves open to organizations in search of advantage. I call this framework the *theory of strategic thrusts*. By supporting or shaping the organization's strategic thrusts, strategic information systems (SIS) support or shape its competitive strategy, its plan for achieving or maintaining competitive advantage or for reducing the edge of an opponent. Strategic thrusts therefore constitute the critical interface that links strategy and information technology.

To prepare for the theory, it will help if we can first develop an intuitive grasp of what is meant by a strategic thrust. A brief review of the strategic evolution of General Motors should serve to identify some of the major strategic thrusts of interest to us. These will reveal the range of opportunities open to the enterprise seeking advantage and provide the basis for a more general discussion of the theory in the last two sections of this chapter.

STRATEGIC THRUSTS AT GENERAL MOTORS

The history of American industry is replete with the kinds of major moves that I count as strategic thrusts: vertical integration along an industry chain, innovation in product or process, diversification or entry into related businesses, expansion to achieve economies of scale or scope, differentiation of product, and acquisitions or other alliances. Each is illustrated in the classic chronicle of William Durant, the founder of General Motors, and by some of GM's actions under Alfred Sloan (Durant's successor) in the embryonic and growth stages of the automotive industry.

Prior to forming GM in 1908, Durant was in the carriage business, having created in 1885 the Durant-Dort Carriage Company with Dallas Dort, a hardware salesman. Durant-Dort began with neither manufacturing facilities nor distribution network. To stimulate business for their product, a new kind of cart, the partners first had to persuade dealers and distributors to promote it. When orders wheeled in, they contracted with a local assembler to produce the carts.

As demand accelerated, Durant-Dort expanded by building its own assembly plant. This move helped reduce costs, putting the company in a better position relative to its direct competitors, the other carriagemakers. Figure 4–1 diagrams the transformation of Durant-Dort's *product network* through the strategic thrust of expansion via vertical integration backwards. It records how this strategic move transformed Durant-Dort from an order-taking enterprise into a producer and captures an important growth stage in the strategic evolution of the firm.

But when demand increased still further, the firm found itself caught in the classic double bind of losing battles simultaneously in supplier and competitor arenas, which in this case were linked. It sacrificed sales to competitors and, hence, market share; it paid premium prices to suppliers who acted oppor-

Figure 4–1   Growth at Durant-Dort

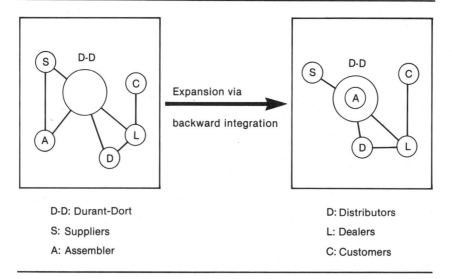

Expansion via

backward integration

D-D: Durant-Dort

S: Suppliers

A: Assembler

D: Distributors

L: Dealers

C: Customers

tunistically toward it. To secure control over the supplier bottleneck and to cut costs, costs that put it at a competitive disadvantage vis-à-vis its direct competitors, Durant-Dort decided to internalize these transactions, this time setting up or financing specialty plants to produce parts needed in its assembly works. From the *assembly* of carts and carriages, Durant-Dort again expanded its operations to include the *manufacture* of bodies, wheels, axles, upholstery, and springs. Expansion enabled it to reduce the advantages held by its suppliers and direct competitors.

Following backward integration, Durant-Dort grew again via moves that extended its product line. By 1900, its factories were manufacturing a full array of carriages, carts, wagons, buggies, and the like, all sold under the Blue Ribbon trademark. Just 15 years after the founding of Durant-Dort, Durant's entrepreneurial acumen had made him a millionaire.

Even though the company became the leading wagon and carriage producer in the United States, its prospects were far from bright. Whatever competitive advantage Durant-Dort may have attained in its marketplace—being the low-cost producer or the manufacturer of the most highly differentiated product inducing the greatest customer loyalty—would be rendered worthless if a new product, the horseless carriage, caught on. Remember, this was the turn of the century, when the automobile industry was moving only in first gear: in 1900, the United States produced fewer than 5,000 cars. In 1902, 12 firms manufactured automobiles; one year later, the total had climbed to 24. The next year, 12 new entrants sprouted. In 1903, the leading manufacturer was Ransom Olds, whose Oldsmobile held 25 percent of the market; 10 years later, Henry Ford produced 182,000 Model Ts, winning 39.4 percent of the expanding automobile market. In 1904, Durant entered the embryonic industry by acquiring the assets of the Buick Motor Company, a bankrupt automobile manufacturer.

This strategic move—prompted by the automobile's threat to carriagemakers as a substitute mode of transportation, by the availability of related managerial and other resources at

Durant-Dort, and by Durant's entrepreneurial and empire-building talents—led in four years to the formation of General Motors. The steps Durant took with Buick reflected the moves he had made previously with Durant-Dort and presaged those he would take as the head of GM.

He redesigned the Buick, built large assembly plants, and established a national marketing and sales network by granting franchises in rural areas to regional distributors (who would be responsible for managing local dealers) and by opening retail outlets to sell directly to consumers in large cities. In both manufacturing and selling, Durant relied on the underutilized, slack managerial and technical talents drawn from his carriage business. Charles Nash, for example, the production manager of the carriageworks, became head of the Buick company.

As the volume of sales orders increased, Durant again initiated an expansion program, integrating backward to cut transaction costs and avoid supply bottlenecks. In the process, for example, he acquired Weston-Mott and Champion, the former a manufacturer of axles and wheels, the latter of sparkplugs. As a result of such acquisitions and other strategic moves, Buick became the leading automobile manufacturer in the United States, increasing its production from 31 cars in 1904 to 8,847 in 1908, with Ford in second place with 6,181 and Cadillac third with 2,380.

Predicting sales of over 1 million cars a year and with the lessons learned at Durant-Dort and Buick imprinted on his mind, Durant concluded in 1908 that the best way to meet this anticipated, unprecedented demand was to grow by forming alliances. Rejected by both Ford and Olds, Durant formed the GM holding company, which in its first two years obtained complete or partial control of Buick, Olds, Cadillac, 8 other automobile companies, 2 electrical lamp companies, and 12 auto and accessory manufacturers.

But Durant's predictions proved erroneous, forcing his resignation from the presidency of GM in 1910. He was replaced by Storrow, who (with the support of GM's bankers) introduced administrative changes aimed at improving efficiency by consolidating joint activities such as purchasing, accounting, and engineering.

Durant, however, was not to be denied. In the years following his resignation, he took control of Chevrolet, an integrated, high-volume automobile company, and developed important financial ties with members of the Du Pont family. Parlaying these resources, he regained control of GM in 1916. Another round of supplier acquisitions followed, among them the Hyatt Roller Bearing Company, which brought with it Alfred Sloan, the organizational wizard who succeeded Durant.

To pave the road for increased sales, GM introduced a radically new entity, the GM Acceptance Corporation, in 1919 (see Figure 4–2). This financial innovation revolutionized the automotive credit business. Prior to the formation of GMAC, dealers, distributors, and consumers had no reliable source of credit for their automobile purchases, as banks seemed to have "a moral objection to financing a luxury, believing apparently whatever fostered consumption must discourage thrift. Conse-

Figure 4–2   Innovation at GM

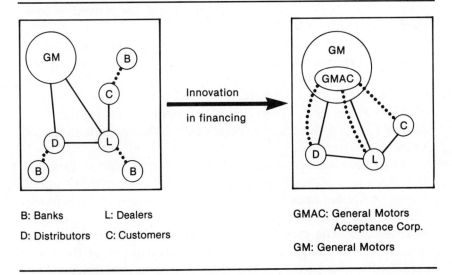

B: Banks   L: Dealers

D: Distributors   C: Customers

GMAC: General Motors
             Acceptance Corp.

GM: General Motors

quently, automobiles were sold to consumers mainly for cash."[1] Dealers and distributors also frequently lacked funds to finance inventories and retail installment sales; local banks were simply too rigid to meet the demand generated by the mass production of automobiles. The GMAC innovation gave GM an advantage in its struggles with other automobile manufacturers and in bargaining negotiation with its distributors and dealers. These latter complained that GM forced them to finance exclusively through GMAC; in 1939, the U.S. government initiated criminal proceedings against GM on this matter. The court found GM guilty; but not until 1952, after a long battle with the Antitrust Division of the Justice Department, did GM consent to change the ground rules under which it and its distributors and dealers operated.

GM's moves to alter business practices and thereby establish competitive advantage were not, of course, limited to the financial area. External competitive threats and internal management crises prompted innovations in organization and product policy that had equally profound effects on the automobile industry. As a result of these strategic moves, GM upset the competitive balance in the industry, securing for itself (at least among its domestic competitors) what has proved to be a decisive advantage.

In the early 1920s, GM viewed the Ford Motor Co. as its principal external threat. Under the aegis of founder Henry Ford, the company had won the top spot in the growing industry, climbing from a 9.7 percent share of the market in 1909 to 55.7 percent in 1921. These figures count only sales for the Ford Model T, first offered in 1908 and essentially unchanged for 19 years thereafter.

Ford, less interested in design innovation than in production advances, pioneered the application of assembly-line operations in the automotive industry, with concomitant standardization and specialization of manufacturing processes and labor efforts. His goal was to provide the most inexpensive, reliable car to the greatest number of consumers at the least cost. In this, he succeeded admirably. In 1909, the price of the

Model T touring car was $950 (12,000 sold); in 1913, $550 (182,000 sold); in 1917, $450 (741,000 sold); in 1921, the height of Ford's supremacy, $355 (845,000 sold). The Spartan Ford firm, which ran a lean, mean operation, was a formidable opponent to the Athenian GM, an organization composed of far too many quasi-independent, freethinking units, each tooting its own horn.

This was the challenge Sloan faced when he took the wheel in 1923. At the time of his ascendancy, GM's market share was 20 percent, essentially unchanged from where it was in 1910 under Durant. By 1929, GM had replaced Ford as the industry leader, capturing 32.3 percent of new car sales to Ford's 31.3 percent; in 1933, the margin widened: 41.4 percent to 20.7 percent.

What did GM do under Sloan to gain such a competitive advantage? Two related innovations were critical. The first dealt with GM's internal management crisis, the second with Ford and the other car manufacturers. GM suffered, Sloan argued, from excessive decentralization as a result of its policy of rapid expansion and acquisition following World War I. The remedy, Sloan concluded, was greater coordination and integration of activities. Without that, top management would never know or prove "where the efficiencies and inefficiencies lay, there being no objective basis for the allocation of new investment."[2] Fundamental to Sloan's view on management problems was his belief that the strategic aim of any business should be to earn a satisfactory return on capital. If not achieved, management must correct the deficiency or dispose of the activity for a more profitable one. Without improved coordination and integration, Sloan contended, GM would never be in a position to make rational decisions about such matters and so would never be able to compete head-to-head with Ford.

Through Sloan's efforts, GM became one of the first businesses in the United States to adopt the multidivisional form of organization. This structure gave GM self-contained divisions (e.g., Chevrolet, Buick, and Cadillac), each having its own engineering, production, and sales functions and an array of corporate staff groups (e.g., R&D, finance) to coordinate and support the activities of the divisions. At the top of the managerial hierarchy, to resolve divisional conflicts and determine corporate policy, was the executive committee.

Prior to the new structure, each unit acted independently, setting its own prices and production rules (which often placed some GM cars in direct competition with others) with no regard for the general well-being of GM. Under Sloan's regime, pricing and product policy became a matter for the executive committee to decide. Through this organizational innovation, GM took the first step toward upsetting the competitive balance.

According to Sloan, "the fundamental conception of the *advantage* to be secured in this business was expressed by cooperation and coordination of our various policies and divisions."[3][Italics added.] Sloan and his colleagues thus rejected the notion that it was essential that GM's production, advertising, selling, or servicing activities for any particular product be more efficient than its best competitor. They assumed that greater efficiency would be achieved through divisional cooperation and coordination once the GM units stopped working at cross-purposes.

Sloan's second strategic move transformed GM's laissez-faire product line policy into a powerful competitive weapon. Where Ford had achieved domination and low-cost producer status through almost fanatical dedication to the production of essentially one product (the Model T), GM sought its competitive advantage through a policy of product differentiation. Sloan's administration formulated a strategy that called for the production of six standard models, distinguished by well-defined price, quality, design, and other features. Each car in the GM product line would now be integral, conceived in relation to other models in the line, with Chevrolet at the bottom and Cadillac at the top—the price range of Cadillac being set at about six times that of Chevrolet.

Sloan was crystal clear about the new product policy and its aim of mass-producing a full line of cars graded upward in quality and price. "This principle supplied the first element in *differentiating* the General Motor's concept of the market from that of the old, Ford Model T concept."[4] The new policy put GM's Chevrolet in direct competition, for the first time, with the Model T.

The strategic move toward product differentiation, coupled with Sloan's multidivisional structural innovation, catapulted GM, within a few years, to the leadership role it then held for decades. The automobile industry is not, as Ford viewed it, a commodity business. Through design, advertising, and the like, manufacturers take great pains to differentiate their products from those of their rivals. They aim to establish long-lasting brand loyalties, for repeat buying is a vital part of the car market. Sloan and GM were the first to realize these truths and to capitalize on them. Through such moves, GM established the competitive edge it maintained until recently.

We conclude our discussion of the Durant-Sloan-GM annals with some strategic moves of another sort: growth via diversification thrusts into nonautomotive markets. Success in diversification often depends on a firm's ability to transfer skills and resources from existing activities to the new venture. For GM, such transfers involved mass-production engineering knowhow and the management expertise accompanying it. According to Sloan, GM had "never made anything except 'durable products,' and they have always, with minor exceptions, been connected with motors. Not even Mr. Durant, for all his expansion and diversification, ever suggested that we should stray into any field clearly outside the boundary suggested by our corporate name, General Motors."[5] GM's interest in diversification seems to have been primarily defensive, either as a hedge against the vagaries of automobile demand or the threat of substitute products that might replace the automobile. But in some situations, GM recognized a growth opportunity and entered the business to exploit it. In any case,

Sloan states, "we never had a master plan for nonautomotive ventures; we got into them for different reasons, and we were very lucky at some critical points."[6]

GM entered the diesel business in the early 30s, at the time when the dominant engine driving the locomotive industry was designed for steam. Prior to GM's entry, locomotives had always been built to a railroad's custom specifications, so that no two in the United States were alike. GM changed this, not through technological innovation but by the transfer of its manufacturing, engineering, and marketing knowhow from the automotive arena to the locomotive. GM manufactured *standardized* diesel locomotives produced in volume, guaranteed to perform at a lower cost per ton mile than steam-driven ones, and maintained by a dedicated service organization using standard replacement parts. In less than a decade, GM's diesels outsold all other locomotives combined. By capitalizing on its own underutilized management and technical resources, GM developed unmatched competitive strength. Through this diversification move, it became the dominant producer in a new industry, selling new products in new markets.

In 1918, GM bought the near-bankrupt firm, Guardian Refrigerator Corporation. After considerable effort by engineers at the GM R&D labs and a name change, the "new" Frigidaire became the market leader in less than a decade. GM stated in its 1925 annual report:

> This apparatus lends itself both from the standpoint of type of manufacture as well as market possibilities to quantity production. The Corporation believes that through its broad experience in quality manufacture, its research activities and through its purchasing ability on account of the large volume of its operations, it can more than maintain the dominating position that Frigidaire now enjoys.[7]

By 1933, GM's Frigidaire Division itself adopted a diversification strategy by increasing the *depth* of its air-conditioning line, offering units for all fields of application (home, office, hotel, hospital, etc.). In 1936, it increased the *width* of its product line by moving into electric ranges and other household accessories and equipment.

Fearing the possibility that personal airplanes might someday replace cars, GM diversified again in 1928, this time into the aircraft industry, purchasing a 40 percent stake in the Fokker Aircraft Corporation of America and a 20 percent interest in the newly formed Bendix Aviation Corporation. A short time later, it acquired a 30 percent share of North American Aviation, a company that once controlled both TWA and Eastern Air Lines.

GM, it seems, was anxious about the possibility of a small plane being produced for everyday family use, a development that Sloan believed would entail, to say the least, large unforeseeable consequences for the automobile industry. To be protected, GM declared itself in the aviation industry. It "felt that, in view of the more or less close relationship in an engineering way between the airplane and the motor car, its operating organization, technical and otherwise, should be placed in a position where it would have an opportunity to come into contact with the particular problems involved in transportation by air."[8]

As it turned out, the threat never materialized, and GM made less of an impact through its engineering genius than through the management expertise it provided to Fokker, Bendix, and North American. Sloan believed that this was perhaps GM's greatest contribution to the airline industry. Through its board memberships and managerial contacts with these aerospace companies, GM was able to transfer some of its managerial skills to its investments. This most likely helped these firms compete more effectively and build commanding positions in their respective segments of the aviation industry.

As they grew, so did the value of GM's investment in them. When, in the late 40s, GM decided to liquidate its aviation holdings, it did so only to release capital to fuel its automotive operations, which after World II were growing rapidly.

THE THEORY OF STRATEGIC THRUSTS

Over the evolutionary span just sketched, GM made major moves related to vertical integration, innovation, cost reduction, product line expansion, diversification, and acquisition. These and countless other moves taken by different enterprises in their endless quest for advantage reflect a daunting multiplicity of strategic actions. The theory of strategic thrusts is intended to simplify this multiplicity by reducing it to five basic actions in terms of which the others can be expressed. These five basic strategic thrusts—*differentiation, cost, innovation, growth,* and *alliance* (see Chapters 5–9)—are adequate to account for most of the moves organizations make in search of advantage within the various arenas, independent or linked, comprising their competitive space.

Strategic thrusts can be thought of as transformations that operate on various states of the enterprise. Thrusts transform an enterprise in state X into state Y, where Y is designed to gain or maintain an edge or to reduce a competitor's advantage. The transformations may apply to product networks, industry or firm value chains, organizational configurations, product lines, and so on. A *transformation diagram* graphically represents the strategic thrust T that transforms state X into state Y.

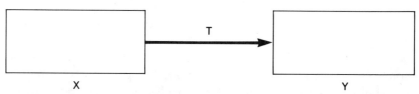

In a transformation diagram, the areas within the rectangles may be filled with appropriate representations of states X and Y. (Figures 4–1 and 4–2 above are examples of such diagrams, where X and Y are product networks representing the flow of goods and information in the business.) This is only one form of representation; other diagrams are possible, of course.

Strategic thrusts are actions intended to support or shape the enterprise's competitive strategy within an arena. In some instances, the thrust can be identified with the strategy. In others, the strategy may be supported and shaped by a family of one or more thrusts. In the case of linked arenas, where action in arena A affects the competitive balance in arena B, thrust T may require cooperation rather than competition in A so that the firm can gain an edge in B as a result of the cooperation.

Relying for a moment on the everyday meaning of these thrusts (each will be described more fully in the next five chapters when I shall show how information technology can be used to support or shape them), let us examine some of their properties.

Properties of Strategic Thrusts

First, they manifest *strategic polarities*. By this I mean that they are capable of assuming opposing sets of attributes, depending upon their strategic use. When GM formulated its product policy under Sloan, it was using differentiation *offensively* to gain competitive advantage vis-à-vis Ford and the other automobile manufacturers. Another company might use this move *defensively* by taking steps to reduce the differentiation advantage of its rivals and thereby advance its own competitive position (see the Honeywell Building Controls Group example in Chapter 5).

Reducing costs and becoming the low-cost producer in an industry often leads to competitive advantage. But a company that can manipulate factors that will *raise* the costs of its competitors may also establish a competitive edge by this maneuver. Alternatively, helping suppliers or customers *decrease* their costs may win the approval of these stakeholders and ultimately serve as an important competitive advantage in battles against direct rivals. Cost may be used *offensively* when a company attempts to reduce its supplier costs so that it can better compete by reducing its prices relative to its direct rivals. Cost may also be used *defensively* by organizations attempting to reduce the leverage that vendors or customers may have over them in their respective arenas.

An innovation in production, processing, or product quality may *increase* the competitive advantage an organization currently enjoys, while another may serve to *decrease* the edge competitors may have. Some may use innovation *offensively* to preempt, while others may exploit it *defensively* to imitate.

Growth via volume or geographical expansion, backward or forward integration, product line or entry diversification may succeed in *increasing* competitive advantage and hence be an *offensive* weapon in an organization's arsenal, or it may be wielded as a *defensive* weapon aimed at *reducing* the opportunities of opponents to gain an edge.

Alliances—joint ventures, acquisitions, and the like—may be arranged to support or shape differentiation, cost, innovation, or growth moves. Hence, they too exhibit the strategic polarities just mentioned.

Second, strategic thrusts frequently occur *in combination.* To gain competitive edge, for instance, a growth-via-backward-integration maneuver, intended primarily to internalize market transactions, may also be aimed at reducing costs (and prices) through innovative applications of technology, made possible by combining acquired and existing resources.

Third, strategic thrusts reflect *a variety of ordering or degree relations.* For example, a cost reduction may be major, medium, or minor; and a differentiation, innovation, alliance, or growth move may be short term or long term.

Fourth, strategic thrusts may be bound together by *dialectical processes,* such as the one illustrated above by Durant's jump from carriages into automobiles. Recall that Durant-Dort had evolved into the leading carriage and wagon producer in the United States. To be in that position, it enjoyed either a price or a features advantage, earned by a cost or differentiation thrust. Yet Durant knew that this edge would be worthless if the automobile replaced the carriage as the primary mode of household transportation. In terms of strategic options, therefore, innovation, growth via diversification, and alliance were open to him as possible moves to transform the nature of Durant-Dort's activities so that it could survive in the new automotive environment. Because innovation in the carriage industry wouldn't be worth the effort, assuming Durant's hypothesis, he therefore had only two options. To build his new enterprise, he pursued both: growth via diversification (making use of resources drawn from Durant-Dort) and alliance formation.

When Durant's empire-building activities came to a close and Sloan was left to rationalize GM's uncoordinated holdings, the dialectical process culminated (temporarily at least) as the focal points of competitive advantage switched from growth and alliance to cost, differentiation, and innovation maneuvers. When these were exhausted, the dialectic resumed.

Chandler and Porter on Strategy

The theory of strategic thrusts sketched above links directly to two important works on strategy: Alfred Chandler's *Strategy and Structure: Chapters in the History of American Industrial Enterprise* (1962)[9] and Michael Porter's *Competitive Strategy: Techniques for Analyzing Industries and Competitors* (1980).[10] Chandler's research on the relationship between an enterprise's growth strategy and the organizational form adopted to execute it led to the rapid expansion of the business strategy field in the 60s and 70s. It was the point of departure for the most influential strategic thinkers of that period (Igor Ansoff, George Steiner, Kenneth Andrews, Seymour Tilles, and others). Porter's application of concepts developed by Joe Bain, and other industrial organization economists, to the competitive strategy area in the late 70s and early 80s sparked another expansion of the field as researchers and practitioners rushed to explore the ramifications of his work.

If, as Chandler suggests, a growth strategy involves "the determination of the basic long-term goals and objectives of the organization"[11] and if "decisions to expand the volume of activities, to set up distant plants and offices, to move into new economic functions, or become diversified along many lines of business"[12] are among the most important strategic decisions an organization can make, then strategic thrusts are those actions associated with such decisions. The strategic thrusts of growth (through expansion, vertical integration, and diversification) and alliance formation (through mergers, acquisitions, and other combinations) are ipso facto tied closely to an organization's growth strategy.

As a result of his studies on the relation between strategy and structure, Chandler hypothesized a pattern of growth and development followed, in varying degrees, by the largest firms in the United States. During Stage 1 in Chandler's growth model, the single-product (-function, -plant, -office, -location, -industry) firm might pursue a growth-via-volume-expansion strategy in response to accelerating demand for its product. Depending on the firm's primary function, this might entail increasing the scale of its sales, manufacturing, or distribution operations. It might also, concurrently or sequentially, follow a growth-via-geographical-expansion strategy, establishing units in different parts of the country. As its scale grew, the firm might decide to participate in other functions along its product network, from supplying raw materials to retail distribution. It would therefore adopt a growth-via-backward/forward-integration (usually through acquisition) strategy, depending on the opportunities open to it. Clearly, each strategic move made during Stage 1 is an instance of either strategic growth or alliance thrusts. The formation of the firm itself might have been due to a new product or a fundamental change in the method of conducting business in an industry. If so, these would be instances of the strategic innovation thrust.

The emergence of the huge, vertically integrated firm marked, for Chandler, the end of Stage 1 and the start of Stage 2. In Stage 2, the sprawling empires that Chandler studied developed strategies to reduce unit costs, enhance product quality and services in response to competitive offerings, improve inefficiently coordinated activities among its functional groups, and so on. Technology often played a critical role during this stage, with firms such as Swift (a gigantic, nationwide distribution and marketing organization in the meat-packing industry at the turn of the century) being the first to move innovatively in the application of the new telephone and telegraph services. These telecommunication technologies enabled Swift to coordinate the activities of its stockyards, packing plants, district offices (which operated warehouses and controlled wholesale, and often retail, outlets), and corporate headquarters. Swift substantially reduced costly errors due to misallocation of supply and demand. Again, as in Stage 1, the strategic actions taken during Stage 2 are instances of strategic thrusts: differentiation, cost, and innovation.

The successful Stage 2 firms established significant and, in some cases, long-lasting competitive advantages. But they couldn't prevent competitors from emulating their efforts and thereby eroding these advantages. There are limits on the efficiencies to be obtained in purchasing, production, distribution, marketing, and so on. As the differences between enterprises receded, profit margins dropped.

> More intensive advertising, product differentiation and improvement, and similar strategies might increase one firm's share of the market, but only major changes in technology, population, and national income could expand the overall market for a single line of products. As the market became more saturated and the opportunities to cut costs through more rational techniques lessened, enterprises began to search for other markets or to develop other businesses that might profitably employ some of the partially utilized resources or even make a more profitable application of those still being fully employed.[13]

For Chandler, this situation signaled the onset of Stage 3: continued growth, essentially reached through diversification. Firms offering a single line might follow a growth-via-full-line-diversification strategy, thus making a range of comparable products available to their customers. In Stage 3, meat packers would diversify into eggs, poultry, and dairy products, taking advantage of economies of scope (see Chapter 6) made possible by excess refrigeration capacity in their distribution network. Others might diversify into international markets. Still others might grow by finding new uses for old products, by developing by-products, by transferring to other areas resources dedicated to one product line or industry, and so on. According to Chandler, "the enterprises whose resources were the most transferable remained those whose men and equipment came to handle a range of technology, rather than a set of end products."[14] Among these were firms involved in the chemical, electrical and electronic, and power machinery industries—industries that also invested the largest percentages of their resources in research and development projects.

Just as Stage 1 (accumulating resources) closed with the need to coordinate inefficiently run operations and led to Stage 2 (rationalizing the use of resources), Stage 3 (continued growth) produced inefficiencies that called for action. It came in Stage 4: rationalizing the use of expanding resources. Organizational innovations—such as Sloan's introduction of the multidivisional structure to handle GM's semiautonomous, diverse operations, and the institutionalization of the strategy of diversification—are this stage's most important features of interest to us.

Other researchers (among them Bruce Scott, Richard Rumelt, and Jay Galbraith) improved Chandler's model by refining his analysis of the stages of growth and the strategy of diversification. But these articulations of Chandler's ideas do not affect the main point being made here: each stage of a firm's evolution fundamentally involves strategic thrusts.

For Porter, recall that competitive strategy involves "taking offensive or defensive actions to create a defendable position in an industry, to cope successfully with the five competitive forces [i.e., threat of entry, intensity of rivalry among existing firms, pressures from substitute products, bargaining power of buyers, and bargaining power of suppliers] and thereby yield a superior return on investment for the firm."[15] It is my contention that strategic thrusts can be used to support or shape the three generic strategies he suggests for outperforming other firms in an industry: *overall cost leadership, differentiation,* and *focus.*

Overall cost leadership requires "aggressive construction of efficient scale facilities, vigorous pursuit of cost reductions from experience, tight cost and overhead control, avoiding marginal customer accounts, and cost minimization in areas like R&D, service, sales force, advertising and so on. . . . *Low cost relative to competitors* becomes a theme running through the entire strategy."[16] [Italics added.] Instances of the strategic cost thrust can be used to support or shape this strategy.

Porter's notion of a generic low-cost strategy to defend against the five competitive forces determining industry profitability differs radically from our concept of cost as a strategic thrust. For Porter, cost as a generic strategy is not a polar concept; it is defined only with respect to cost reduction efforts on the part of a firm following the "overall cost leadership" strategy, a strategy designed to provide a sustainable advantage vis-à-vis rivals. The strategic cost thrust suffers no such limitation. It may operate in any competitive arena, offensively or defensively, aimed at sustainable or contestable advantages, and so on (see Chapter 3).

The "second generic strategy is one of differentiating the product or service offering of the firm, creating something that is perceived *industrywide* as being unique. . . . It should be stressed that the differentiation strategy does not allow the firm to ignore costs, but rather they are not the primary *strategic target.*"[17] [Italics added.]

Again, note that Porter's notion of a generic differentiation strategy differs radically from our concept of differentiation as a strategic thrust. For Porter, differentiation as a generic strategy is not a polar concept; it is defined only with respect to *increasing* the differentiation advantages enjoyed by a firm following this strategy. The strategic differentiation thrust suffers no such limitation (for the same reasons as given above for the cost thrust).

The final strategy, focus, has as its target a particular industry segment. "The strategy rests on the premise that the firm is thus able to serve its narrow *strategic target* more effectively or efficiently than competitors who are competing more broadly. As a result, the firm achieves either differentiation from better meeting the needs of the particular target, or lower costs in serving this target, or both."[18] The points made above with respect to Porter's other generic strategies apply here as well, because the focus policy relies ultimately on a firm's resolve to be either the low-cost or a highly differentiated producer, albeit in a market segment rather than industrywide.

I have taken pains first to connect strategic thrusts and then to distinguish them from generic strategies. This done, let us consider another aspect of Porter's work relevant to this book. Recall that generic strategies are designed to cope with the five forces shaping competition and determining (assuming, as Porter does, the applicability of the industry structure → behavior → performance model, the fundamental paradigm of industrial organization economics) industry profitability. A firm defends itself against these forces or takes steps to influence them in its favor by adopting a generic strategy that, in Porter's view, will lead to a long-term, sustainable price or feature competitive advantage, industrywide or in a segment.

The five forces Porter posits derive their strength, which ranges from intense to nil, from a variety of sources. The strategist needs to investigate these sources, for they reveal the strengths and weaknesses of industry participants and environmental opportunities and threats. This study, called structural analysis, provides the base upon which competitive strategy should be formulated. The strategy will attempt to deal with the forces through programs aimed at manipulating their sources.

Strategic thrusts play a critical role in this process. For example, erection of barriers against new entrants, if taken as a strategic move, can be expressed in terms of our strategic thrusts of differentiation or cost. (This will become clearer in the next two chapters as these latter concepts are defined and illustrated.) Alternatively, the strategic thrusts of differentiation, cost, innovation, growth, and alliance can be used to affect bargaining relations between buyers and suppliers.[19]

This completes the description of the theory of strategic thrusts, the conceptual underpinning for the strategic perspective on information technology presented here. The theory spotlights two complementary lines of strategic thought: Chandler's work on organizational growth and Porter's on competitive analysis. We might visualize these as converging to form a kind of matrix from which the firm fashions its major strategic moves, its strategic thrusts. For, as we have just shown, strategic thrusts are linked directly to Chandler's growth strategies and to Porter's generic strategies and industry forces. They are the basic moves an enterprise can execute in pursuit of advantage. Part II will show how information technology is used to support or shape competitive strategies by supporting or shaping strategic thrusts. Strategic thrusts constitute, therefore, the vehicles for harnessing strategy and information technology.

STRATEGIC OPTION GENERATOR

The theory of strategic thrusts enables us not only to illustrate strategic connections but also to design a conceptual instrument, the *strategic option generator* (see Figure 4–3), to identify SIS opportunities and thrusts.[20] But a user of the instrument must be familiar with the theory of strategic thrusts, just as an experimental physicist who uses a bubble chamber in searching for fundamental particles must grasp the atomic theory of matter. If not, the scientist would, like the layman, see only meaningless patterns instead of particle tracks. (See the introduction to this book for more on this point.)

The option generator rivets the mind on a range of strategic targets and then on the strategic thrusts used to reach them. By prompting a series of questions related to targets and thrusts,

Figure 4–3   Strategic Option Generator

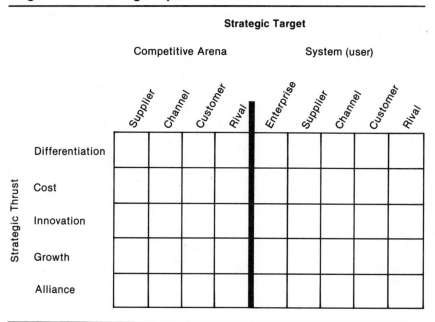

the generator encourages its users to search systematically for SIS opportunities and threats. (See Chapter 10 for an account of how this approach was successfully applied at GTE.)

When discussing targets, thrusts, and information technology, we need to distinguish (1) the target(s) of the system from (2) the target(s) of the competitive arena. The former, called *system (user) targets*, are those entities involved with using the application; the latter, called *competitive arena targets*, are those competitors of the enterprise within supplier, channel, customer, or rival arenas whose competitive position is affected by the firm's use of information technology and the thrust(s) it supports or shapes. In some instances, the system and the arena target(s) are one. But this is not always the case.

A firm might, for instance, develop an application to monitor inventory and product quality among its suppliers. Since both the firm and its vendors would use it, they are both targets of the system. But the application would provide no edge to the firm in the supplier arena. Rather, it would, for instance, enable the firm to satisfy customer needs for the timely delivery of a top-quality product. This ability would earn the firm an advantage over its direct rivals, the arena targets at which the thrust is pointed.

Classifying Strategic Targets

Five classes of system or user targets should be explored: the enterprise (firm, company, organization) itself, suppliers (vendors), channels (intermediaries between the firm and its suppliers and customers), customers (end users, consumers), and rivals. Also needing exploration are four classes of competitive arena targets: suppliers, channels, customers, and rivals. It is with respect to arena targets that the enterprise may gain or maintain competitive advantage or reduce a target's edge.

Enterprise targets.   Enterprise targets comprise internal groups involved with the enterprise's product network. These include functional units (e.g., manufacturing, marketing, and finance) as well as business units that may serve as internal suppliers or buyers of the enterprise's product.

Supplier targets.   Supplier targets are organizations providing what the firm needs to make its product(s) ready for sale, where product is understood to be any good or service offered to satisfy a want or need. This definition is intended to net such diverse production factors as those providing raw materials, finished goods, labor, capital, utilities, insurance, information, advertising and public relations services, energy, permission(s), medical services, and transportation.

Channel targets.   These targets comprise organizations acquiring the firm's product so that they can arrange for its sale to end users or to other channel members. This captures a wide assortment of intermediaries that includes, but is not limited to:

- *Middlemen:* Organizations assisting the firm in its search for customers or in its attempt to close sales with them. Examples include both retailers (specialty, department, convenience, combination, discount warehouse, and superstores; supermarkets, service businesses, mail- and telephone-order, vending machines, buying services, door-to-door, chain, franchise operations), and wholesalers (full service, including wholesale merchants, industrial distributors; limited service, such as rack jobbers, mail-order, truck jobbers; brokers; agents).
- *Physical distributors:* Organizations assisting the firm in stocking and moving its products. Examples include truckers, railroads, pipeline companies, airlines, inland and oceanic shippers, bus companies.
- *Financial institutions:* Organizations assisting the firm in acquiring supplies or in financing its sales or insuring risks associated with their purchase or sale. Examples include banks, credit companies, and insurance companies.

Customer targets.   This class of targets includes individuals or organizations that purchase the firm's product for their own use. Depending on how the product is used, this class may be divided into five categories: consumers (who use it for personal consumption), industrial buyers (who use it to produce other products), resellers (who use it, after adding value, for resale), governments (who either use it to produce public services or transfer it to others who need it), and international customers (i.e., foreign consumers, industrial buyers, resellers, and governments).

Rival targets.   Rival targets comprise organizations selling (or potentially selling) products judged to be the same as, similar to, or substitutable for the firm's. Granted, this is not the most precise of definitions. Yet, for our purposes, it is adequate, for it identifies at least three recognizable subclasses: *direct rivals*, those selling the same or similar products, also known as the industry (e.g., Ford, GM, and Chrysler); *potential rivals*, those who may enter the industry to sell the same or similar products; and *substitute rivals*, those that may or do sell substitute products. To these subclasses, a fourth, the *indirect rivals*, can be added by extending the definition of rival targets to include those entities that may not sell the same, similar, or substitutable products but that may use the same resources (e.g., labor, components) as the firm. Note that I do not count suppliers, channels, and customers among the rival classes, yet each is a potential *competitor* (adversary, opponent) of the firm in its respective competitive arenas.

Transactional Relationships

With the diversity of possible supplier, channel, customer, and rival targets, it is not surprising to find between the enterprise and these entities a variety of transactional relations ranging from long-term contractual to short-term perfunctory, from vehemently competitive to intimately cooperative. Nor is it unusual to discover within the firm specialized groups dedicated to dealing with different kinds of suppliers, channels, customers, and rivals. On the supplier side, for example, the human resources department bargains with labor, telecommunications with long-distance telephone carriers, and purchasing with raw materials or finished goods vendors. On the channel or customer side, we find internal groups dedicated to handling the special needs and desires of intermediary or end-user buyers. In some negotiations, gaining competitive advantage is the main objective; in others, no such concern dominates.

The same kind of channel (agent or intermediary) structure may exist between suppliers and the firm as exists between the firm and its customers. Thus, the firm sometimes deals directly with manufacturers and at other times with sales reps or retailers who may carry the manufacturer's products

One should note too that a firm's suppliers may be its channels, customers, or rivals; its rivals may be its suppliers, channels, or customers; and its channels or customers may be its suppliers or rivals. This kind of overlap often makes for interesting strategic plays—some legal, others less so.

Finally, the major points on the enterprise's product network—its suppliers, channels, and customers—and their relations need to be analyzed to determine those of strategic importance that can be managed by the firm to achieve its ends. I shall return to this subject in Part III, "Implementation."

The option generator concentrates attention on important elements (targets and thrusts) in the firm's *strategic mix*. It should not, however, be taken as a rigid scheme for classifying strategic uses of information technology. (Indeed, the same SIS may be assigned in some cases—with good reasons—to different cells in the matrix by different people.) Rather, it is intended to function more as a heuristic device to aid in the process of identifying SIS, comparable in this regard to some of the general-purpose schemes suggested recently by F. Warren McFarlan, James Cash and Benn Konsynski, Michael Porter and Victor Millar, and Michael Hammer and Glenn Mangorian.[21]

In my experience, not one firm that seriously attempted to identify SIS opportunities and threats through the use of the option generator (after completing a preliminary analysis of the firm's targets and thrusts; see Chapter 11) failed to do so. This does not mean that the options discerned could be realized without the commitment of resources. But the generator helps systematically to create a substantial number of possibilities suitable for attack by strategic thrusts supported or shaped by information technology.

Having described the strategic target dimension of the option generator, let us turn now to the strategic thrusts, devoting the next five chapters to showing how information technology can be used to support or shape each of them.

NOTES

1. Alfred Sloan, *My Years with General Motors* (Garden City, N.Y.: Doubleday Publishing, 1963), p. 304.

2. Ibid., p. 48.

3. Ibid., p. 66. See also Walter Adams, ed., *The Structure of American Industry*, 6th ed. (New York: Macmillan, 1982); Leonard Weiss, *Case Studies in American Industry* (New York: John Wiley & Sons, 1971).

4. Sloan, *My Years*, p. 69.

5. Ibid., p. 340.

6. Ibid., p. 341.

7. General Motors Annual Report, 1925.

8. Sloan, *My Years*, p. 363.

9. Alfred Chandler, *Strategy and Structure: Chapters in the History of American Industrial Enterprise* (Cambridge, Mass.: Harvard University Press, 1962). See also Alfred Chandler, *The Visible Hand: The Managerial Revolution in American Business* (Cambridge, Mass.: Harvard University Press, 1977).

10. Michael Porter, *Competitive Strategy: Techniques for Analyzing Industries and Competitors* (New York: Free Press, 1980).

11. Chandler, *Strategy and Structure*, p. 13.

12. Ibid., p. 13.

13. Ibid., p. 391.

14. Ibid., p. 392.

15. Porter, *Competitive Strategy*, p. 34.

16. Ibid., p. 35.

17. Ibid., p. 37.

18. Ibid., p. 38.

19. Readers familiar with Porter's work should note that I have omitted discussion of strategic groups, mobility barriers, and such to avoid unnecessary complexity. These concepts can be easily grasped once the five forces and their sources are understood. Strategic thrusts probably play a more significant role in relation to the industry's strategic groups than they do vis-à-vis the industry itself.

20. For an earlier form of the strategic option generator, see Charles Wiseman and Ian MacMillan, "Creating Competitive Weapons from Information Systems," *Journal of Business Strategy*, Fall 1984. See also Alfred Oxenfeldt and Jonathan Schwartz, *Techniques for Analyzing Industries and Competitors* (New York: American Management Association, 1981).

21. See F. Warren McFarlan, "Information Technology Changes the Way You Compete," *Harvard Business Review*, May–June 1984, pp. 98–103; James Cash, Jr., and Benn Konsynski, "IS Redraws Competitive Boundaries," *Harvard Business Review*, March–April 1985, pp. 134–42; Michael Porter and Victor Millar, "How Information Gives You Competitive Advantage," *Harvard Business Review*, July–August 1985, pp. 149–60; Michael Hammer and Glenn Mangorian, "The Changing Value of Communications Technology," *Sloan Management Review*, Winter 1987, pp. 65–71.

II

Strategic Thrusts

5

Differentiation

PRODUCT DIFFERENTIATION

Potato farmers from Idaho worry about the weather, the cost of new equipment, and the latest government regulation bearing on their crop. Unlike economists, they don't lose sleep computing complex trade-offs between cost and price. If a farmer took his Idaho Grade A's to market and asked for more than the going price, he wouldn't do any business. Buyers don't pay premiums for items they can't distinguish, differentiate, or otherwise discriminate one from the other. Just as the truth value of the sentence "John is a bachelor" remains unchanged when the term *unmarried man* is substituted for *bachelor,* the value for the buyer stays the same when Farmer Jones's peck of Idaho A's is substituted for Farmer Smith's. If you sell a commodity—a standardized, homogenized, substitutable product—you lack the freedom to raise your price above the going rate, assuming you prize solvency. Your customers, moreover, have no reason beside price to prefer your generic product over another's.

For economists, *product differentiation* indicates the degree to which buyers perceive imperfections in the substitutability relation between items offered by sellers in an industry. It is measured by the cross-elasticity of demand. If Product X is highly differentiated from Product Y, a small price reduction in X will not affect demand for Y; if X and Y are close substitutes, a small reduction in the price of X will result in a small increase in the demand for X *and* a small decrease in the demand for Y (assuming the price of Y remains constant), since some customers will switch from Y to X due to the incentive to buy at a reduced price.

Sellers of differentiated goods and services, on the other hand, need to spend time assessing trade-offs between cost, price, and product variation. Differentiation confers on the seller power over these factors, power that can significantly affect profit margin. Yet differentiation has its cost, the price producers must pay when indulging their desire for distinction.

Buyers of differentiated wares also must pay a price when satisfying their preference for something special. Sellers tag differentiated products not only with a price premium but frequently with a loyalty tax, tribute customers may have to pay if they decide to switch from one vendor to another, from Product X to Product Y. The tax will be high if the customer's investment in learning to use X is high, and because it will ipso facto be lost when Y replaces X. In addition, the customer who switches may have to make new investments in learning to use Y. To prevent such infidelities, sellers scheme to raise their customers' *switching costs*; the latter, naturally, take whatever steps they can to minimize such costs.

This situation often creates an opportunity for an enterprising firm to introduce a Product Y designed to reduce the switching costs of prospective customers moving from X to Y *and* to offer desired features or services not associated with X. In the early 60s, Honeywell's Building Controls Group, a supplier of thermostatic and other control systems, seized just this kind of opportunity.[1] Prior to making its strategic move, Honeywell offered to its over 5,000 independent distributors a long line of 18,000 items targeted at both the new and replacement markets. To meet the needs of its intermediaries and their customers, Honeywell maintained a nationwide network of warehouses, for no dealer wanted to stock such a large inventory from a single vendor. Moreover, dealers needed space for competitive lines containing items incompatible with Honeywell's.

To reduce the product differentiation advantages of its competitors as well as its own inventory-carrying and transaction costs, Honeywell executed a bold strategic plan. It redesigned its product line by replacing the 18,000 parts and pieces with 300 interchangeable, standard items. The kicker here was that not only were these interchangeable across Honeywell's product lines but also across those of its major competitors. Through standardization, Honeywell eliminated the differential advantages enjoyed by its rivals.

After this innovation, Honeywell closed its warehouse network and thereby shifted inventory-carrying costs to distributors. The latter assumed the added expense of carrying *all* 300 interchangeable items but would need now to carry fewer items overall. For there was no longer any reason to stock as many competitive substitutes.

Not all distributors went along with Honeywell's strategy, but those that did recorded large sales increases. Honeywell's replacement market share doubled, and its new product sales rose almost 50 percent. Transaction costs declined: prior to the move, 90 percent of Honeywell's sales had been to 4,000 distributors; within 10 years, that same percentage was sold by 3,100 fewer distributors. This group of 900 also benefited from increased sales volume.

Product differentiation has long been recognized as an important competitive weapon.[2] Indeed, economists who study competitive behavior identify it as one of the principal determinants of advantage. Suppose, for example, that a firm seeks opportunities to diversify into another industry (call it A). By analyzing the competitive structure of A, it might find that its potential rivals have neither (1) absolute cost advantages (due to patented-production techniques, unique access to supplies, cheap labor, and so on) nor (2) significant cost advantages (due to economies of scale in production, purchasing, advertising, and the like) nor (3) sustainable product differentiation advantages (due to preferences of buyers for brand name items, superior quality, location, services, and the like). If A is such that participants enjoy neither 1 nor 2 nor 3, the firm can enter A at no disadvantage: competition is pure; no one has an edge (see Chapter 3).

On the other hand, entry will be blocked or deterred if at least some participants enjoy 1, 2, or 3. To enter this game, a prospective competitor must scale *entry barriers*. And these generally entail costs that put the new entrant, at least initially, at a disadvantage. Product differentiation, in this sense, is a barrier to entry, a long-term deterrent that protects industry incumbents from invasion. It is the study of such barriers and the sources from which their power emanates that occupies a good portion of the industrial economist's time. Among the important sources leading to product differentiation advantages, they have hypothesized such factors as services, physical differences, and subjective image due to brand labeling, advertising, and the like.

Of course, what is one firm's barrier may be another's gateway. When Philip Morris entered the brand-differentiated beer industry through its acquisition of Miller's, it used the advertising hurdle not as a barrier but as a platform, a veritable launching pad for its subsequent conquests. While this obstruction blocked some entrants, it enabled Philip Morris, with its deep financial resources and well-honed marketing skills, to raise Miller's 4 percent market share to well over 20 percent in less than a decade.[3]

The economist's view of product differentiation, reflecting the strong, narrow sense of the term, differs from the somewhat weaker, wider meaning ascribed to it by marketers. The latter have operationalized the economist's theoretical insights by deriving a variety of schemes, all going under the name "marketing mix," aimed at systematically uncovering opportunities to make their products unique and thereby establish *differential advantage* over their rivals.

When first proposed by Neil Borden in 1964,[4] the term *marketing mix* covered not only possible combinations of such marketing elements as product quality, price, and channel of distribution but also the market forces determining management's choice of a combination to satisfy the firm's profit and growth objectives. For Borden, the *elements* comprised policies and procedures related to product planning (product lines offered, markets to sell, new products), pricing, branding, distribution channels, personal selling, advertising, promotion, packaging, display, servicing, physical distribution, and fact-finding and analysis (securing, analyzing, and using the facts needed to make marketing decisions). The *forces* determining a mix of the elements included consumers' buying behavior and its determinants, the trade's (wholesalers', retailers') behavior and its influences, competitors' position and behavior and their influences (e.g., industry structure, relation of supply to demand, degree to which competitors compete on a price versus nonprice basis, technological trends), and government behavior and its market impact.

Since Borden's work, others have attempted to refine the notion, restricting its sense to the marketing-mix elements. Albert Frey, for example, proposes two categories: the offering (product, packaging, brand, price, and service) and methods and tools (distribution channels, personal selling, advertising, sales, promotion, and publicity). William Lazer and Eugene Kelley suggest three: goods-and-services mix, distribution mix, and communications mix. Jerome McCarthy touts four: product (quality, features, options, style, brand name, packaging, sizes, services, warranties, returns), price (list, discounts, allowances, payment period, credit terms), place (channels, coverage, locations, inventory, transport), and promotion (advertising, personal selling, sales promotion, publicity).[5]

By adopting one of these marketing-mix schemata, the firm positions itself to manipulate a large number of variables. This yields an even larger number of possible marketing combinations, each capable of establishing a differential edge. Take the case of a single product. If its quality can be excellent, good, or fair; if its price ranges from $50 to $150 in increments of $10; if it is distributed through retail, wholesale, or company-owned outlets; and if its promotion takes the form of either local demonstrations or advertisements via newspaper, magazine, radio, television, or mail; then there are 594 ($3 \times 11 \times 3 \times 6$) possible marketing mixes, that is, ways to establish differential advantage.[6]

This brief review of the concept of product differentiation, from first the economist's and then the marketer's perspective, is sufficient to elucidate the strategic thrust of differentiation and show how information technology can be used to support or shape it. The cases described below fall into three classes: differentiation of expected product, differentiation of aug-

Figure 5–1   SIS Differentiation Opportunities

Product Offering

	Expected product	Augmented product	Marketing support
Product			
Price			
Place			
Promotion			

(Rows labeled along left side: Marketing Mix)

mented product, and marketing support for differentiated products. Each class may be crossed with a marketing-mix element, following McCarthy's categorization (see Figure 5–1).

DIFFERENTIATION: EXPECTED PRODUCT

Information systems used to support or shape the firm's expected product do so with respect to the marketing-mix elements:

- *Product:* Is it modifiable, compatible, extendable?
- *Price:* Is credit extended? Are allowances made?
- *Place:* Are customers' expectations met with respect to time of delivery, channel of distribution, quantity of product?
- *Promotion:* Is advice available before, during, and after sale?

The firm's *expected product,* the offering it designs to satisfy the customer's minimal buying conditions (as just indicated), includes all those characteristics intrinsic to the *generic product,* the basic, plain vanilla offering that competitors may find no difficulty in emulating. Even at the generic level, opportunities to differentiate exist. But they are much more plentiful once one moves beyond the unadorned to the anticipated (i.e., expected), as suppliers of perfumes and other cosmetic products seem to understand intuitively. According to Theodore Levitt, "the generic product can be sold only if the customer's wider expectations are met. Different means may be employed to meet these expectations. Hence differentiation follows expectation."[7]

Clairol uses information technology to support its segmentation strategies. Through telemarketing applications like 1–800–HISPANA or 1–800–GRAY WAR, the hair-products firm takes direct aim at the fast-growing Hispanic and "graying" baby-boomer niches. These 800-telephone numbers constitute "an integral part of our marketing mix," notes the director of consumer satisfaction at Clairol. "Consumers need help in choosing the right hair-coloring products. Once they have the advice and reassurance they need, they're far more likely to purchase, and then repurchase, the products we recommend."[8]

Clairol's customer information hot lines receive more than 500,000 calls annually, with over 80 percent classed as inquiries, not complaints. And surveys confirm that most callers are prospective customers who become buyers after talking to Clairol's consultants, experts who spend their days in front of video display terminals, digging up the answers to caller questions. Moreover, these telemarketing applications, programmed to gather and analyze inquiry and complaint data automatically, help the firm's line managers—in packaging, advertising, and product formulation—read the constantly changing, highly segmented, hair-products marketplace.

Niche marketing of course is not limited to the hair-products industry. Truck manufacturers have become keenly aware of segmentation techniques, in part because of the erosion of their traditional customer base, the freight haulers. Ever since the deregulation edict of 1980, the trucking industry has been on the skids, what with intensified foreign competition from

European and Japanese manufacturers and brutal cost-cutting strategies, strategies dictating that the purchase of new trucks be postponed for as long as possible, with the average life of a truck estimated to be 14 years.

Navistar (formerly International Harvester) responded to this treacherous new competitive landscape by developing a strategic information system (SIS) to meet the special, market-niche strategies of its customers, existing and potential. The Navistar system, called Focus, assists fleet managers who must decide on the appropriate mix of vehicles for a particular business segment. When a Navistar sales team visits a prospect, it takes along a portable computer programmed to accept customer requirements and produce a report specifying how these requirements should be met—not necessarily by Navistar's trucks, but generically. According to its chief architect, Focus "gives customers the opportunity to reliably evaluate equipment purchases before they spend that first dollar."[9]

Is the system an effective weapon in the battles Navistar faces with its industry rivals? One measure of success can be calculated from the competitive responses, if any, to Focus. If rivals are investing to match or leapfrog Navistar's SIS, this is a sure sign that it's having the desired strategic impact. From the informal, off-the-record talks I've had with managers from other trucking manufacturers, it is clear that Focus has become an effective competitive weapon—so effective, in fact, that others are scrambling to match it.

When industrial buyers, and perhaps others as well, assess a vendor's offering, they weigh heavily such virtues as reliable delivery, prompt quotation, technical advice, discounts, maintenance, sales representation, credit, and ease of contact. Each should be carefully explored as a potential SIS opportunity area.

In the 70s, Warren Communication, a manufacturer of power supplies for telephone systems, and Corning Glass, a multiproduct manufacturer of glass-related products, learned the same lesson: prompt delivery is an aspect of service in which a firm can use information systems to support a differentiation thrust and gain an edge. Both companies discovered this truth only after suffering the pangs of competitive disadvantage. Warren—with a 12 percent share in an industry led by AT&T's Western Electric—supplied telecommunications companies, governments, and others. Its former president recalls that because of late and generally mediocre delivery performance, Warren paid $140,000 in 1980 in late-charge penalties, infuriated customers like GTE and MCI, and lost $3 million in contracts canceled by the governments of Taiwan and Puerto Rico for failure to deliver.

At Corning's Erwin ceramics plant the story was slightly different, but the pressure to produce on time was just as, if not more, intense. Erwin, a major source of catalytic converter components, supplied parts to manufacturers such as Ford and Chrysler for use in their automobile emission control systems. In 1979, a Japanese-based division of NGK–Locke Inc., with a 20 percent share of the market, introduced an improved version of its product and gained an additional 10 percent share. Erwin, the market leader, had to act to protect its position.

At Warren and Erwin, the response was the same. Both installed information systems to improve the management of their manufacturing operations, from loading to shipping dock. At Warren, the system eliminated late-delivery penalties, restored customer confidence, and led to a doubling of plant capacity. At Corning, enhanced quality control *plus* improved performance in delivery (the delivery success rate for the first three quarters of 1983 was measured at 99.8 percent) enabled the firm to repulse the Japanese attack. According to NGK's Ceramic Division manager, "We cannot offer the same lead time as Corning. Our product is produced overseas, and it is shipped by boat. The shipping, customs, and trucking slow delivery."[10]

Savvy customers often apply another test to the offerings of suppliers: Can they provide prompt, clear, and accurate quotations? This condition tends frequently to separate winners from also-rans. Taking the hint, firms large and small have developed information systems applications to satisfy precisely this service need of their clients.

The president of Rehler, Vaughn, Beaty & Koone, an architectural firm based in San Antonio, Texas, knew that "to get ahead of the competition, we would have to learn to use a microcomputer."[11] His firm developed cost-estimating and income property analysis applications so that it could generate for prospective clients estimates for different structures occupying the same space. After collecting client responses to questions about quality of materials, location, building type, and so forth, Rehler's program produced detailed reports on costs, schedules, projected income and expenses, return on investment, and the like. Because of its ability to provide quick, reliable quotes, Rehler recovered from customers attracted to its service more than 10 times what it had invested in systems.

For Setco Industries, a supplier of machine-tool components, the speed of its computer-aided engineering system means the difference between winning contracts or losing them. Due to Setco's ability to generate quotations in hours rather than days, sales have doubled. Its president notes that on one job, "we had the order before our competitor ever had a chance to quote it."[12]

Continuing now in a more theatrical vein, Olesen of Hollywood, a rental supplier of lighting equipment to film production companies, uses its minicomputer system not only to handle inventory but also to build customer credibility and avoid confrontations. Prior to implementing the application, according to Olesen's president, "the same information scribbled on a piece of paper would most likely initiate an argument. The system convinces the customer that we are a first-class operation and that they are dealing with professionals. This makes them happy and comfortable."[13] Olesen's information system gives it a differential edge in the fiercely competitive theatrical rental equipment business.

Body shop companies tell a similar tale. In Bakersfield, California, the president of Maaco Auto Painting and Body Works says the software package he bought gives the firm a significant advantage over competitors. "It has given us tremendous credibility with our insurance customers and our retail customers. We look more professional. You don't get a hand-scribbled estimate that looks like a prescription some doctor wrote. They come out very clean. When an adjuster gets it, he can read it first off. Since it's computer-printed, the arithmetic is right."[14]

Friedman & Associates, a custom software vendor based in Deerfield, Illinois, develops order entry, manufacturing control, purchasing, and related on-line applications. It differentiates these offerings from the hundreds of similar if not identical products on the market by providing a special feature. Instead of having users carry, store, and search through thick manuals of documentation, Friedman in 1982 became one of the first firms to offer an on-line documentation feature with its packages. For any of the applications just mentioned, puzzled users need only press a HELP key on the terminal and easy-to-read text is flashed on the screen to aid them.

A somewhat more controversial use of information systems to differentiate a firm's expected product comes from the securities industry. Portfolio managers hired by corporations, unions, and state and local governments to invest money for pension funds can accumulate "soft dollars" from brokers who charge more than the lowest possible rate for a securities transaction. This practice is justified because the law doesn't require money managers to trade with the broker offering the smallest commission, as long as investment research is included.

Inventive brokers have interpreted the term *investment research* broadly to include one-week, all-expenses-paid trips to Paris, Madrid, and Milan; tickets to sports and cultural events; meetings with influential political and government figures; and so on. Others have seen an opportunity to enhance their expected research offering by providing computer terminals with sophisticated analytical investment programs. For some clients, it seems, such rewards are more appealing than a week on the French Riviera.

Up to this point, I have presented only examples of the offensive use of information technology to support or shape strategic differentiation thrusts. The air traffic controller's strike of 1981 illustrates the defensive use of information systems to reduce the differentiation advantages of labor—in this case, the controllers.

The federal government based its decision to dismiss the strikers in part on the availability of a computer application for controlling the flow of aircraft. According to labor relations expert Harley Shaiken, what doomed the strike was the "government's skillful use of a new weapon—information systems technology—-to keep air traffic moving, gutting the strikers' leverage."[15] Soon after the walkout, 75 percent of the commercial flights were operating while 75 percent of the controllers were marching on the picket line.

Prior to striking, controllers were considered to be highly trained specialists, in short supply. By performing many of the controller's tasks, the flow-control system would, it was believed, dramatically reduce their bargaining power, making their skills less valuable. For as labor's skill differentiation advantages erode, its price on the market drops. The system was also expected to widen the pool of new applicants by reducing the level of expertise required.

While this new competitive weapon certainly was used to justify and support the Reagan administration's strike policies, it seems not to have achieved its long-term objectives. After more than a dozen air crashes in 1985 and an increase in near-collisions on the ground and in the air, Transportation Secretary Elizabeth Dole announced plans to add nearly 1,000 controllers over the next two years. It seems that the skill level for becoming an air traffic controller, despite the flow-control support system, is still high enough that 40–50 percent of the applicants fail the course conducted at the controller's academy in Oklahoma.

DIFFERENTIATION: AUGMENTED PRODUCT

Information systems used to support or shape the firm's *augmented* product do so with respect to marketing-mix elements that reach beyond the customer's minimal expectations. Whatever benefits the customer and can be added to the expected product should be examined by the firm as an opportunity for a differentiation thrust. From this set of options, those that can be supported or shaped by information technology should be identified and assessed.

Pacific Intermountain Express (PIE), a large trucking firm based in California, competes in the deregulated, commodity-like trucking industry. It developed an application for tracking the status of a shipment at any point along its route from origin to destination. A PIE customer checks on its misplaced or delayed shipment by querying the PIE computer, using its own computer terminal.

Through this information system, PIE differentiates its shipping service from the noncomputerized ones offered by its rivals. As the company's president put it, "In trucking today, we all use the same highways and the same freight terminals. Our only competitive advantage is to stand out technologically."[16]

Back in 1971, PIE seized the opportunity to set itself apart from the 15,000 competing firms in the industry by investing in an on-line computer system for shipment tracing and freight billing. Today, PIE offers to its customers reports on over-the-road costs and empty-mile cost allocation. It allows them to send and receive a variety of messages related to their shipments. When PIE's vice president for marketing visits clients, he discusses not only shipping volumes and rates but also information system requirements. These meetings inspire many of the system's enhancements. At the request of a GM plant manager in California, for instance, PIE developed an application that lists all inbound shipments due on its trucks. Like Metpath in the clinical laboratory business (see Chapter 1), PIE raised the information systems ante for other trucking firms through the strategic use of computer technology.

But raising the ante in information technology, as in poker, doesn't guarantee advantage in a competitive arena. Consolidated Freightways and Leaseway Transportation have matched PIE's investment and now feature information-based services to distinguish themselves from other 18-wheelers on the road. Consolidated, with an on-line system called Direct, provides critical data to more than 1,500 shippers (via computer terminals at their locations) on the progress of shipments. It also produces customized reports for large customers like American Hospital Supply, itself an information technology powerhouse (see Chapter 7). For American, Consolidated breaks down shipments by origin and destination points and gives a complete history that lists purchase order numbers, freight charges, pickup and delivery dates, total service time, and so on. The report enables American to pinpoint opportunities for productivity improvements in distribution and in some cases to reduce inventory by taking advantage of Consolidated's excellent service.

Leaseway expresses its message in full-page *Wall Street Journal* advertisements with headlines such as "The key to better-integrated transportation services lies in integrated circuits."[17] Leaseway claims to have "quietly pioneered the technological revolution in transportation." "Only Leaseway," the copy runs, "can bring your company the benefits of strategic tools like Computer-modeled mode-mix analysis. . . . Computer lane balancing. Electronic routing and scheduling. . . . Our technological advantage over other transportation companies enables us to custom-tailor packages of services more productively so that your company can maximize both service and savings. And get unmatched management and cost control."[18]

Whatever the truth of these claims, one thing is certain: Leaseway's marketing team is aware of the strategic use of information technology in differentiating the firm's offering from those of its rivals. Whether Leaseway actually delivers on its high-tech rhetoric remains a question the answer to which only its customers and competitors really know.

In the past, furnituremakers competed against one another on the basis of style, color, price, and other features. Today, a new source of competitive advantage is emerging in the service area. With computer-aided design (CAD) systems, interior designers can simulate alternative furniture arrangements from a variety of perspectives. Manufacturers view CAD systems as important new marketing tools. "We're doing this to support our business," says a vice president and director of marketing for Steelcase Inc., a large, Michigan-based furniture company.[19] Steelcase developed software to display its product line and sell to its dealers. A competitor, Herman Miller, decided to go toe-to-toe with Steelcase, implementing a $250,000 top-of-the-line system. With it, designers can pan across a roomful of furniture. According to Herman Miller's program manager, to compare other systems to it "is like comparing snapshots to a movie."[20]

Milliken, a textile manufacturer, also attracts interior designers and decorators, but not with a channel-located system. Instead, designers and decorators visit Milliken's plant in Georgia to use a powerful graphic-design system that triggers the production of the item specified. For those involved with carpet projects in which the customer desires an original design and wants to see a sample before proceeding, this capability distinguishes Milliken from its rivals. Decorators who need color printouts of new office configurations involving carpets, furniture, and the like can also use the system to meet the demands of their clients.

Epson, a manufacturer of dot-matrix printers, personal computers, and handheld computers, offers a set of computer-based services to its distributors, retailers, and end users. To strengthen its bonds with these groups, Epson contracted with CompuServe, Inc. for space on its new videotex network. Callers connect their computers with CompuServe through a local dial-up number. Only Epson's intermediaries can download technical and pricing information about product lines, read Epson's electronic newsletter, and correspond via electronic mail. Others can access public files for news and feature stories about Epson's products or participate in conference calls to exchange information. These services help Epson differentiate its product line by augmenting it through the use of information systems provided by CompuServe.

Hertz, the car rental agency, and Owens-Corning Fiberglas, the home-insulation company, also use systems to augment their expected products. Each offers its customers reports pertaining precisely to their needs. The Hertz customized printout explains in English, French, German, Italian, or Spanish (depending on the language preference of the traveler) how to reach hotels, office buildings, convention sites, and sports arenas in major U.S. cities. Once the traveler specifies the destination desired, it details expressways and exits, where to turn, and how long the trip should take.

To differentiate its commodity-like product line, Owens-Corning hit upon a distinctive computer-based service. Home buyers, it knew, wanted well-insulated houses. But they lacked convenient, inexpensive tests for assessing the energy efficiency of designs proposed by builders. This presented a challenging opportunity for Owens-Corning: What can we do to satisfy the obvious consumer want and get our buyers, the builders, to select our products rather than those of our competitors?

By design or chance, it responded to this challenge ingeniously with an information system for cranking out energy efficiency ratings for new home designs. Owens-Corning offers the package "free" to builders as a service for their customers, the home buyers. In return, Owens-Corning makes two demands on builders: carry only our insulation materials and meet minimum efficiency standards in design.

Built in 1983, this SIS has become an essential part of the firm's marketing effort. Witness the remarks of an Owens-Corning marketing manager, quoted in the *Whale,* a local Long Island, New York, newspaper: "This program lets you determine, before you buy your home, approximately how much your energy bill will be. Ask your builder—or prospective builder about how you can take advantage of it."[21] While some may believe that the jury still sits on this attempt to build channel loyalty and increase sales, I believe it represents a strategic thrust warranting emulation in other industries as well.

Along these lines, Benjamin Moore, the paint company, developed a computerized paint analyzer for retail stores selling its products. Janovic/Plaza, an independent paints and papers, blinds, and fabrics store in New York City, recently ran an advertisement headlined "Get 50 percent off Levolor Blinds and a Computer to Match."[22] What Janovic meant here was that a customer could select any of Levolor's 100-plus colors and then use Moore's computer color-matching system to determine the exact paint-mix formula needed for matching the blinds with Moore's paint. Janovic also offered this augmented service for matching fabric swatches, wallpaper, or whatever. This turnkey SIS, which Benjamin Moore introduced in 1983 and sells to paint outlets for about $25,000, combines a personal computer and a spectrophotometer, a device capable of analyzing *any* color sample.

For those more inclined to change the world than merely to paint it over, W. R. Grace, one of the largest home-center operators in the United States, with 201 Channel and Central Region Home Center stores in 1985, offered not only Black and Decker drills and Homelite chain saws but also useful computer-generated information as well.

When the do-it-yourselfer specified measurements and other pertinent data, the Grace computer cut a well-honed report on cost, materials needed, and advice on how to proceed. As a senior vice president at the firm put it: "Sometime the customer is just interested in buying a drill, but more likely he's concerned with doing a project. If you teach him how to do the project, you can sell him the power drill in addition to a hammer, blades, and nails."[23] Grace also invited its customers to call a toll-free telemarketing number for do-it-yourself project information. (At the end of 1986, the firm agreed to sell its home-center units in a leveraged buyout. The new company, Channel Home Centers Inc. will be headed by managers from the units.)

W. R. Grace, Benjamin Moore, Owens-Corning, and others have gone beyond the call of duty to provide their customers with more than the bare bones of a product. They have differentiated their lines from those of their rivals through the strategic use of information technology. Other firms see opportunities to provide a full line of computer-based services that aid customers in managing the resources they purchase from the vendor.

Take, for example, the PHH Group, formed in 1946 by three former retailers named Peterson, Howell, and Heather to manage large corporate automobile fleets. From a relatively small, local operation based in Hunt Valley, Maryland, PHH today manages over 300,000 cars for more than 800 U.S., British, and Canadian customers. This growth, which has made PHH a relatively large service company with over $2 billion in assets and close to $1 billion in revenues, was fueled in large part by the firm's ability to satisfy its customers' needs through the use of information technology.

PHH developed SIS that enabled it to (1) manage fleets of cars at 10 to 15 percent less than its customers could through self-management and (2) satisfy the resource life-cycle needs of its customers. The notion of the *customer resource life cycle* (CRLC), which provides a useful model for describing what PHH has done, derives in part from IBM's information systems planning methodology. Blake Ives and Gerard Learmonth applied it imaginatively as an instrument for identifying product differentiation opportunities backed by information systems.[24]

As defined by Ives and Learmonth, the CRLC comprises 4 primary phases and 13 subphases. The primary phases are:

1. Determination of resource requirements.
2. Acquisition of the resource.
3. Ownership of the resource.
4. Disposition of the resource.

Information technology may find a use at one or more points in the CRLC. For instance, in Phase 1, where customer requirements for the resource are determined, the Benjamin Moore SIS establishes the kind of paint needed to match a customer's furnishings and the Owens-Corning Fiberglas SIS helps home builders determine insulation requirements.

Applying the CRLC model to PHH, we find that the firm keeps elaborate, computerized records of the entire automobile marketplace, tracking items such as model types and prices. Coupled with input from the customer on its needs, PHH develops a detailed plan to fit the customer's automobile fleet requirements and specifies precisely what is needed. Once the plan is accepted by the customer, PHH selects the appropriate sources for the resources, acquires the desired mix of cars, and processes the required tax, insurance, and title forms. After the customer takes possession of the vehicles, PHH monitors usage, notifies the customer when maintenance should be performed, and in general manages the fleet. When the customer is ready to dispose of its vehicles, PHH is there to sell them, arranging the best terms because of its intimate knowledge of the market, based on its extensive automotive-market data base. In effect, PHH offers systems support at every point on the CRLC.

According to PHH's president, originally trained as a computer analyst and hired over 30 years ago to set up the firm's first data processing center, "people are starting to focus on the dollar value of information and the notion that information can be sold. Well, that's always been our business. We help corporations mind their own business."[25]

Consider now a use of information systems to reduce the differentiation advantages of competitors. In the cosmetics industry, firms such as Chanel, Estée Lauder, and Revlon spend millions each year on advertising to establish brand name identity, to differentiate themselves from the swarms of other companies in the business. Without a large advertising budget, a new firm (so the conventional wisdom goes) would find it difficult to enter this highly competitive marketplace.

In 1984, three cosmetics companies introduced computer systems to analyze human skin, simulate how different makeup will look, and instruct on applying their products. Two Japanese firms, Shiseido and Intelligent Skincare (hardly household words in the United States at the time), unveiled their systems at Bloomingdale's, the large New York City department store. According to the store's executive vice president, customer response was remarkable. "Yesterday, 70 people were standing around looking at the demonstrations. Shiseido has quintupled its sales. And to our astonishment, I.S.—a totally unknown company—has been very strong."[26] It seems that these two companies have learned the trick of effective retailing: getting customers to their counter, not to their rival's.

Shiseido operates a line of four "cosmetic computers": Shiseido Face, Shiseido Eyes, Shiseido Makeup Simulator, and the Replica Skin Diagnosis System. Each augments the selling efforts of Shiseido's beauty consultants, who evaluate a customer's needs and prescribe the company's products based on the computer's analysis.

Intelligent Skincare's systems, on the other hand, do not rely on human intervention. Once the customer enters her skin type and makeup preferences, for example, the system takes close-up pictures of her skin and then prescribes a skin care regimen and color palette using IS's products. The system also records all purchases and maintains a customer database for marketing purposes.

The marketing component of these SIS may ultimately prove to be as important as the system's ability to induce sales at the counter. Special promotions can be targeted at women with light or dark, sensitive or robust, dry or oily—you name it—skin. Or reminders and announcements of sales can be sent to those who might be running low on the company's product, assuming the prescribed regimen has been followed. Shiseido, for example, formed a customer service group for just this marketing purpose. With the aid of a database that includes not only data on a customer's physical attributes and cosmetic purchases but also information on her hobbies and lifestyle preferences, this group fashions mail-order campaigns (offering, for example, free samples of new products and health and style reports) tailored to fit a customer's special needs. In addition, like Clairol's line managers who exploit its telemarketing database gathered from its special 800-numbers, the heads of Shiseido's R&D, market analysis, and other functions also reap the fruits of their unique source of customer information.

What is the value of this augmented differentiation thrust? One way to calculate it is to look first at the costs associated with putting it into place and then to estimate some of the benefits. The manufacturer bears development costs and the cost of a makeup simulator (about $1 million). It shares promotional costs with department stores. A cosmetics SIS like Shiseido's Replica system can perform up to six makeovers an hour, for 8 to 10 hours a day. Customers who use the system pay a fee that is applied to any purchases they make. Average sales at Shiseido counters equipped with Replica are said to average $100 or more, with some stores reporting a 40 to 50 percent increase in sales.

Not only the cosmetic firm and the store benefit from these SIS. Customers receive a personalized, objective analysis and have the ability to test a great variety of makeovers, something impossible to achieve with a makeup consultant trained to duplicate only a few standard looks.

Cosmetic SIS also raise interesting competitive dynamics (see Chapter 11) and global growth (see Chapter 8) issues related to the strategic use of information technology. Elizabeth Arden, a veteran cosmetics manufacturer, created a system to *match* Shiseido's makeup simulator. Its president reports that "we're capable of generating over $40,000 in one week when these computers are in a cosmetics department. The problem is the limited number of customers we can handle. . . . There is such a receptive customer response, we can't keep up with it."[27] Arden's hair care affiliate, Philip Kingsley, developed a system to take pictures of a customer's hair, perform an analysis, simulate styles, and recommend (in the form of a printout the customer can take with her) Kingsley products to achieve the desired results. With the success of these two systems and its skin analysis application, Arden has taken steps recently to integrate these SIS to provide "total care" and service for those desiring ("needing" might be the wrong word here) it. Arden has decided to invest in information technology, taking seriously the threat posed by the Japanese invaders and the prediction by Bloomingdale's divisional manager and operating vice president for cosmetics: "The computer concept for treatment and color is the way all cosmetics companies will go in the future. Its possibilities are endless."[28]

But other rivals face a far greater challenge. For the success of the cosmetic SIS threatens their marketing strategies. Take Estée Lauder, a leading manufacturer, for example. Central to its marketing strategy is the beauty advisor concept and the promotion of the makeup process as an intensely pleasurable, personal experience. Its vice president of marketing has expressed concern about the sterile, impersonal nature and perception of computers. How can Lauder, he reasons, invest large sums in cosmetic SIS without eliminating its advisors and losing the differential marketing advantage it has cultivated successfully for years. Such dilemmas represent classic cases for strategists who wish to design strategic moves that force rivals to choose between no response at all or a response that will destroy their reason for being.

Finally, there is the global growth dimension of cosmetic SIS to consider. As Japan's largest cosmetics manufacturer, Shiseido has created a luxury image for its products, selling them in the United States only through fashionable department stores (e.g., Bloomingdale's) and advertising in quality magazines (e.g., *New Yorker*). It has also pursued an aggressive and imaginative marketing strategy, making it the world's largest cosmetics manufacturer in 1987 (it was third in 1985) with about 90 percent of its revenue derived from sales in Japan. Yet its global growth ambitions are evident from the moves it has made in the United States. Will it use its line of cosmetic SIS to support its global growth thrust to penetrate the lucrative national markets of France, Germany, Italy, and England, as well as the United States? Its success in the United States indicates an affirmative answer to this question.[29]

Shoppers satisfied by a cosmetic SIS might also be inclined to try another system catering to their personal needs, one designed to differentiate the department store rather than the manufacturer. Suppose, for example, you need to buy a gift for a special occasion. You, like many others in your position, face a number of daunting questions: Will the recipient like it? Is it needed? Will it duplicate items already possessed or planned? In some situations, questions like these are relatively easy to answer. But in others (weddings, housewarming parties, and bar mitzvahs come to mind), gift givers have been known to suffer not a few anxious moments.

To reduce this anxiety and to increase sales, Dayton's, a 13-unit department store chain in Minneapolis, introduced two innovative computer-based registry systems. Both attempt to reduce gift-giving risk by ascertaining the recipient's desires in advance. The first, called the Bridal Registry, offers, to those who need to purchase but are undecided about wedding presents, a user-friendly terminal that displays the bride's wish list and items already acquired. At any Dayton's store, gift givers can peruse the list and place orders from the terminal. Following the Bridal Registry's success, Dayton's gave birth to a similar system designed for expectant mothers, the Stork Club Registry.

AT&T's promotion of its Unix operating system in the early 80s suggests another example of a defensive differentiation thrust involving an augmented product. Somewhat analogous to Honeywell's strategic move in the control market (described earlier), this also had an offensive kicker.

Unix emerged from research by two computer scientists in one of the back rooms at Bell Labs during the late 60s. It has two remarkable strategic features: horizontal and vertical portability. This means that Unix runs on the machines of competing computer manufacturers (horizontal portability) and on micros, minis, and mainframes (vertical portability). Defined on over 70 different types of computers, it can be used to operate IBM, Sperry, Amdahl, and Honeywell mainframes; Digital Equipment, Data General, and Hewlett-Packard minicomputers; and microcomputers driven by Intel, Zilog, and Motorola chips. AT&T's announced lines of mainframe and minicomputers, not surprisingly, run under Unix.

Why did AT&T hawk the virtues of Unix? Listen to the explanation proffered by the vice president of computer systems at AT&T Technologies, Inc.:

> We're anxious to see IBM and other companies go with our *standard*. We think it's good for the whole industry. A lot of the industry infrastructure—the value-added resellers—agrees with that. It's been our product for a long time, and I think the industry has been pretty successful going with our *standard*. If IBM goes another way, that will be unfortunate because it will have a diversifying effect on the industry.[30][Italics added.]

AT&T's beneficence rang even more resonantly in the words of the head of Unix Systems Planning at Bell Labs:

> The Bell system telephone network is made up of many different machines running many different operating systems. It is a distributed operating system that we have managed to develop and continue to evolve. The Unix system is like that. It provides a uniform tying factor from micros to mainframes which the industry can capitalize on to get to the consumer market.
>
> And consumers can capitalize, too, because now they have access to microcomputers. There are different machines, different operating systems, different interfaces—they're very confusing to customers. The automobile industry solved that problem quite well—that's a very complex device that many of us can run. There are not that many people who can run computers. I think we need to provide a basis for solving that problem, and I think the Unix system provides that basis very well.[31]

But was this the whole story behind AT&T's extraordinary advertising and public relations campaign on behalf of its Unix baby, Ma Bell's first legitimate offspring since divestiture? Not by a long shot. The computer industry recognizes no operating-system standards except local, de facto ones, primarily established by IBM. Why? Because operating systems are one of the best investments a computer vendor can make in locking in its customer base, in raising customer switching costs to a painfully high level. Imagine what it would be like if a firm could move all its applications from, for instance, IBM to AT&T computers, with no switching cost except small change? As the poet Ezra Pound once mused: "America, America. Think what America would be like if the classics had a wide circulation." IBM, I'm sure, has thought about what the world would be like if AT&T's Unix had a wide circulation. I leave it as an exercise for the reader to predict the final outcome of this bold strategic thrust by the former monopolistic giant, reincarnated now as the information industry's David.

DIFFERENTIATION: MARKETING SUPPORT

Finally, information technology used to support or shape other marketing efforts may do so with respect to activities related to the firm's differentiated product(s). As the following cases show, these activities include but are not limited to product line planning, market planning, media selection, product promotion, R&D, and production.

According to E. F. Hutton, packaged investments accounted for 30 percent of its commission revenues in 1983, up from 4 percent in 1978. Unlike traditional stocks or bonds, these bundled, often unique products target competitive offerings. Financial service firms like Hutton use information systems as integral parts of their product creation or "manufacturing" processes.

Consider, for example, how one large firm created a new certificates of deposit (CD) fund. At 6 A.M., traders at the brokerage house called London to order sheaves of CDs from foreign banks, which often pay higher rates than their U.S. counterparts. By 11 A.M., they had accumulated $50 million of the paper. The next step in the fund creation process depended on an information system that took the prices and rates, juggled them according to the firm's objectives and constraints embodied in its computer program, and arrived at management fees and commissions. Thirty-six hours after the start of this production run (job-shop style, to be sure), brokers were selling the fund.

Behind all the promotional hoopla surrounding such products, there is generally an information system playing a critical role in product development, processing, or distribution. A computerized portfolio management system, for example, directs Shearson/Lehman Brothers' managed-commodity account. Merrill's cash management account (see Chapter 7) depends for its existence on database and laser printing technology.

Scholastic Magazine, unlike the financial services firms just mentioned, uses its information system to support product- and market-planning efforts. Due to decreasing school enrollments and budgets, the 60-year-old publisher of elementary and secondary school materials faces mounting pressures to develop and market new products.

To meet the challenges, the company compiled an automated database with information on its product sales, on 16,000 school districts, on teachers and students who have bought its products, on millions of U.S. households (obtained from data on census tracts), and so on. This marketing information system produces sales penetration ratios (e.g., sales/teacher, sales/student), district profiles, and the like.

Scholastic uses the system to fine-tune the personal selling efforts of its approximately 100 sales representatives. But its most critical application relates to direct mail campaigns, the firm's major method of reaching the school market. *Scholastic* posts over 50 million items a year, using its marketing information system as one would a rifle's telescopic lens. Without it, like competitors who lack such a system, *Scholastic* would be shooting in the dark. But with it, *Scholastic* can, with a high degree of confidence, support efforts to develop differentiated products and the plans to market them to well-defined segments and customer groups.

Along similar lines, the United Church of Christ (UCC), faced with declining membership, has put its faith in the power of information systems to attract new or past members to its flock. Using 1980 census data on such variables as age, income level, ethnic background, and so on, the UCC can, with a few simple computer programs, create a demographic profile of a community. With this profile as a guide, the UCC pastor can devise targeted programs to capture recent immigrants, the elderly, yuppies, or what have you. But the UCC doesn't have an exclusive here. Religious battles for market share are brewing as other church groups mobilize their forces. The United Presbyterian Church, for example, has its own programmers and access to computers at Concordia College in River Forest, Illinois. According to the director of research for the church, "We can build an age-sex pyramid [an interesting idea as such], determine how many people are bilingual, and determine the educational level in any census tract."[32]

While demographic analysis suits the needs of *Scholastic* and the UCC to identify prospects, Manufacturers Hanover Trust (MHT), the nation's fourth largest bank-holding company (based in New York), takes a different track. In 1977, it sponsored the first corporate challenge race (3.5 miles) in Central Park, attracting 600 entrants. Within six years, it ran (at the New York City Park Department's behest) three heats of no more than 10,000 runners each and started races in Los Angeles, San Francisco, Houston, Dallas, Atlanta, Albany, Buffalo, Syracuse, and Chicago.

What happened at a recent run in Houston is typical of the entire MHT program. The race turned up 12 companies considered to be active prospects. After-race contact could be easily established, as MHT people knew members of the target's running team personally. This isn't a random kind of thing—it's designed into the program. According to a senior vice president and director of marketing for the bank, the name, company, and corporate position of all runners in a race become part of a database from which MHT and its subsidiaries in factoring, international banking, leasing, and the like, draw leads. At $30,000 a shot, the vice president claims that these races provide "the biggest bang for the buck in our whole marketing effort."[33] It must be particularly gratifying for MHT to see runners from its competitors—Citibank, Chase, and Chemical—pin "Manufacturers Hanover Corporate Challenge" identification tags to their running outfits and give their all for good old Manny Hanny.

To support the promotional component of the marketing mix—advertising, personal selling, sales promotion, and publicity—firms use information systems in a variety of inventive applications. In the increasingly international and competitive game of commercial real estate, developers new to an area help prospective tenants visualize structures still on the drawing board by inviting them to elaborate shows held at "marketing centers." To induce tenants reluctant to lease space unseen," builders create Hollywood-style productions to simulate planned structures. Gerald Hines Interests, a Houston-based developer seeking a foothold in the Manhattan market, was the first to use this new marketing tool to sell space in large commercial complexes. Recently, to attract New York City tenants to its site on 53rd Street, Hines presented a show driven by 24 computer-controlled slide projectors. According to some in this field, "If we lease the project three weeks sooner because of the marketing center, we've paid for it."[34] In southern and western markets, builders view marketing centers as essential. Indeed, they would not initiate a project without them. And information systems have become indispensable to these elaborate promotional efforts.

For companies that must undergo the rigors of competitive bidding, the bid itself can be viewed as a product, intermediate to be sure, but just as important (if not more so) as the final product. For if the bid is not bought, everything else must remain on the shelf. This applies to products the firm offers for sale as well as to those items it seeks to acquire through the bidding process. Firms engaged in competitive bidding battles must be adept at the intricate details of negotiating, entertaining, politicking, maneuvering, and analyzing. Some, like Sun Oil and Otis Elevator, learned to use information systems in supporting their winning bids.

Sun competed against other oil exploration firms for offshore leases. This is not a game for the timid or the ignorant, involving as it does huge amounts of money and high levels of risk. When the U.S. government sold $1 billion worth of offshore tracts in the Gulf of Mexico, Sun successfully bid on 35 of the 48 blocks it wanted, paying $22 million. To "take the risk out of the crapshoot," says the manager of planning and analysis,[35] Sun developed an information system application to help price its bids, taking into consideration such variables as reserve estimates, oil price forecasts, and drilling and development costs. The system acted as a filter, eliminating as too costly tracts that had satisfied geological criteria as possible sites for exploration.

Otis, on the other hand, developed an application to provide strategic intelligence on its rivals. The system tracks all elevator sales put out for bid, about 50 a day, in the United States. The national sales director for Otis says that "when we know that a job exists, it is posted on the system, and we start negotiating. When it is in the budget stage, we give it a dollar value and then keep track of it through the bid and contract dates."[36] Having this information available, Otis is able to compare systematically its prices with those of the competition and thereby to improve significantly its chances for developing winning bids.

NOTES

1. Theodore Levitt, *Marketing for Business Growth* (New York: McGraw-Hill, 1974).

2. Joe Bain, *Barriers to New Competition* (Cambridge, Mass.: Harvard University Press, 1956). See also Joe Bain, *Industrial Organization*, 2nd ed. (New York: John Wiley & Sons, 1968); Richard Caves, *American Industry: Structure, Conduct, Performance*, 4th ed. (Englewood Cliffs, N.J.: Prentice-Hall, 1977).

3. George Yip, *Barriers to Entry: A Corporate Strategy Perspective* (Lexington, Mass.: D. C. Heath, 1982).

4. Neil Borden, "The Concept of the Marketing Mix," *Journal of Advertising Research*, June 1964.

5. See Philip Kotler, *Marketing Management: Analysis, Planning, and Control*, 5th ed. (Englewood Cliffs, N.J.: Prentice-Hall, 1984), for more on these categorizations.

6. Ibid.

7. Theodore Levitt, "Marketing Success through Differentiation—Of Anything," *Harvard Business Review*, January–February 1980, p. 87.

8. Rheva Katz and Julie Knight, "Telemarketing and Technology: A Strategic Investment," *Forbes*, October 7, 1985.

9. Kurt Hoffman, "Trucking: Corporate Managers Capitalize on Their New Options," *Fortune*, September 30, 1985.

10. "Manufacturing Technology: A Report to Management," undated.

11. "Texas Architect Builds Business with Micro Software," *Output*, June 1981.

12. *American Machinist*, June 1982, p. 141.

13. "Theatrical Supplier Raises Curtain on Minicomputer Use," *Office*, September 1981.

14. Steven Burke, "Specialized Packages Help Increase Profits," *InfoWorld*, July 15, 1985.

15. Marguerite Zientara, "Computer as Strikebreaker? Labor Relations Expert Says Yes," *Computerworld*, April 5, 1982.

16. Jill Cortino, "Trucking Firm's Load Monitor Shifts into High Gear," *Management Information Systems Week*, March 24, 1982.

17. Leaseway advertisement, *The Wall Street Journal*, September 10, 1985.

18. Leaseway advertisement, *The Wall Street Journal*, March 14, 1985.

19. "Rearranging the Office Furniture—On a Screen," *Business Week*, July 5, 1982.

20. Ibid.

21. "Hints for Homeowners: How to Buy an Energy Efficient Home," *Whale*, January 2, 1987.

22. Janovic/Plaza advertisement, *New York Times*, 1984.

23. Hank Gilman, "Hardware Stores Forced to Alter Marketing Tack," *The Wall Street Journal*, August 13, 1985.

24. Blake Ives and Gerard Learmonth, "The Information System as a Competitive Weapon," *Communications of the ACM*, December 1984.

25. James Cook, "The PHH Factor," *Forbes*, November 4, 1985.

26. Anne-Marie Schiro, "The Computer Is a Hit at the Cosmetics Counter," *New York Times*, October 29, 1984.

27. June Weir, "Computing Skin Care," *New York Times Magazine*, December 9, 1984.

28. Anne-Marie Schiro, "The Computer Is a Hit at the Cosmetics Counter," *New York Times*, October 29, 1984.

29. Charrisse Min, "The Computer and the Cosmetics Industry," Research paper prepared for a course on the strategic use of information technology, Columbia University Graduate School of Business, 1987.

30. John Gallant, "AT&T's Scanlon Details the Future of Unix," *Computerworld*, March 12, 1984.

31. George Harrar, "Bell Labs Version of the Unix Story," *Computerworld*, August 22, 1983.

32. Charles Austin, "Churches See Computer as a Tool to Lure Flock," *New York Times*, October 23, 1982.

33. "What Makes Manny Hanny Run?" *Business Week*, August 22, 1983.

34. Robert Guenther, "Builders Using Fancy Marketing Centers to Draw Tenants to Commerical Projects," *The Wall Street Journal*, August 7, 1984.

35. Bryan Burrough, "Sun's Quest for Offshore Oil Leases Demands Preparation, Huge Risks," *The Wall Street Journal*, July 19, 1984.

36. Joseph Kelley, "Distributed Processing at Otis Elevator," *Output*, May 1981.

CASE REFERENCES

DIFFERENTIATION: EXPECTED PRODUCT

Clairol

Rheva Katz and Julie Knight. "Telemarketing and Technology: A Strategic Investment." *Forbes,* October 7, 1985.

Navistar

Kurt Hoffman. "Trucking: Corporate Managers Capitalize on Their New Options." *Fortune,* September 30, 1985.

Alex Kotlowitz. "Truck Maker's Road Is a Rough One." *The Wall Street Journal,* November 20, 1985.

Warren Communications and Corning Glass

"Manufacturing Technology: A Report to Management." Undated.

Rehler, Vaughn, Beaty & Koone

"Texas Architect Builds Business with Micro Software." *Output,* June 1981.

Setco Industries

American Machinist, June 1982, p. 141.

Olesen

"Theatrical Supplier Raises Curtain on Minicomputer Use." *Office*, September 1981.

Maaco

Steven Burke. "Specialized Packages Help Increase Profits." *InfoWorld*, July 15, 1985.

Friedman & Associates

Lois Paul. "Software House Puts Documentation On-Line." *Computerworld*, August 16, 1982.

Brokers

Randall Smith. "Pension Funds Feud with Money Managers over Brokers' Rebates." *The Wall Street Journal*, October 4, 1984.

Bruce Ingersoll. "SEC May Broaden Services Managers Get from Brokers." *The Wall Street Journal* (European Edition), April 23, 1986.

Air Traffic Controllers

Marguerite Zientara. "Computer as Strikebreaker? Labor Relations Expert Says Yes." *Computerworld*, April 5, 1982.

Reginald Stuart. *New York Times*, September 20, 1985.

DIFFERENTIATION: AUGMENTED PRODUCT

Pacific Intermountain Express

Distribution, September 1981, pp. 68–69.

Jill Cortino. "Trucking Firm's Load Monitor Shifts into High Gear." *Management Information Systems Week*, March 24, 1982.

David Stamps. "Bottle Firm: 'Trac' Spots Lost Loads Fast." *Management Information Systems Week*, March 24, 1982.

Consolidated Freightways

Consolidated Freightways, Annual Report, 1984.

Leaseway

Leaseway advertisement. *The Wall Street Journal*, March 14, 1985.

Leaseway advertisement. *The Wall Street Journal*, September 10, 1985.

Herman Miller and Steelcase

"Rearranging the Office Furniture—On a Screen." *Business Week*, July 5, 1982.

Milliken

Peter Petre. "How to Keep Customers Happy Captives." *Fortune*, September 2, 1985.

Epson

Eric Arnum. "Epson Offers Product News on Data Bases." *Communication Week*, July 16, 1984.

Hertz

Hertz advertisement. *The Wall Street Journal*, April 24, 1984.

Owens-Corning Fiberglas

"Business Is Turning Data into a Potent Strategic Weapon." *Business Week*, August 22, 1983.

"Hints for Homeowners: How to Buy an Energy Efficient Home." *Whale*, January 2, 1987.

Benjamin Moore

Janovic/Plaza advertisement. *New York Times*.

Peter Petre. "How to Keep Customers Happy Captives." *Fortune*, September 2, 1985.

W. R. Grace

Hank Gilman. "Hardware Stores Forced to Alter Marketing Tack." *The Wall Street Journal*, August 13, 1985.

"Grace Will Sell Home Centers." *New York Times*, December 2, 1986.

PHH

James Cook. "The PHH Factor." *Forbes*, November 4, 1985.

Blake Ives and Gerard Learmonth. "The Information System as a Competitive Weapon." *Communications of the ACM*, December 1984.

Elizabeth Arden, Intelligent Skincare, Estée Lauder, and Shiseido

"Face by Arden . . . and IBM?" *New York Times*, October 21, 1984.

Anne-Marie Schiro. "The Computer Is a Hit at the Cosmetics Counter." *New York Times*, October 29, 1984.

June Weir. "Computing Skin Care." *New York Times Magazine*, December 9, 1984.

Susan Chira. "In Cosmetics: The Japanese Connection." *New York Times,* May 12, 1985.

Susan Chira. "A Fresh Thrust by Shiseido." *New York Times,* December 16, 1985.

Charrisse Min. "The Computer and the Cosmetics Industry." Research paper prepared for a course on the strategic use of information technology, Columbia University Graduate School of Business, 1987.

Dayton Stores

David Roman. "MIS on the Attack." *Computer Decisions,* February 26, 1985.

AT&T

Philip Gill. "Bell to Offer Fixed Unix Kernel, System Suport." *Information Systems News,* February 7, 1983.

George Harrar. "Bell Labs' Version of the Unix Story." *Computerworld,* August 22, 1983.

Philip Gill. "Unix Gains as Micro Standard." *Information Systems News,* December 12, 1983.

Jeffry Beeler. "Unix and the New Contenders." *Computerworld,* December 26, 1983, and January 2, 1984.

John Gallant. "Unix: The Operating System of the 80s?" *Computerworld,* January 23, 1984

Greg Leveille. "1984: The Year of Unix." *Information Systems News,* January 23, 1984.

John Gallant. "AT&T Keynoter Lauds Unix." *Computerworld,* January 30, 1984.

Jack Scanlon. "Industry 'Unixization' Traced from Guru Days." *Information Systems News,* February 6, 1984.

John Gallant. "AT&T's Scanlon Details the Future of Unix." *Computerworld,* March 12, 1984.

DIFFERENTIATION: MARKETING SUPPORT

E. F. Hutton

Tim Carrington. "Big Brokers Shift Attention to Packages." *The Wall Street Journal*, March 29, 1983.

Scholastic Magazine

"*Scholastic Magazine* Reads the Competition by Using DBMS to Keep Track of Market Shares." *Computerworld*, November 30, 1981.

United Church of Christ

Charles Austin. "Churches See Computer as a Tool to Lure Flock." *New York Times*, October 23, 1982.

Manufacturers Hanover Trust

"What Makes Manny Hanny Run?" *Business Week*, August 22, 1983.

Gerald Hines

Robert Guenther. "Builders Using Fancy Marketing Centers to Draw Tenants to Commercial Projects." *The Wall Street Journal*, August 7, 1984.

Sun Oil

Bryan Burrough. "Sun's Quest for Offshore Oil Leases Demands Preparation, Huge Risks." *The Wall Street Journal*, July 19, 1984.

Otis Elevator

Joseph Kelley. "Distributed Processing at Otis Elevator." *Output*, May 1981.

Richard Layne. "Otis MIS: Going Up." *InformationWeek*, May 18, 1987.

6

Cost

COST ECONOMIES

Just as competitive advantage may flow to the firm concentrating its strategic moves on product differentiation, it may also issue to the organization focusing its thrusts on cost economies. For the imaginative enterprise, the latter presents a fertile field of opportunity. Rather than attempt to map it completely (which would require us to cover such economic exotica as X-efficiency theory, a theory that attempts to account for the difference "between the value of maximizing the opportunities open to the firm and those actually utilized"[1] by it), I shall limit the discussion to three important kinds of cost savings: economies of scale, scope, and information. It is with reference to these that enterprising firms can fashion a variety of strategic thrusts, thrusts that frequently can be supported or shaped by information technology.

Strategic cost thrusts are strategic moves intended to reduce or avoid costs the firm would otherwise incur; to help suppliers, channels, or customers reduce or avoid costs so that the firm receives preferential treatment or other benefits it deems worthwhile; or to increase the costs of its competitors.

Following the pattern established in the preceding chapter, I shall review the basics of scale, scope, and information economies and then show through examples how information technology is used to support or shape thrusts based on them.

COST: SCALE

Scale economies enable relatively large firms to acquire, produce, process, store, ship, or sell products at lower cost per unit than relatively small ones. Opportunities to reap the rewards of economies based on size may be seen from the perspective of the firm's functional activities (e.g., manufacturing, marketing, and purchasing) or may be viewed from the vantage point of its products, plants, or multiplant operations. In most industries, up to a certain point, economies of scale may be attained if the firm is willing and able to make the necessary investments. Once minimum optimal scale—the smallest size at which average cost per unit is at its lowest—is reached, however, any move to increase the size of a firm's operation would most likely result in *diseconomies of scale,* higher costs caused by such factors as rising transport charges, lack of local labor, and bureaucratic inefficiencies.

What accounts for the possibility of scale economies? What kinds of action are open to a large firm but closed to a small one? What are the sources of increased efficiency, of lowered average unit cost? Among the factors most frequently cited by economists are the following:

Specialization. As Adam Smith observed over 200 years ago, efficiency can be increased if labor is divided. Ideally, the firm meshes requirements of the job, abilities of the worker, and wages paid, so that employees are kept busy all the time at tasks demanding all their faculties. By taking advantage of Smith's division of labor principle, large firms avoid the waste and cost of having skilled, highly paid employees performing tasks which less-qualified, lower-paid workers could do as well if not better. Size enables them to employ specialized labor for well-defined jobs.

Automation. With ever-finer divisions of labor and concomitant specialization, opportunities increase to automate particular tasks or entire processes. Large firms can take advantage of these opportunities more readily than their smaller counterparts, as they have the resources to invest in specialized equipment designed to increase efficiency.

Bargaining power. Large firms, because of the size of their orders, shipments, or service needs, frequently are able to cut better deals with suppliers, customer intermediaries, and end users than those negotiated by their smaller rivals. Volume discounts on purchases, transportation, and so on are well-known instances of this source of scale economy.

Failures of proportionality.   A large firm can frequently capitalize on certain failures of proportionality. Capacity increases can often be achieved at less than proportionate rises in equipment or labor costs. As the number of machines at a facility increases, the number of technicians needed for maintenance usually rises less than proportionately.

Experience.   Large firms are able to take advantage of unit cost declines due to cumulative volume increases—the so-called experience curve effect. Such declines are the result of learning, of the experience workers gain in mastering their jobs, the machines they use, and so on. Their learning generally results in increases in the rate of output and in decreases in the rate of errors.

But we must remember that these and other sources of scale economies may also turn into sources of diseconomies. The large firm with a highly specialized labor force cannot easily retrain it if forced by a drastic decline in demand to exit from its primary business and enter a new arena. The long-term price contract that was the envy of the industry when consummated between the largest manufacturer and its principal raw material supplier may not be worth the paper it's printed on, indeed may cost the manufacturer far in excess of the price of the contract, if technological innovation makes a cheaper, easily substitutable material available. Similarly, the newly built, 20-acre rural processing plant that takes optimum advantage of a proportionality failure may find it lacks the labor willing to work in such an environment. Or the firm that has invested heavily in technology designed to improve the productivity of its labor force, and hence its opportunity to ride the experience curve, may find other firms using new and less costly techniques to produce in far greater volume, with order-of-magnitude increases in quality. Like other strategic thrusts, moves to exploit economies of scale cut both ways. Caveat emptor.

While the idea of scale economies may bring forth images of gigantic blast ovens and massive rolling mills, it would be a mistake to believe that such savings were restricted to heavy industry. Through the strategic use of information technology, banks, hospitals, and other organizations have capitalized on scale economies inherent in their lines of business.

In 1982, Chase Manhattan Corporation acquired the Visa traveler's check business of the First National Bank of Chicago. In this activity, profit comes mainly from the float, the funds that issuing institutions like American Express, Citicorp, Barclay's, and Chase invest between the time a traveler's check is purchased and redeemed. According to banking sources, industry leader American Express has at its disposal on an average day $2 billion in float; invested at 15 percent, this would yield a gross of over $300 million a year.

But since check-processing overhead is high, large volume is necessary to clear a significant profit. This reason evidently motivated Chase's purchase decision, for the acquisition doubled its annual traveler's check sales volume to over $1 billion and its sales outlets (primarily other banks) to about 10,000. According to a Chase vice president, it "gives us *economies of scale* faster than we could get through internal growth. It will reduce our cost per check by 20 percent."[2] [Italics added.] Like the expensive steel press whose cost is spread over as many units as possible, the cost of Chase's large-scale information systems operation can be spread over a volume sufficient enough to reduce its average cost per transaction by one fifth.

Taking advantage of proportionality failures in data processing operations and a fortuitous chain of events, General Bancshares Corp., until recently a relatively small, St. Louis–based bank engaged primarily in selling home mortgages and local loans, has also benefited from scale economies. When federal law prohibited interstate banking in 1956, a loophole permitted banks with interstate holdings at the time to keep them. General Bancshares opted to retain its units in Illinois and Tennessee. In 1982, these two states passed laws permitting bank-holding companies within the state to expand. General Bancshares acquired Belleville National Bank of Illinois and reduced local marketing and auditing expenses, using corporate resources. In addition, it eliminated the redundant data processing operation at Belleville and thereby cut over $750,000 from Belleville's annual overhead because of the services its centralized, large-scale information systems group could offer.

American Medical International, a large hospital management firm, saw a similar opportunity to exploit a failure of proportionality when it acquired Lifemark, another concern in its industry. According to the president of Lifemark, "the key to understanding this transaction is the rather dramatic *economies of scale* that will result. Over $20 million of Lifemark headquarters expense will be eliminated annually. There'll be a $10 million saving in data-processing costs.[3] [Italics added.] Indeed, rising costs in the health care industry have, according to some, made size an essential ingredient for survival.

Humana, the second largest hospital chain in the United States, certainly appreciated the opportunities for scale economies supported by information systems. A senior vice president noted that "a key element in our growth is the computer."[4] He expected the information systems staff to increase from its 1983 level of 350, a sevenfold jump from 1973, to at least 700 in another 10 years. This group enables Humana to develop large, centralized information systems and to spread costs over the more than 89 hospitals Humana runs. A system installed to manage inventory was expected to save Humana over $85 million in labor and reduced expenditures in three years.

Regional securities firms face rising competition from commercial banks and national brokerage houses. A significant revenue source, the underwriting of municipal revenue bonds, is threatened by the entry of banks into their business with the advent of deregulation. Customer bases face erosion as growing numbers are lured by costly, technological-based products offered by such firms as Merrill Lynch. When Merrill was attracting 10,000 customers a week with its cash management account (see Chapter 7), the president of a regional acknowledged that his firm didn't have the resources to offer a similar product.

Situations like this represent opportunities for growth-minded companies like Shearson/Lehman Brothers, the brokerage subsidiary of American Express. In 1982, Shearson acquired Foster & Marshall of Seattle, the Northwest's leading regional. According to Mr. Foster, the head of the company, plans for expansion and the need to enhance its data processing system were among his most important merger motives. From Shearson's point of view, the acquisition expanded the market for its products (by adding Foster's customer base) and enabled it to achieve economies of scale by integrating Foster's data processing operations into its own.

Levitz, the large furniture retailer, capitalized on information systems to support a strategic cost thrust that dramatically improved its bargaining position with its suppliers. Rather than have its local outlets (cash-and-carry warehouses stocking items on display) deal directly with vendors, Levitz established a 12-person buying department at corporate headquarters in Miami. Supported by a system that allows local store managers to identify slow-moving items, cut prices, and increase turn ratios, the central staff can restock simply by checking items off a master list. The president at Levitz, in commenting on the strategic significance of the system, remarked rhetorically, "What kind of clout can you have with manufacturers if you have 55 buyers?"[5]

In the emerging world of electronic publishing, where industry structure has yet to solidify, some organizations have succeeded in the pursuit of cost economies based on scale while others have tossed in the towel. The New York Times' Books, Information, and Education Group falls into the latter category while Mead Corp.'s Data Central regards itself as one of the winners. In 1983, the Times' group concluded that it had had enough of electronic distribution, at least for the immediate future, having lost $3–4 million in this area between 1981 and 1982. Recognizing the group's limits, its vice president noted that "we don't bring anything unique to the distribution business. But we bring a lot to the business of collecting information."[6] In effect, he was admitting that the Times had failed in its attempt to become a vertically integrated information services firm providing *both* the information or content *and* the information systems to store, process, and distribute it. The Times discovered that large capital investments in information technology, as well as experience obtainable only through years of operating electronic distribution facilities, were required before it could be a profitable participant in this industry.

When the Times exited, it gave its distribution business to Mead's Data Central, a company with a long track record in the field of electronic distribution, having successfully supported Lexis, Mead's innovative database service for the legal profession. Independent firms like Lockheed's Dialog Information Services, which distributes over 120 databases, and Data Central are able to amortize the cost of running their systems to a far greater extent than could the Times. Both independents achieved economies of scale, based on experience, specialization, and automation, that gave them a distinct advantage over their less fortunate rivals.

COST: SCOPE

In 1975, economists John Panzar and Robert Willig coined the term *economies of scope* to describe cost savings that result from the scope of the firm's activities rather than from the scale of its operations.[7] Roughly speaking, scope economies arise when it is less costly to combine the production of two or more product lines in a single firm than it would be to produce them separately.

More formally, firm F is said to enjoy the benefits of economies of scope with respect to product or products x/y (here x/y stands for either a single product with features x and y *or* for separate products x and y) and input i if F's total cost of producing x/y from i, $C_F(x/y, i)$, is less than firm A's cost of producing x from i, $C_A(x,i)$, plus firm B's cost of producing y from i, $C_B(y,i)$:

C_F (x/y,i) is less than C_A (x,i) plus C_B (y,i)

An economy of scope may develop, for example, when a given input (factor of production) cannot be divided but is only partially consumed or occupied and, hence, free for other uses. Or, it may appear when a single service is offered to replace previously separate services, provided the cost of the new is lower than the sum of the combined costs of the old. In this latter case, either the producer of the service or the consumer of it may be the beneficiary of a scope economy.

Economies of scope, we will see shortly, have a specific relevance in the information systems field. To sharpen the sense of this concept, consider the following examples of scope economies, based in general on sharable inputs:

By-product.   It is generally accepted that the cost of raising one flock of sheep for wool and another for mutton is higher than raising one for both. The farmer who raises sheep for both purposes enjoys the benefits of scope economies.[8]

Fixed factors.   If a passenger railroad is underutilized, use of the railroad for passengers *and* freight will provide economies of scope, all things being equal.

Reuse.   The firm that creates a general index of articles published in the sciences benefits from cost advantages due to scope economies when it reuses the general index to derive particular listings for sale to physicists, chemists, biologists, and the like.

Knowhow.   A firm's knowhow represents a shared input that may be used in producing a variety of products. If the firm can find ways to transfer proprietary knowledge or experience from its various activities at low costs, it may be able to enjoy the benefits of scope economies. On the open market, firms attempting to obtain proprietary knowledge face high acquisition costs.

Combinations. The cost of manufacturing an AM/FM clock radio, by all reports, is less than producing *separately* an AM radio, an FM radio, and a clock, all things being equal.

Sears, Roebuck & Co. takes advantage of scope economies based on knowhow and a fixed factor of production to pursue its objective of providing customers with a full line of financial services. A Sears spokesman says that by virtue of its size, the company has considerable technological knowhow in data processing and telecommunications and intends to develop and market this capability.

In 1983, Sears negotiated an agreement with the Mellon Bank to process retail remittances for certain customers of the bank. In 1984, it arranged a test with the Phillips Petroleum Company to process credit card transactions involving 28 service stations and 12 stores in Oklahoma. Using its excess telecommunications and computer capacity, Sears developed an information system to authorize and record credit card transactions at the stations and stores. Upon completion of these steps, it transmits the data to a Phillips computer center for further processing.

How can we get a better return from underused assets? Answers to this not so uncommon question may represent economy-of-scope opportunities for the imaginative firm. When Allen Neurath, the chief executive officer of Gannett Company, posed it, he had in mind printing plants in 38 states used only a few hours a day and 84 local reportorial staffs capable of writing more stories than ever made it into print. Neurath believed Gannett could launch a national newspaper supported by a computerized satellite network linked to local printing plants to take advantage of the evident scope economies. The result was *USA Today*, an innovative venture that found itself in the black in 1987.

Metropolitan Life Insurance Co. saw an economy-of-scope opportunity for a new, fee-based service aimed at corporations and other purchasers of group health insurance dedicated to curbing the rising cost of medical services. Metropolitan, one of the largest health insurance carriers in the country, developed a system for monitoring out-of-hospital medical care, which amounts to about 50 percent of the total claim dollar. By matching its electronic claim files against a standard "pattern of treatment" file developed by Concurrent Review Technology Inc. of California, Metropolitan can spot abnormal numbers of office visits, X rays, laboratory tests, and other procedures "used by doctors for each of several common illnesses."[9] The system identifies physicians who consistently exceed the normal patterns of treatment, so that steps can be taken to eliminate such medical profligacy.

Japan Airlines flies an economy-of-scope route when it finds fee-generating applications for its underutilized worldwide computer-based reservation system. Instead of using it exclusively for its original purpose, seat reservations on JAL flights, the airline now employs it to book tickets around the world for sports events, concerts, plays, and the like. Commenting on the scope economy, a JAL official said, "Why can't we buy Wimbledon tickets for our passengers who are flying to London and dream of watching the matches?"[10]

From satisfying the dreams of JAL passengers to responding to the desires of hog farmers and cattle ranchers, economies of scope based on information systems are playing an increasingly important role. The farmers, it seems, would rather hear about changes in sow mating behavior due to variations in barn illumination than the newest strain of alfalfa and its effect on the portliness of calves. The ranchers, need it be said, have just the opposite preferences. To meet the needs of its multiple readerships, *Farm Journal* (the largest farm publication in the United States) publishes 1,134 different versions for its over 1 million subscribers.

Farm Journal divides its target audience into five major producer categories—cotton, dairy, beef, hogs, and livestock—and partitions the United States into 26 regions. For each of the 14 issues that an $8 annual subscription brings, about 20 percent of the editorial content remains the same in all versions. The rest combines 32 supplements, depending on the subscriber's profile. The journal realized this opportunity to exploit scope economies based on the reuse of material when it switched to a new computer-controlled system offered by its printer, R. R. Donnelley & Sons in Chicago. Capitalizing on the new technology, *Farm Journal* can print, for example, 150,000 beef-only copies, 7,000 beef and dairy copies, and 25 copies for top producers of cotton, hogs, and dairy cows. Without this system, the journal could not afford to meet the increasingly specialized needs of its readers. Unlike subscribers to *The New Yorker* or *Reader's Digest*, "a farmer," according to *Farm Journal's* president, "doesn't pick up a farm magazine to be entertained."[11]

Leaving the farm and moving to the factory, we encounter another form of scope economy, flexible manufacturing. By integrating information systems, robotics, and other forms of automation, firms like Deere & Company no longer find themselves limited to particular product lines rigidly determined by highly specialized manufacturing equipment. In the flexible factory, firms can produce custom-made products in low volume at a profit. To duplicate this in a conventional factory would require several different assembly lines, each with its own costly set of machinery and specialized human resources.

In the Deere plant in Waterloo, Iowa, for example, tractors in more than 5,000 different configurations are produced for farmers desiring not only specialized publications but also custom designs. Deere saves on direct labor costs, since numerically controlled (NC) machines have replaced highly paid machinists. NC machines also lower the costs of retooling and finished-parts inventory. More significantly, the company can reprogram its machines for entirely different purposes. A Deere manager notes that "we can make aircraft parts or washing machine parts or almost anything within a certain size range."[12] Racing to exploit its scope advantages, Deere formed a group to seek opportunities in defense and other nonfarm business areas.

Petroleum companies like Exxon, Texaco, and ARCO pioneered the development of sophisticated information systems to analyze geological data generated by satellite reconnaissance, seismic probes, and the like. To further refine their search for oil and gas formations, these companies compile extensive geological databases. As a result, they have acquired unparalleled expertise and knowledge in a highly specialized field.

This technological knowledge, the oil giants discovered, is not limited to locating oil. It can be used by their geologists to help in the search for coal, uranium, and oil shale. For these alternative energy sources lie buried in sediment formations similar to those bearing oil and gas. When such crude-oil producers pursue these new veins, they benefit from scope economies based on their information systems knowhow. Some economists have even suggested that scope economies, together with considerations such as managerial discretion and the regulatory climate, may have fueled oil firms' diversification moves in the 70s into the coal, uranium, and oil shale industries.[13]

Information technology knowhow enabled Citibank to develop, as a by-product of its massive credit card–processing activities, a new service for retailers. With over 15 million Visa, Master, Diners and Carte Blanche cardholders, Citibank processes vast pools of transaction data. Pumping from these inexhaustible reservoirs, it created a series of marketing reports on customers for retailers intent on improving their merchandising, promotion, and advertising operations. These reports present summary statistics on buying patterns, customer groups, local demographics, and so on. The cost of creating this information on the outside would be prohibitive. Scope economies make it possible for Citibank and, by the way, for others similarly situated on top of valuable, essentially untapped databases.

As a final, double-entry scope economy, consider the cost savings associated with automatic teller machines. For banks, ATMs clearly cut labor costs for routine transactions like deposits and withdrawals. But more importantly, just as flexible manufacturing enables innovators like Deere to offer a variety of products and lines, ATMs provide enterprising banks such as Citibank, Banc One, and others with an opportunity to create new fee-generating financial services based on scope economies obtained through combinations of previously discrete services or of entirely new ones. Bill payment, money market fund transfers, discount brokerage, and cash management accounts are all available—if not today, then tomorrow—on your bank's ATM network. (See Chapter 9 for the market share advantages Citi realized from its ATM net.)

Not only the banks enjoy the rewards of scope economies gained by combining services. Customers, too, benefit. Under the assumption that time is money, customer transaction costs can be substantially reduced when multiple financial services are obtained at an ATM. In the future, "home banking" will offer the same kind of scope economies.

COST: INFORMATION

Information economies enable relatively knowledgeable firms to acquire, produce, process, store, ship, or sell products at lower average cost per unit than relatively ignorant ones. Opportunities to benefit from economies of information may be found in each of the firm's functional areas. Like economies of scale and scope, economies of information have a price, which must be paid before the information advantage can be gained.

The sources of information economies run the gamut from intelligence on the costs, prices, and policies of the firm's strategic targets to data on economic, social, political, and technological trends affecting its products. Consider, for example, the cost reduction or avoidance opportunities arising from the organization's knowledge of such items as:

1. The costs and benefits of matching a competitor's promotional campaign wherever it is launched.
2. A competitor's advertising, credit, or pricing policies.

3. The prices charged by independent vendors who deal separately with the firm's local purchasing agents across the country.
4. The rules suppliers use to estimate, calculate, or otherwise determine the price you will pay for their product.

For each of these items, and countless others as well, knowledge could lead to advantage by enabling the firm to achieve economies of information. Not in all cases, of course. But there seem to be a sufficiently large number of possibilities—caused in many instances by opportunistic behavior on the part of the firm's suppliers, customers, or rivals—to make investments in the appropriate resources worthwhile to acquire such knowledge.

For example, Qantas, the Australian airline, suspected that its insurance premiums were too high. It checked by developing an information system to model three types of risk—accidents in the air, on the ground, and to passengers—and their costs. By comparing what was paid to what the model said should be paid, Qantas accountants confirmed their suspicions. Armed with this information, they renegotiated with the insurer and obtained lower rates. While insurers must protect themselves against customers who fail to disclose risk-related facts, clients, in turn, need to defend themselves against opportunistic insurance companies preying on the ignorant.

Inland Steel built a system to help both itself and its customers reduce inventory-carrying costs. Ford Motor Co. uses it to order specialty steels directly from the mill and then monitor the manufacturing process from beginning to end. Keeping tabs on when the order will be completed enables Ford to schedule deliveries so that its just-in-time production schedules can be met. Inland invested $10 million in developing this application first for internal and then for external use. It claims the application can save customers more than the 10 percent price advantage now enjoyed by foreign suppliers over their U.S. rivals.[14]

The Aluminum Co. of America (Alcoa) purchases over $100

million worth of metals each year for its 13 processing plants. Making imaginative use of a graphics package in conjunction with a popular spreadsheet (Lotus 1-2-3), Alcoa discovered how to increase rivalry among its vendors and gain substantial savings in price negotiations with them. Key plant personnel are asked to rate each vendor with respect to "product quality, quality of paperwork, technical service and support, delivery performance, sales performance, and innovation or inventiveness."[15] This data serves as input for a graphical report displaying summary rankings for the three top vendors. Alcoa uses the report to make vendors focus their attention on areas deemed important—to compel them, in effect, to compete on its rather than their terms. Indeed, this SIS provides, on the one hand, a recipe for how the superior vendor ought to differentiate its offering from the rest of the pack. But on the other hand, it tends to reduce systematically the differentiation advantage that a vendor might enjoy. For it explicitly makes it a target for the others to match or exceed.

Equitable Life Assurance, the nation's third largest insurer, developed an on-line inventory control and purchasing system to tie the firm's field offices with its seven regional offices, four warehouses, and corporate headquarters in New York City. The warehouses stock paper clips, stationery, and other office supplies.

In the past, purchasing agents at the warehouses often lacked information to analyze vendor bids and determine the best buy. With the new system, Equitable corporate now purchases supplies from a distributor in New York and offers them to the warehouses at a bit above cost. The purchasing agents are free to buy from corporate or go outside. The system gives agents leverage during vendor negotiations, since they can access the system's database to learn the terms of recent deals for items they want. With this SIS, Equitable reduced the bargaining power of its office-item suppliers. The system saved Equitable over $2 million a year, according to company sources.

While Equitable protects itself against vendors hawking goods, other organizations aim their information systems at those selling services. Xerox, Digital Equipment, and General Motors among others—all concerned about rising business travel expenses, estimated as the third largest controllable cost of doing business (after salaries and the cost of computers and related equipment)—have taken steps to reduce their costs in this area. New policies, backed by applications designed to aid in travel planning *and* to monitor travel expenses, give them an information advantage when negotiating corporate discounts with hotels, airlines, and car rental agencies and encourage employees to comply with organizational guidelines. Systems report to management, for example, on whether employees take advantage of the lowest fares and rates available to the firm. This tends to have a dampening effect on those employees whose tastes do not match the corporate pocketbook or culture.

And if the firm prefers not to establish its own system, American Express offers a customer-resource-life-cycle (see Chapter 5) service to seal what it dubs the "black hole of American business," the bottomless pit that swallows travel and expense dollars. Called the travel management system (TMS), it provides savings on regular coach fares, hotel rates, interest income on cash advanced to traveling employees, administrative costs related to reconciliation of expense reports and statements, and time associated with bookings of flights, hotels, and automobiles. TMS "manages and controls every phase of a company's travel, from ticketing to cash advances, straight through to reconciliation."[16]

The rising costs of telephone services have prompted many organizations to defend themselves by becoming more knowledgeable, through the use of information systems, about calling and circuit activity. Sometimes, the mere distribution of a report detailing data on the time, type of call, number dialed, location, direction, cost, and account number to department heads causes impressive reductions in telephone expense. A Connecticut manufacturer found that such distribution reduced (in one of its departments) nonbusiness-related calls by 50 percent and the total monthly phone bill by $4,500. Such systems can also be employed to prevent blatant misuse, such as frequent calls to dial-a-joke, the weather or time, dial-a-porn messages, and the like. The state of Washington claims that it saved over $300,000 annually by programming its system to block such calls.

In addition to reducing telephone service expense vis-à-vis providers, some organizations use information systems to stem losses due to clients or customers. A Chicago law firm recovers about $2,500 a month in hourly charges after examining print-outs highlighting clients that its attorneys had not billed for time spent telephoning on their behalf.

Avoiding costs induced by the behavior of opportunistic customers motivates many to develop inventive applications designed to reduce such abuses. In the parking lot business, Edison Parking spent four years devising a system to prevent the loss of up to 20 percent in revenues due to customers who park illegitimately. Now customers must use a plastic identification card before gaining admittance to the lot. They insert the card into an optical reader linked to a central processing unit. The computer checks the validity of the account number, whether last month's bill has been paid, and so on. The garage door opens only if the card passes all tests.

To prevent "customers" who abuse refund policies from continuing their activities, a group of New York City department stores—Bloomingdale's, Gimbel's, and others—banded together, with the aid of an information system, to reduce their losses. What caused this rare act of solidarity were mounting losses due to fraudulent returns. These large retailers were being taken by a varied group of abusers:

- Shoplifters who remove sales tags and ask for refunds at the checkout counter.
- Models who purchase clothes, wear them for a shooting session, and then return them.
- Employees with discount privileges who buy merchandise at discounts and have friends return the items for cash at the regular price.

To meet the challenge posed by these individuals, the stores channeled all refunds through a single information system. In this way, the special customers could be identified by inspecting frequency-of-return reports generated by the system. By warning letters and the threat of more serious actions, the stores were able to stem their losses.

While department stores use information technology to cut their losses by detecting, after the fact, acts committed by opportunistic customers, others have adopted the practice of screening prospects before they have a chance to take advantage of them. Isolating the high-risk customer, they believe, can prevent substantial losses. The 10,000-member Los Angeles County Medical Association (LACMA) subscribes to Physicians Alert, a service offered by a unit of the Chicago-based Docket Search Network Inc. Docket Search, as its name implies, collects court records and organizes them into a number of database services. Physicians Alert sells a computerized record of malpractice suits filed over a 10-year period, which may be used by physicians to identify "patient plaintiffs, the slip-and-fall people," in the words of LACMA's president.[17]

But the story doesn't end here. The slip-and-fall people play their game with teammates, attorneys who provide expert legal counsel. Taking the high ground in this competitive battle, the Los Angeles Trial Lawyers Association, together with some consumer groups, decided to start "a rival computer service for patients that will identify doctors who have been targets in malpractice suits."[18] As the headline reads, "In this battle, it's hard to decide which side we'd rather see lose."[19]

Not so in this next cost-related application, which provokes pressing questions about the exercise of legally sanctioned tenant rights. Landlords in New York, to protect themselves against tenants with certain kinds of undesirable habits—namely, those known for bouncing checks, past evictions, non-payment of rent, credit problems, or complaints against landlords (that appear on Housing Court records)—subscribe to database companies specializing in this kind of information.

Certainly landlords have a right to check certain facts about prospective tenants. In this regard, such inquiries resemble those handled by credit-rating agencies. But "the danger of unfair blacklisting, harassment, and other abuses of the rights of tenants"[20] alarms renters and those individuals or groups who work to protect them. "If you don't get heat or hot water, you have the right to withhold your rent. These computerized systems will tend to make people very uneasy about exercising fundamental rights guaranteed to them under law," noted a representative of a group providing legal assistance to the poor.[21] In Washington, Representative Charles Schumer, a Brooklyn Democrat, introduced a bill "to protect tenants against abusive inquiries," which he called "a genuine threat to all tenants, especially for New Yorkers."[22]

A similar argument has been made by the American Civil Liberties Union in response to a new U.S. government program that uses telecommunications software to spot suspicious telephone calls or calling patterns made by federal employees from their offices. The government's long-distance phone bill comes to about $500 million annually. Federal auditors suspect that 30 to 40 percent of these calls are personal. For the Reagan administration's Office of Management and Budget (OMB), the monetary benefits of the application appear to have outweighed questions of privacy. But not for civil libertarians, who argue that "the audit will have a potentially chilling effect on government whistle-blowers and will create a climate of distrust among personnel in the workplace."[23] The OMB has denied these charges, and the president's Council on Integrity and Efficiency is responsible for carrying out the audit.

A cooperative effort under way in California targets another kind of telephone thief, those who cancel their service without paying their bills. Initiated by the California Public Utilities Commission, which requested of Pacific Bell and six other telephone companies in the state that they form a joint venture to develop and operate a centralized credit check system (CCCS) to track down the cheaters, the effort is expected to save ratepayers about $60 million a year. For in California, ratepayers pick up the tab on uncollectable expenses incurred by the "telcos."

At the center of this cooperative SIS sits a combined telco database containing names and other identifying information for all ratepayers in California. If customers move without paying their last bill, a situation that evidently occurs with some frequency in California, telcos can use the system to track them down and collect the unpaid balances. CCCS also sets deposit rates for new service, calibrating the rate to the degree of ratepayer risk as determined from payment records.

Another interesting game played between a business and its customers occurs most baldly at Atlantic City gambling casinos. To lure its best customers—the high rollers (i.e., those having the greatest probability of losing the most)—Caesar's Palace, Bally's, Harrah's, and other houses offer a well-orchestrated array of complimentary enticements ranging from free drinks, food, and room accommodations to transportation via private jet.

The object of the game, from the casinos' point of view, is to maximize the spread between the high roller's losses and the amount spent on the complimentaries tailored to the desires of the individual. To improve its chances of winning, casinos keep elaborate customer records on game preferences, betting patterns, favorite drinks, restaurants, entertainers, and so on. Not content only with the advantage guaranteed by the odds at the gambling table, casinos employ information systems to help improve their chances of selecting precisely those players who will yield the most net to the house. For gaming marketers, the opportunities are limitless. Yet, there are also risks. By designing an expensive package of complimentaries for a gambler, the house will lose if the player doesn't play as expected. To prevent this possibility, the casinos attempt to refine their analyses of the best prospects and weed out those who don't play by the "rules."

From information systems intended to get the upper hand in buyer relations, we turn now to a few designed to help customers reduce their expenses and, in the process, to advance the interests of the system supplier. To support a cost reduction thrust in the customer arena (in contrast to Equitable's cost reduction thrust described above vis-à-vis its suppliers), the Hartford Insurance Company provides customers who have complex exposures and multiple claims with a computer-generated loss control analysis. Breaking out losses by location, time of day, type of accident, and so on, this information system pinpoints accident causes and, after preventive measures are taken, can lead to substantially lower premium costs for customers and more business for Hartford.

To help its customers improve their operations, Packaging Corporation of America (PCA), a large paperboard supplier, offers a host of specialized services. Knickerbocker Toys, one of PCA's customers, certainly was grateful for the assistance it received when it confronted a complex and costly packaging puzzle. Knickerbocker ships over 22 million individual items each year, with each toy requiring a different display carton, and each primary package a corrugated shipping container. It was the latter that caused the problem, for each primary package needed its own customized corrugated container. Before PCA offered its assistance, Knickerbocker juggled nearly 400 containers of varying sizes and shapes.

PCA's marketing services group designed an information system to solve Knickerbocker's puzzle. This enabled the toy company to cut its warehouse space by 50 percent and to reduce container setup costs by 75 percent. Moreover, with larger-volume container orders, the firm now enjoys substantial savings in unit costs. In helping Knickerbocker better manage its costs, PCA gained the respect and confidence of its customer, an important factor in the commoditylike packaging business.

Strategic information systems may also be used to secure an edge with more than one target or to support activities in one arena so that advantage may be gained in another. The manager of General Electric's distribution center for large appliances in Kentucky uses an application to help GE keep down its substantial shipping costs so that its retailers can maintain competitive prices. Xerox, Pratt & Whitney, General Motors, and others require their suppliers to provide computer-generated data on product quality, inventory levels, and the like, for the goods they supply. The desire to produce more efficiently rather than to gain advantage over suppliers motivates such initiatives. These new information-based demands, however, open competitive advantage opportunities for suppliers: As large customers formulate supplier plans in response to more intense competition, their strategies often aim at reducing the number of suppliers to a select few who can provide not only the desired components but also value-added services like computer-generated quality control reports. In this environment, a supplier's information system expertise can create a decisive edge in securing long-term contracts, which could pre-empt the business from competitors.

The use of information systems offensively against competitors is illustrated by some of the extensions of the airline reservation systems (see Chapter 1). For example, the cut-rate airlines contend that American and United use traffic information obtained from their systems to overcharge them just for being listed. Airlines without their own systems complain that the intricacies of Sabre and Apollo often stymie attempts to create innovative packages. As one rival put it, "If you're out of sync with their reservation system, then whatever you're doing won't exist."[24] Finally, Braniff and Continental have argued that their cash flow problems were due in part to these automated reservation systems: When multiple carriers are involved, the first carrier in the itinerary is considered the ticketing airline, so it collects all the revenues, but repays the others only when the flight is over.

Economies of information, of course, are not limited to the profit sector. Government agencies have strategic targets also, and some of the latter have on occasion tried to beat the system. Recently, however, agencies have started to fight back, aiming computer-based weapons at those seeking to collect benefits they are not entitled to. Several examples follow.

Massachusetts saved $56 million in 1983 by automating its $1.2 billion Medicaid budget, formerly monitored by staff members adept at index card manipulation. The economies achieved were not due to personnel reductions. Rather, the state discovered that doctors, hospitals, and others were over-billing it.

California devised a system in 1978 to eliminate jobless-benefit payments to those attempting to rip off the state through the "fictitious-employer scheme."[25] The scheme works like this: The thieves set up a phony business, pay some unemployment insurance taxes for fictitious employees, lay them off (so to speak), and then collect jobless benefits by posing as laid-off employees. This fraud certainly isn't limited to the inventiveness of Californians. A New Yorker formed 28 corporations, created 168 aliases, and collected $600,000 before he was caught. Through the use of information systems modeled after California's, states have significantly reduced their losses in this area.

The Boston-State Retirement Board knew something was amiss when it, after asking its 14,500 pension recipients to submit proof that they were still among the living, received responses from 13,994. Inspired by this saving of over $700,000 from the $85 million it pays each year, the board contracted with Hooper Holmes, a company that supplies continuously updated magnetic tape listings of the social security numbers of some 12 million deceased persons. With these listings, the Board has written a program to detect those illicit claimants from another world.

Since 1981, New York City's Tax Division has run a computerized program to catch evaders of city taxes. At the end of 1983, it had aided in the collection of more than $40 million from over 55,000 individuals and businesses. By simple file-matching procedures, the division identified those who failed to pay taxes on commercial rent, business income, and personal income.

NOTES

1. Harvey Leibenstein, *Beyond Economic Man: A New Foundation for Microeconomics* (Cambridge, Mass.: Harvard University Press, 1980).
2. Robert Bennett, "Chase Agrees to Buy Traveler's Check Unit," *New York Times*, January 28, 1982.
3. Steven Grover, *The Wall Street Journal*, October 29, 1983.
4. *New York Times*, May 8, 1983.
5. "Levitz Furniture: Sitting Pretty as It Waits for the Recovery," *Business Week*, February 7, 1983.
6. "Can an Electronic Publisher Be Its Own Delivery Boy?" *Business Week*, March 7, 1983.
7. John Panzar and Robert Willig, "Economies of Scale and Economies of Scope in Multioutput Production," *Bell Labs Economic Discussion Paper* 33, 1975. To contrast scope and scale economies, see E. A. G. Robinson, *The Structure of Competitive Industry*, 2d ed. (Chicago: University of Chicago Press, 1958); William Shepherd, *The Economics of Industrial Organization* (Englewood Cliffs, N.J.: Prentice-Hall, 1979); F. M. Scherer, *Industrial Market Structure and Economic Performance*, 2d ed. (Skokie, Ill.: Rand McNally, 1980); Robert Hayes and Stephen Wheelwright, *Restoring Our Competitive Edge: Competing through Manufacturing* (New York: John Wiley & Sons, 1984).
8. Elizabeth Bailey and Ann Friedlaender, "Market Structure and Multiproduct Industries," *Journal of Economic Literature*, September 1982.
9. Jerry Bishop, "Metropolitan Life Offers New Service to Monitor Claims," *The Wall Street Journal*, June 25, 1986.
10. "Asian Report," *The Wall Street Journal*, February 17, 1984.
11. Jeffrey Birnbaum, "With 1,134 Editions, *Farm Journal* Labors to Please All of Its Readers," *The Wall Street Journal*, January 21, 1983.
12. John Holusha, "The New Allure of Manufacturing," *New York Times*, December 18, 1983.
13. David Teece, "Economies of Scope and the Scope of the Enterprise," *Journal of Economic Behavior and Organization* 1 (1980). See also Oliver Williamson, *Markets and Hierarchies: Analysis and Antitrust Implications* (New York: Free Press, 1975).
14. Peter Petre, "How to Keep Customers Happy Captives," *Fortune*, September 2, 1985.
15. "Alcoa Rates Vendors' Mettle," *Computer Decisions*.
16. American Express advertisement, *The Wall Street Journal*, September 9, 1985.
17. Bill Johnson, "In This Battle, It's Hard to Decide which Side We'd Rather See Lose," *The Wall Street Journal*, November 14, 1985.
18. Ibid.
19. Ibid.
20. David Burnham, "Landlords Using Computer Services to Screen for 'Troublemaker' Tenants," *New York Times*, February 25, 1986.
21. Ibid.

22. Ibid.
23. Mitch Betts, "U.S. to Use Program to Audit Federal Employees' Calls," *Computerworld*, March 25, 1985.
24. "Do Airlines Play Fair with Their Computers?" *Business Week*, August 23, 1982.
25. Joann Lublin, "States Using Computers to Battle Growing Thefts of Jobless Benefits," *The Wall Street Journal*, July 20, 1983.

CASE REFERENCES

COST: SCALE

Chase Manhattan

Robert Bennett. "Chase Agrees to Buy Traveler's Check Unit." *New York Times*, January 28, 1982.

General Bancshares Corp.

John Curley. "General Bancshares Corp. Gets Head Start in Building Interstate Banking Network." *The Wall Street Journal*, December 12, 1983.

American Medical International and Lifemark Corp.

Steven Grover. *The Wall Street Journal*, October 29, 1983.

"Why Private Hospitals Are Checking into the Chains." *Business Week*, November 7, 1983.

Humana

"A Pricing Revolution Aids the Big Guys." *Business Week*, January 9, 1984.

New York Times, May 8, 1983.

Foster & Marshall and Shearson/Lehman Brothers

Tim Carrington. "Regional Brokerages Are Selling to Giants as Earnings Sag and Big Offers Are Made." *The Wall Street Journal,* January 8, 1982.

Levitz Furniture

"Levitz Furniture: Sitting Pretty as It Waits for the Recovery." *Business Week,* February 7, 1983.

Mead Data Central and the *New York Times*

"Can an Electronic Publisher Be Its Own Delivery Boy?" *Business Week,* March 7, 1983.

"Mead Stresses Data Growth." *New York Times,* April 23, 1984.

Zachary Schiller. "Mead Makes Information Pay—Most of the Time." *Business Week,* August 25, 1986.

COST: SCOPE

USA Today

Myron Magnet. "How Top Managers Make a Company's Toughest Decision." *Fortune,* March 18, 1985.

Metropolitan Life

Jerry Bishop. "Metropolitan Life Offers New Service to Monitor Claims." *The Wall Street Journal,* June 25, 1986.

Japan Air

"Asian Report." *The Wall Street Journal,* February 17, 1984.

Farm Journal

Jeffrey Birnbaum. "With 1,134 Editions, *Farm Journal* Labors to Please All of Its Readers." *The Wall Street Journal*, January 21, 1983.

Deere & Company

John Holusha. "The New Allure of Manufacturing." *New York Times*, December 18, 1983.

David Teece. "Economies of Scope and the Scope of the Enterprise." *Journal of Economic Behavior and Organization* 1 (1980).

COST: INFORMATION

Qantas

"The Qantas Way of Financial Modeling." *ICP Interface: Administrative and Accounting*, Autumn 1982.

Inland Steel

Peter Petre. "How to Keep Customers Happy Captives." *Fortune*, September 2, 1985.

Alcoa

"Alcoa Rates Vendors' Mettle." *Computer Decisions*.

Equitable Life

Bob Johnson. "Tracking Stock Inventory Saving $2 Million Yearly." *Computerworld*, May 10, 1982.

American Express

"Business Travel: Amenities Curbed." *New York Times,* June 15, 1983.

American Express advertisement. *The Wall Street Journal,* September 14, 1985.

Connecticut Manufacturer and Chicago Law Firm

John Detler. "Telephone Information Systems: Five Management Applications." *Office,* April 1982.

State of Washington

Claudia Ricci. "Personal Use of Company Phones Is Target of Cost-Cutting Efforts." *The Wall Street Journal,* April 11, 1984.

Edison Parking

"Computer Attendants Cut Parking Lot's Losses." *Computerworld,* November 21, 1983.

New York City Department Stores

Brad Altman. "Note to Refund Abusers: The Check Is in the Mail." *Chain Store Age Executive,* May 1982.

L.A. Trial Lawyers Association and L.A. County Medical Association

Bill Johnson. "In This Battle, It's Hard to Decide which Side We'd Rather See Lose." *The Wall Street Journal,* November 14, 1985.

Landlords and Tenants

David Burnham. "Landlords Using Computer Services to Screen for 'Troublemaker' Tenants." *New York Times,* February 25, 1986

U.S. Government

Mitch Betts. "U.S. to Use Program to Audit Federal Employees' Calls." *Computerworld*, March 25, 1985.

California Telcos

Bob Violino. "California Telcos Ordered to Join Plan to Catch Cheaters." *CommunicationWeek*, March 18, 1985.

Atlantic City Casinos

"Caesar's Boardwalk: Accounting in Color." *ICP Interface: Administrative and Accounting*, Summer 1982.

"How Casino Computers Stretch the House Odds." *Business Week*, July 30, 1984.

Hartford Life Insurance

Hartford Life Insurance advertisement. *The Wall Street Journal.*

Packaging Corporation of America

"Computer Solves Packaging Puzzle." *Paperboard Packaging*, August 1982.

GE

Michael King. "Transportation Official at GE Finds His Role Rises with Fuel Prices." *The Wall Street Journal*, December 31, 1981.

Xerox

Business Week, August 22, 1983.

James White. "Xerox Expects to Learn a Thing or Two from Some Successful Japanese Imitators." *The Wall Street Journal*, July 30, 1982.

GM and Pratt & Whitney

Ralph Winter. "Concerns' Push to Improve Quality of Products Puts Heat on Suppliers." *The Wall Street Journal,* September 20, 1983.

American Air and United Air

"Do Airlines Play Fair with Their Computers?" *Business Week,* August 23, 1982.

State of California

Joann Lublin. "States Using Computers to Battle Growing Thefts of Jobless Benefits." *The Wall Street Journal,* July 20, 1983.

State of Massachusetts

The Wall Street Journal, November 27, 1984.

Boston

Bill Laberis. "Mass. Finds Way to End Pensions for the Dead." *Computerworld,* January 17, 1983.

New York City

"NYC Computerized Tax Program Collects $40 Million from Evaders." *Computerworld,* January 9, 1984.

7

Innovation

KINDS OF INNOVATION

In 1959, when Xerox introduced its first copier, the 914, it realized the dream of Chester Carlson, the patent attorney who conceived the basic idea 20 years earlier. The 914 product was an innovation, invented by Carlson and imitated (in one form or another, in due course) by a long line of competitors who entered the industry Xerox created.

While it took Xerox two decades to bring Carlson's idea to market, Dr. L. A. B. Pilkington saw his dream become reality in just seven years. In 1954, he thought of a new way to make plate glass, then manufactured by grinding the surface of a continuous glass ribbon until the desired thickness and quality were reached. To replace this rather wasteful and costly process, Pilkington imagined an entirely different procedure, one that eliminated grinding altogether by floating a continuous feed of molten glass on a layer of molten tin.

Invented by Pilkington and developed by Pilkington Brothers Ltd., a British glass manufacturer, the float-glass process was an industry-transforming innovation, making this relatively small firm a leading player. Shortly after its commercial introduction in 1961, the process was licensed to Pittsburgh Plate Glass in the United States and to St. Gobains in France. Within a few years, all major producers, under agreements with Pilkington, manufactured plate glass by the float process, which enabled them to reduce production cost substantially.

Innovation, as these examples show, involves the *adoption* of new products or processes. A product innovation satisfies customer needs or wants previously unmet. A process innovation improves the efficiency or effectiveness of a process associated with a product. An innovation may relate to one or more links on the product network (industry or value chain), which typically covers product and process R&D, purchase and transportation of raw materials, manufacturing of parts and components, assembly, testing and quality control, marketing, sales, wholesale distribution, and retailing. It may stem from technological, organizational, or other sources.

Innovation is the middle stage in the sequence that starts with invention (creation) and ends with imitation (diffusion). *Invention* is the first confidence that something should work, "the stage at which the scent is first picked up."[1] *Innovation* is the first commercial application of an invention, "the stage at which the hunt is in full cry," comprising such activities as refining the initial idea, prototyping, engineering and design, tooling, manufacturing setup and start-up, and marketing. Economists estimate that invention consumes 5–15 percent of the total cost of realizing new products or processes, while innovation takes the remainder. *Imitation,* the final stage, signals the success of the innovation.

The 914 copier and the float-glass process were major innovations. Other product and process changes may not have such far-reaching consequences. Yet these qualify as innovations if they bring into existence a new product that catches on or they alter (to a degree often difficult to determine) the established conduct of business in an industry. This implies that innovations may either be unprecedented (like the two just mentioned) or be new applications of concepts developed in other contexts.

While the boundary between a slight modification and a prior innovation may be difficult to perceive, we need not be troubled here by this failure of vision. For I am not so much concerned with drawing theoretical lines as with uncovering opportunities to use information technology strategically. To this end, we need to understand the various sources of product and process innovations, since these are the ingredients of innovative strategic thrusts.

Strategic innovation thrusts are moves intended to increase the firm's competitive advantage or reduce the advantage(s) of its strategic targets. An innovation thrust can be defensively employed by a firm to imitate a competitor's innovation by introducing its own variant, not precisely the same as the pioneer's but different enough to be considered a minor innovation in its own right.

A firm may introduce a process innovation that simultaneously reduces cost and improves quality to such an extent that customers perceive its product as far superior to the competition's. Finally, like its close relatives, differentiation and cost, innovation often goes hand in hand with other thrusts.

INNOVATION: PRODUCT

Like most religious rituals, the process of identifying innovation opportunities remains a mystery, defying rational explanation. And their development is largely an act of faith, vision, and energy. Before Xerox launched the 914 copier, it commissioned three independent studies to determine market demand. Two major consulting firms reported that demand was so low the project ought to be scrapped. The third was more optimistic, projecting cumulative totals of 8,000 placements (maximum) and 3,000 (minimum) by the end of six years. Yet within three years after launch, 80,000 914s were in place.[2]

Beyond the eternally black bowels of the earth from which revolutionary products like the Xerox 914 emerge as major innovations, lies a region of opportunity far more amenable to conceptual understanding. Assume for a moment that a product exists. Ask the question: What can I do to ensure the continued life of this product? Answers to this question, I suggest, will provide a rich source of product innovation ideas.

Begin by reviewing the main features of the current product. Can any be modified to create a new version? Can performance be improved? Can the product be put to other uses? Can it be enlarged? Miniaturized? Rearranged? Concatenated with other products? Second, ask customers about improvements they would like or problems they've encountered. Third, consider competitors' products. Can you differentiate your offering from theirs? Can you provide a new combination of product features and services? Answers to such questions may lead to a product innovation opportunity.

In 1977, Merrill Lynch, the largest U.S. brokerage house, announced a new product, the cash management account

(CMA), offering under one umbrella three appealing services to investors: credit through a standard margin account, cash withdrawal by check or Visa credit card, and automatic investment of cash, dividends, and so on in a Merrill-managed money market fund.

Hawked by its brokers to clients with minimum balances of $20,000, CMAs moved slowly during their first few years. Brokers couldn't see what was in it for them. Realizing this lack of incentive, Merrill dangled free trips to Hawaii and Puerto Rico as rewards for attracting the greatest number of CMAs. The troops responded by running CMAs up the exponential curve: 1980/180,000 accounts, 1981/560,000 accounts, 1982/900,000 accounts, 1983/over 1 million accounts. The average balance in 1984 was $70,000.

These efforts brought in over 450,000 new accounts, accounts that had not been with the firm previously. Merrill reaps over $60 million a year in fees ($4.17 a month in 1986, up from the $2.33 initially charged) from the more than $20 billion it manages in the three money market funds associated with the CMA product.

The CMA is an innovative product, providing scope economies to customers as well as to Merrill. The product would never have left the launching pad without a 162-step (subsequently patented) computer program; the help of Banc One, a bank-holding company (see Chapter 1) that processes CMA checking and Visa card transactions; and Merrill's resources in database and laser printing technology.

The deal with Banc One enabled Merrill to circumvent federal regulations prohibiting brokerage houses from offering their customers checking account privileges or unsecured loans via credit card transactions. Banc One processes checks written by Merrill's customers and issues a Visa credit card to them. But Merrill developed the software to keep track of all customer transactions: brokerage, credit card, and check cashing. Running on Merrill mainframes, the application performs daily sweeps of cash into money market accounts, complex database searches, and antifraud routines to protect against scams such as check kiting.

With this product-based strategic innovation thrust, made possible by information technology, Merrill preempted the market from a monopoly position for four years. Competition from other financial services organizations did not appear until 1981; and at the close of 1983, Merrill's closest rival, Dean Witter, had only 125,000 customers for its active asset account. Only in 1984 and thereafter did Merrill's premier position begin to erode as banks and other financial service organizations finally entered the market with similar products and the information systems technology needed to support them. By 1987, Merrill's share had dipped to about 50 percent.

An enterprising market research firm, National Decision Systems of San Diego, captured another form of product innovation opportunity. The U.S. Constitution mandates a population count every 10 years to reapportion seats in the House of Representatives. Not content to tally only heads, the decennial census has developed over the years an insatiable appetite for data, from the basics of age, sex, and race to the number of holes drilled or dug (if your water comes from wells) and babies had (if you're a householder).

In 1980, the data collected by the Census Bureau filled 38 reels of computer tape. By 1983, the bureau had still not issued its report on the 226 million Americans who had completed questionnaires. But it offered to sell the raw results of this $1 billion survey sponsored by the American taxpayers to anyone willing to pay $38,000 for the tapes.

The purchaser could, for example, use them for its own purposes or merely package the tapes in attractive containers and advertise their availability. This would add some value but not much; it certainly wouldn't count as an innovation. Or the purchaser might divide the data on the 38 reels into (say) 3,800 different categories and offer each for sale in diskette form suitable for microcomputer analysis. This, too, adds value to the raw data but wouldn't (except under the most liberal interpretation) be considered innovative, since the distributor's function of "breaking lots" is not something that ordinarily turns heads. But an illuminating transformation of the raw data through analysis and a presentation of the results in a readily available form should, I suggest, count as an innovation.

This is precisely what National Decisions did with the 1980 U.S. Census data. It purchased (at less than cost) a complete set of tapes and developed information systems to process the raw data and present it in attractive form. What National did, anyone with the requisite expertise could have done with this uncopyrighted material.

National added value to the raw computer tapes by preparing a five-volume compendium of the 1980 census, offering it for $395 as a set. It sells to those involved in market research, demographic analysis, and so on. It's a value-added product that could only be produced through the aid of information systems designed to analyze and report on the 1980 tracts. National Decisions saw an opportunity and pursued it. In this marketplace, National Decisions enjoyed first-mover advantages.

The innovations of Merrill Lynch and National Decisions, while noteworthy, pale beside the achievement of Federal Express (FE). In 1986, just 13 years after it got off the ground, this overnight, door-to-door air delivery service of business goods and messages flew past the $2.5 billion revenue mark. Carrying close to 50 million packages, serving more than half a million customers in over 40,000 communities across the United States, and still expanding domestically and internationally, Federal represents a by-now legendary case of business innovation, innovation that depends essentially on the strategic use of information technology.

The company operates an armada of over 75 aircraft, a fleet of more than 5,000 delivery vans, and a central sorting facility, the hub, located in Memphis, Tennessee. Each day, couriers pick up shipments from senders and load them on planes bound for the hub. Most planes arrive between midnight and 1:00 A.M. After their cargoes are unloaded and sorted, they are reloaded to return to their points of origin carrying only shipments addressed to locations in these areas. Couriers at the destination points deliver priority packages by 10:30 A.M.

The hub-and-spoke idea, applied for the first time by Fred Smith, the founder and chief executive officer (CEO) of Federal, to the overnight delivery of packages transformed the airfreight business. Smith conceived the idea while enrolled in an undergraduate course at Yale. But he couldn't sell it to his professor, who gave him a C on a paper describing it. After graduation from Yale in 1966, service in the Marine Corps as an officer, and a sales job with an airline company, Smith founded Federal Express in 1973 at the age of 29 with the help of a $4 million trust fund left by his father.

Far from taking off like a rocket, Federal's future in the early days was questionable at best. But Smith believed in his idea and was willing to risk all to achieve it. Federal was once so low on funds it was unable to meet the payroll. Undaunted, Smith flew to Las Vegas, parlayed his last few hundred dollars into $30,000 and returned to ignite Federal on its meteoric rise. Or so the legend goes.

The success of Smith's entrepreneurial venture depends on interrelated networks of ground, air, and electronic (computer and telecommunications) systems. Consider, for example, how the ground and air networks are linked by the electronic network when a customer calls to request a pickup:

1. The customer's call is switched automatically to one of FE's three centers, where a service representative receives it.

2. The request is then transmitted to the Memphis computer system, where it is printed and displayed on a terminal screen.

3. If the request is for a package in a major city, it is routed by FE's digitally aided dispatch system (Dads) to a courier (van driver) in the field. Dads consists of a small computer and a video display terminal attached to a digital radio in the van. It enables drivers to communicate with an FE dispatcher electron-

ically linked to the hub computer. When a driver signs on to a mobile terminal, orders for the day are displayed on the screen.

4.   After the courier picks up the package, he or she enters identifying data into the terminal so that a dispatcher can close out all requests at the end of the day.

5.   Before the package is shipped, its airbill number is scanned electronically and transmitted via FE's satellite net to the Memphis computer. Frequent electronic monitoring is one of the features of FE's offering that differentiates it from the competition. It enables customers who inquire about their shipment to determine its status along the way as well as the date and time of its delivery.

6.   At each embarkation point and airport ramp, there is a computer terminal connected to FE's data network. By taking the pulse of its packages at various checkpoints along the shipment chain, FE can compute individual flight plans to accommodate variations from anticipated volumes. Such computer-generated plans also take into consideration weather conditions, traffic delays, rerouting of trucks to alternative airports, and the like.

7.   Upon arrival at the hub, packages are sorted in FE's half-million-square-foot building along 17½ miles of automated, high-speed conveyor belts.

With its innovative, computer-shaped service, Federal captured an estimated 50 percent share of the air express market by the mid-80s. In June 1986, Smith was presented with the Gartner Group's annual "Excellence in Technology" award at the National Computer Conference. The award "was created to recognize CEOs who within their industry have championed and utilized information technology in exceptional ways."[3] The previous winner was Robert Crandall, CEO of American Airlines, the guiding force behind American's Sabre system (see Chapter 1). Smith was the unanimous choice of the 1986 selection committee, composed of information management professionals from a variety of industries. If anyone possessed SIS vision, it was Smith. If any organization was aware of the strategic use of information technology, it was Federal.

But there is more to the Federal Express story than its spectacular rise to domination. Federal has also participated in one of the greatest SIS failures in recent years, dwarfing by far the total losses of such illustrious firms as IBM/Merrill Lynch with Imnet (the SIS-backed service intended to replace Quotron in broker's offices; see Chapter 1) and Citibank/McGraw-Hill with Gemco (the SIS-backed service intended for traders in petroleum and other commodity futures; see Chapter 9). Federal's answer to Imnet and Gemco was called ZapMail, an SIS attempt that resulted in an over $400 million operating loss in less than three years.

In mid-1984, Federal launched ZapMail, a system designed to transmit facsimile copies of documents over a nationwide packet network called ZapNet. By July 1986, Federal had leased to customers 6,000 ZapMail facsimile machines (ZapMailers), which transmitted documents to other ZapMailers or to Federal's locations where they were printed and then delivered by courier. Over the next eight years, Federal expected to spend over $1 billion on three satellites, four earth stations, and as many as 50,000 ZapMailers on customers' premises.

But in September 1986, Federal pulled the plug on its Zap-Mail service, taking a $190 million write-off. Why did this innovative attempt to preempt the facsimile network marketplace fail? Didn't it have everything going for it, including a man with certifiable SIS vision and an organization that had proven beyond any doubt that it could deliver the technological goods? Scanning the history of the ZapMail venture, it is hard to fault the planning and implementation steps followed.

Consider, for instance, the initial decision to develop Zap-Mail. Smith assembled his senior management team around the table and outfitted each with *consensors,* two-knobbed devices that register either approval or disapproval, and, depending on how hard they are pressed, the degree of intensity or feeling associated with a decision. According to Smith, "we used a lot of those methods to surface things and to help us develop our strategy."[4] When the final decision on ZapMail was made, there was no dissension among Federal's top executives.

Observe also how Federal handled the huge internal education challenge posed by the new ZapMail service. In July 1984, according to Federal's chief operating officer, "we ran a worldwide video teleconference to tell our employees why we were doing this."[5] This effort required seven origination points, 240 downlinks, and an expense of $1.1 million. This "family briefing" employed the very satellite technology that ZapMail would use and "was one of the largest corporate satellite meetings ever held."[6]

Nor can Federal be blamed for being insensitive toward its customers or for lack of commitment and belief in the ultimate success of ZapMail. As its chief operating officer said, "I've always believed that the user will tell you what he wants. Don't go in there and tell him what he needs. That's where a lot of mistakes are made."[7] Or listen to its senior vice president for electronic products, who figured in 1985 that there would be 1 million ZapMailers within the next decade: "People's views about whether to have a telephone once depended upon whether they thought nobody had one or everybody had one. The same with office copy machines and overnight express. Once the habit was accepted, it became an expected way of doing business."[8]

Finally, hear what Fred Smith told people about the secret for Federal's success in overnight express. He claimed it was having the delivery system in place before demand accelerated and before competitors could build a comparable network. "Only 16 packages showed up on the first night of operations in 1973, but when the market suddenly exploded, Federal was poised on the high ground."[9] Is it any wonder Smith and others at Federal believed ZapMail would follow a similar evolutionary path?

SIS vision, technological smarts, commitment, dedicated employees, sensitivity to user needs: all the ingredients for SIS success. Despite these, ZapMail still failed. At Federal's 1986 annual meeting, Smith explained ZapMail's demise to stockholders as a combination of the following factors:

- Insufficient demand.
- Technological problems (e.g., the unreliability of ZapNet).
- Cost problems (e.g., the cost of ZapMailers did not decrease as anticipated, because the yen-dollar exchange rate made it impossible for NEC, Federal's Japanese supplier, to reduce its prices; the cost of launching satellites rose more than 50 percent after the U.S. space shuttle disaster).
- Competitor problems (e.g., low-cost facsimile machines became available within the last year).

"We found," Smith said, "that this market was much harder to stimulate than the research had indicated."[10]

Why did Federal persist in the face of mounting losses? Smith's gambling instincts and previous experience with pioneering the overnight delivery service seemed applicable. Also, belief in false analogies about telephones, copiers, and so forth, and faith in the rationality of success as reflected in the use of such "scientific" decision-making tools as consensors may explain a large chunk of it. But in the end, it comes down to one thing: a blindness to the reality that was plain for others to see and a form of arrogance nourished by the extraordinary success of the express business. Customers weren't interested or ready for the service. The writing was on the wall. The facts were there, but executives at Federal were caught up in a myth about excellence, a belief that they could do anything. But don't you need such a myth to succeed? That, I'm afraid, is the subject for another book.

INNOVATION: PROCESS

Like preemptive strikes—major moves made ahead of competitors, through which the firm secures an advantageous position by being the first mover and from which it is difficult to be dislodged (see Chapter 10)—opportunities for process innovation may occur up and down the constantly evolving industry chain. Indeed, many preemptive strikes are major process innovations related to manufacturing (Japanese improvements in the production of 64k RAM chips), distribution (BIC ballpoint pen and L'eggs pantyhose sales in supermarkets, a channel never used for such products previously), and so on.[11]

The process innovator therefore must look systematically at the chain of activities, goods, and services associated with the development, production, distribution, sale, financing, maintenance, and so on of a particular product. At one or more points, opportunities for an innovative strategic thrust might arise. Promising sites to explore, which are illustrated by the cases to follow, include:

- *Resource identification/selection:* Opportunities to develop innovative procedures to identify or select resources critical to the development, manufacture, distribution, and so forth of the product.
- *Distribution:* Opportunities to provide innovation distribution channels, services, and the like.
- *Retailing:* Opportunities to alter the normal procedures for retailing products, affecting both customers and suppliers.
- *Service processing:* Opportunities to provide a firm's service at substantially lower cost or higher quality because of processing innovations associated with it.

This list is not exhaustive. As usual, targets for possible innovative strategic thrusts may be selected from among the firm's suppliers, channels, customers, or rivals (see Chapter 4).

Resource Identification/Selection

Suppose the basketball coach of the men's U.S. Olympic team picked his players according to the following criteria:

> *Identification:* Height—at least 6'10".
> Weight—between 180 and 250 pounds.

Scoring average—18 points/game.
Team winning ratio—greater than .500.

Selection: After observing identified prospects perform in practice games, decide intuitively.

Now, suppose the coach of the French team identified and selected prospects strictly in terms of their ability to pass an intricate series of speed, dexterity, and intelligence tests. As a result, the French team consists of 10 extremely quick, nimble, and bright players whose average height, it turns out, is 5'6" and whose basketball experience is one to three months. Against the U.S. team, it is safe to say, France would be at a competitive disadvantage. We know this immediately, the results of the contest having been determined by the identification and selection criteria used by each coach.

This hypothetical case underlines the importance of identifying and selecting the right materials for the task at hand—the ingredients, as it were, of success. In sports, money management, and politics—to name but three areas in which this principle rules—enterprising organizations seek innovative strategic thrust opportunities to transform (to their advantage) traditional ways of identifying and selecting the ingredients of success. The examples to follow show how these may be supported or shaped by information technology.

Moving from the ridiculous to the sublime, consider the Dallas Cowboys, pro football's most successful team (between 1960 and 1984) with 18 consecutive winning seasons, 12 division championships, and two Super Bowl victories in five appearances. When the Cowboys' franchise was created in 1960, president and general manager Tex Schramm had a vision about improving the player identification and selection process. He believed that through the use of computers (then applied in pro football, if at all, for the most mundane accounting and payroll functions), Dallas could gain a competitive edge. Together with a friend at IBM's Service Bureau Company, he initiated a project to define those player attributes, position by position, that made a good football player.

By 1965, after four years of research and development, a system for evaluating and selecting players was up and running. As experience with the system grew, being enriched by feedback on what particular factors led to success once a player was selected and playing on the team, management confidence in this new competitive weapon grew. It enabled the Cowboys to improve the accuracy of scouting reports, often biased by personal preferences for factors such as speed or hitting power, by assigning weights based on past performance to each scout.

While it is impossible to determine the precise value of the Cowboys' strategic information system, the testimony of its vice president for player development (the principal user) serves as a reliable proxy.

> Today I am very excited about the system, and how we now can get the percentage a player has of playing in the league, what percentage he has of starting, and what are the most and least important qualities that make up a successful football player. When we started, we had a four-room house of grey vanilla— and it ended up a mansion. . . . Life is percentages. If we can arrive at a 52 percent possibility rather than 50 percent, we will be that much better off.[12]

Schramm echoed this sentiment, saying, "We have an *advantage* because we've been doing it the longest. Other teams take a simplistic approach and don't specifically rank players the way we do. They may use the computer more in terms of simply listing what players are available in which positions, and their size."[13]

In pro football, advantage is determined in large part by the talent assembled on the field; in money management, by the investments in the portfolio. Expertise in the processes of identification and selection, while important in the former, is absolutely essential in the latter. For more conventional money managers, portfolio construction proceeds stock by stock. One learns the pros and cons of individual companies by visiting plants, assessing competitors and patterns of industry evolution, listening with a third ear to public relations announcements, and the like.

Not so with Batterymarch, the path-breaking money management firm from Boston led by Dean LeBaron, a contrarian. From 1970 to 1983, Batterymarch exceeded or matched the Standard & Poor's 500 Stock Index 12 times. The firm's 15 percent annual rate of return topped the market rate by 6 percent.

LeBaron's method for identifying and selecting investments prescribes two steps: (1) formulate a general investment strategy and (2) use the computer to identify and select investments conforming to the dictates of the strategy.

Since its formation in 1970, Batterymarch has pursued 12 strategies, couched in such terms as:

- Invest in small to medium-sized companies selling at low price-earnings ratios and owned by less than 10 percent of other money managers.
- Invest in companies with new plant and equipment, which have greater tax deductions (due to depreciation) and whose reported earnings are therefore artificially low.
- Invest in companies with low ratios of price to sales value, as an inflation hedge and a bet that asset-rich companies might be taken over.

These investment strategies translate into computer programs written to search through 4,000 or so issues, make arcane calculations consistent with the guidelines, and ultimately identify and select all and only those stocks satisfying strategic criteria. Computers suggest and execute all trades at Batterymarch; only one technician monitors the system. This innovative strategic use of information systems catapulted Batterymarch in less than 15 years into the nation's 11th largest stock market investor, the sixth largest excluding banks, with over $11 billion in assets.

LeBaron's innovation transformed a critical industry process. Listen to what peers have said about the changes wrought by Batterymarch.

They're reinventing virtually every part of the investment process.[14] [Charles Ellis, financial services consultant from Greenwich, Connecticut.]

LeBaron has probably set the pace for large money managers in America. He has a *process* for managing large sums of money, which have historically been the downfall of money managers.[15] [Roger Hertog, executive vice president at Sanford C. Bernstein & Co., a $2.3 billion money manager based in New York City.]

From the stadium and the trading room to the political ring, astute professionals gain an edge by using computer technology imaginatively. To complete this triad of examples illustrating strategic innovation thrusts related to sports, money, and politics, we turn to the role played by systems in fundamentally transforming aspects of the American political scene.

The Republican Party pioneered in the application of computers to the processes of identifying and selecting contributors. Traditionally, Republicans paid their bills by digging into the pockets of a small group of wealthy individuals. Democrats, on the other hand, covered their costs from the nickels and dimes contributed by the masses. At least that's how the story used to run. But by 1983, after applying the fruits of information processing technology to support their fund-raising campaigns, the Republicans claimed that over 70 percent of their national committee's revenues came from contributions of less than $25.

Even the Democrats agreed that the Republicans had established a major competitive advantage in this area. According to a statement made at the time by the former executive director of the Democratic National Committee:

> The various wings of the national Republican apparatus are now raising at least 10 times more money than the various segments of the Democratic National Committee. Now, when you include the money raised by the Republican and Democratic candidates, the spread is considerably less, but there is a threshold, a financial critical mass, which the Republicans already have and the Democrats have not.[16]

The Democrats were fully aware of the bind their strategic information systems blindness had imposed upon them. "We saw the result in 1981 when the Republicans harvested the product of a decade of systematic and disciplined investment in the new technology: A Reagan presidency, a Republican-led Senate, and a working Republican minority in the House."[17]

In the 1984 elections, the Republicans moved beyond the use of information systems to identify potential contributors. They extended their innovations to three other critical areas:

1.   Unregistered voters likely to support Republican candidates. The Republican National Hispanic Assembly, an arm of the Republican National Committee, used an assortment of lists to generate the names of "upwardly mobile Hispanics," according to the group's executive director.[18]

2.   Potential Republican voters who might be away from their residence on election day. Members of this group were sent applications for absentee ballots.

3.   Voter concerns on a day-to-day basis in every state. The results of such poll watching enabled Republican candidates to fine-tune their messages and arrange their promotions and advertising accordingly.

But in the Congressional elections of 1986, despite some noteworthy new applications of information technology, Republican efforts to regain control of the Senate and win a majority in the House failed. Not even President Reagan's persuasive pitch—transmitted from a computer located in a Chicago suburb to 400 other computers around the country, which in turn initiated a telephone-calling process intended to reach hundreds of thousands of registered Republicans urging them to vote for candidates of the party—could turn the tide.

Neither could the computerized services of a small, Virginia-based political consulting firm, National Media Inc., which bought radio and television time for Republican candidates in search of political advantage. Using a bank of personal computers programmed to analyze Nielsen and Arbitron rating data, coupled with demographic information, National selected the best programs and times for handcrafted campaign commercials aimed at particular audience segments. Incumbent Senator Paula Hawkins hired National to choreograph her $5 million media campaign in Florida, a campaign that employed a great variety of recorded political messages to reach its target audiences. Yet, for Senator Hawkins, not even the most sophisticated use of information technology could save her from defeat.

Other candidates took advantage of the Republican Information Network, hooked to an extensive database that included, among other things, the voting records of Democrats, campaign organizational tips, and environmental legislation. A spokesperson for the Republican National Committee claimed that "this is the biggest technological edge we have with the Democrats."[19] But like Paula Hawkins, the Republicans were beyond technological salvation in 1986. How much greater their losses might have been without the aid of information technology is an open question.

On the other hand, the Democrats had made significant strides by 1986 to reduce their information technology–induced political disadvantage. One Democratic innovation, code-named "Avenel" (after the consulting firm that suggested it), identified Democratic incumbents who might be the targets of special Republican efforts to unseat them. Avenel is a diagnostic tool, the political equivalent of a physical examination, that assesses the incumbent's strengths and weaknesses. The "Democrats believe that many of the participants in the Avenel [project] so improved their performance that the Republicans were unable to mount strong campaigns against them."[20]

In another competitive arena, organized labor is capitalizing on information technology in its corporate battles with management. Cesar Chavez, the head of the 30,000-member United Farm Workers of America (UFW) union, argues that "we need to *innovate* and take risks with new ways of doing things or we'll go out of business. Way deep inside me, there is something about computers I don't like. I seldom go into the computer room. *But the other side has them, and we need to compete.*"[21] [Italics added.]

The UFW purchased a mainframe in December 1984. They use it in direct mail campaigns to compile target lists by sorting through census and other demographic data. Just as the Republicans targeted Hispanics and executives who might need an absentee ballot, the UFW sets its sights on, say, liberals and middle-class blacks in New York and San Francisco for grape boycott or fund-raising campaigns.

Distribution

In the health care industry, the innovations of American Hospital Supply are, by now, classic exemplars of the strategic use of information technology. The company manufactures, markets, and distributes health care products to hospitals, laboratories, and medical specialists worldwide. In 1976, it introduced a computerized order-entry system, dubbed ASAP (American's analytical systems automated purchasing system), for customer use. Using an ASAP terminal, hospital staff members placed orders directly for any of American's full line of over 100,000 products. By 1984, over 4,200 customers were tied to American electronically via ASAP.

If American had lost access to ASAP for a period of only five days, according to a senior executive at the firm, the consequences would have been dire: loss of market share and control of its business. To protect itself from the loss of so integral a part of its operations, American established a backup site capable of handling all ASAP transactions and normal company processing.

As American sees it, ASAP "helps customers by simplifying the ordering process and permitting customers to reduce their inventories."[22] American consultants are available to assist customers in learning to use ASAP, "improve the hospital's purchasing procedures, reduce on-hand inventory, standardize their use of supplies, and implement improved patient-change procedures."[23] With a more recent version of

ASAP, the purchasing process can be reduced to only one manual step: approving the order. Everything else is linked by ASAP to the hospital's computer system and by high-speed telephone lines to American's processing facilities and through them to over 122 distribution centers nationwide.

To get a better sense of the strategic significance of one of the first uses of an information system as a competitive weapon, listen to what the competition has said about ASAP. Industry executives claim that "ASAP was largely responsible for driving competitors like A. S. Aloe Company and Will Ross Inc. from the national hospital supply distribution business. Once a hospital got an ASAP terminal, American couldn't be budged."[24] As a director at rival United Hospital Supply put it, "There will never be another American Hospital Supply. Who's kidding who? It's almost impossible for a hospital to avoid doing business with them."[25] One former employee says it's like having the fox in the hen house but admits that American saves its customers money also.

ASAP shaped an innovative strategic thrust that transformed a basic point—order entry—on the product network and, in the process, raised customer switching costs. American seized an opportunity for using information technology to win a significant competitive advantage.

While American's advantage made it the leader with about one third of the hospital supply market, it wasn't enough to defend itself against the forces of change and consolidation spreading epidemically through the health care industry. Cutbacks in federal medicare payments under the Reagan administration forced hospitals to perform radical surgery on their cancerous expenditure growth. And among the primary victims of the massive cuts were suppliers like American. The situation had become so desperate for the firm in 1985 that it was willing to give up its independence and merge with its biggest customer, Hospital Corporation of America (HCA), the largest publicly owned chain in the country.

However, as talk of the impending marriage reached some of American's other customers, HCA's rivals, a strange thing happened. The seemingly sustainable advantage enjoyed by American with its ASAP system started to deteriorate. Customers began finding new suppliers, swiftly overcoming the "substantial switching costs" hypothesized by Eric Clemons and Steven Kimbrough (see Chapter 3) as one of the conditions necessary for sustainable competitive advantage. Fearing that the proceeds from their business with American would be used by HCA to fund its drive for industry domination, hospitals moved with surprising speed to extricate themselves from their electronic bondage.

As the senior vice president of the Good Shepherd Medical Center in Longview, Texas (located but a few football fields away from a 100-bed HCA-owned hospital), put it: "I am not going to do business in any way that will strengthen my direct competitor."[26] Prior to the merger announcement, Good Shepherd acquired more than a third of its supplies from the large distributor. Immediately after it, purchasing managers were instructed to buy as little as possible from American.

Others feared that the merger would give HCA unique access to ASAP-related information. If so, HCA might use this advantage to analyze hospital buying patterns and spot trends for new lines of business or candidates for takeover. Both possibilities, and others as well, raised serious questions in the minds of American's customers about the proposed merger.

But these questions became moot once Baxter Travenol Laboratories, a hospital supply company half the size of American and suffering from the same cost-squeeze condition ravaging its customer base, made a bid for its larger rival in June 1985. After a protracted struggle, Baxter won control of American in a $3.7 billion deal that made it the largest hospital supply company in the nation.

Three months prior to its bid for American, Baxter had acquired Compucare, a firm providing "information processing services and software products, with financial, administrative, and clinical applications, to the health care industry."[27] Vernon Loucks, Baxter's president and CEO, said that "the acquisition of Compucare will allow Baxter Travenol to play an increasingly important role in several key areas of the rapidly growing hospital–information systems market."[28] Baxter, which had been diversifying into this line of business for the past few years, now ranks as one of the largest players.

In 1987 it acquired Caremark, a health care company specializing in home-care treatment. Part of the attraction, industry analysts suggest, was Caremark's Health Data Institute subsidiary, a unit providing "management and analytical systems to health insurance companies and others involved in alternate-site care."[29]

The SIS vision of Karl Bays, American's president and CEO, inspired the company to develop ASAP, which led to its leading position. But when the winds of change rocked the industry, his vision proved inadequate to handle the new turbulence. Baxter's Loucks, on the other hand, saw the importance of information technology in a different light. He viewed ASAP as an underutilized channel of distribution, as a source of scope economies that could handle Baxter's supplies as well as American's. Moreover, he saw ASAP as a powerful asset that could enhance Baxter's new information systems business by providing an unmatched market intelligence opportunity similar in some respects to the market intelligence derived by United and American Airlines from their Apollo and Sabre systems, respectively.

Retailing

From resource identification/selection and distribution, we move now to retailing. As one of the major processes in the consumer product chain, retailing comprises all the activities involved in selling goods or services directly to customers for personal, nonbusiness use. When an organization—be it a manufacturer, wholesaler, supermarket, or department or specialty store—engages in this kind of selling, it is retailing. Retailers may ply their trade in a store, on the sidewalk, at a concert. Products may be sold in person, over the telephone, through vending machines. It's all retailing.

Ever since the establishment of Bon Marché, the first department store, retailing has witnessed one innovation after another, from mail order to catalog showroom, from gas station convenience store to community shopping center. Two recent examples are of interest to us because they use information technology to support or shape strategic innovation thrusts.

Founded in the early 70s, Comp–U–Card International turned a profit for the first time in 1983. Its original business provided a telephone-based service to shoppers who wanted to compare prices of brand name products across the country. By paying an annual membership fee (in 1987, $39), a shopper could call a CUC representative, ask for the price of an item, and (if it is acceptable) place an order. CUC, having neither inventory nor warehouse, would forward the order to the manufacturer, distributor, or other intermediary offering the product at the price the consumer had agreed to pay. In effect, CUC acted as the shopper's agent. As such, it received a small percentage of each sale. But this wasn't its main source of revenue. That came from fees paid by over 3 million CUC members.

The original CUC service kept tabs on products manually. In 1979, CUC automated its database of over 60,000 items, which by 1987 had reached over 250,000 items and hundreds of brands, and launched the first interactive home computer shopping service, a strategic innovation thrust shaped by information systems. CUC markets this service, called Comp–U–Store, itself and through the Source, Dow Jones, and Compu-Serve information services to members with micros and modems. This affluent group, in 1987 totaling 75,000, counts as CUC's best customers, purchasing on average five times more than pure telephone customers.

The Comp–U–Store innovation led in 1984 to Comp–U–Mall, a browsing service for subscribers who wish to explore CUC's name brand items or stroll electronically through a mall whose "stores" offer such lines as discount drugs, flowers, and specialty items from Neiman-Marcus.

To expand its product line (see Chapter 8), CUC acquired

Financial Institution Services in 1985 for $56.8 million in stock and Certified Collateral Corp. in 1986 for $98 million in stock. Financial, based in Nashville, Tennessee, markets insurance, travel, shopping, and other services through banks. Collateral assists insurance agencies in claims processing and has built a database of vehicle identification numbers from 5,000 car dealers. CUC capitalizes on Financial's bank network and Collateral's dealer network to gain new customers for itself and to provide new electronic services to help them (e.g., finding the lowest available car prices). These, together with other acquisitions, enable CUC to offer a growing list of fee-based services such as credit card protection and travel. For an additional $39 annually, for example, CUC members can subscribe to Travelers Advantage, a service that guarantees "the cheapest fares available and a 5 percent rebate."[30]

In 1986, Comp–U–Card joined with the Financial News Network to create Telshop, a new electronic home shopping service. Cable television viewers can purchase goods by telephone, with Comp–U–Card providing the items for sale and processing the orders.

Can information technology be used to change our normal patterns of supermarket shopping? In West Los Angeles a few years ago, one firm believed that the answer to this question was yes. The Phone In–Drive Thru Market offered shoppers an opportunity to call in orders for over 4,000 grocery and general merchandise items (each having a five-digit code) appearing in a bimonthly catalog. The listing included national brands and generics if available. Operators accepted the orders and entered them on computer terminals. At this point, the Phone In–Drive Thru information system took over.

The system batched orders, analyzed them, and generated a bulk pick list and an optimal route for employees wheeling large carts through the Phone In–Drive Thru warehouse. Exhibiting a modicum of intelligence not always found at supermarket checkout counters, the system determined packing sequences that placed, for instance, canned goods at the bottom of the bag and bread, grapes, and potato chips on top.

When customers arrived to pick up their orders, they first stopped at a terminal station that displayed instructions. After they entered their IDs, the screen listed the items ordered and prices. The customer wrote a personal check (approved in advance) and drove to a designated pickup lane (the place where the computer had instructed the picker to leave the order), received the order, paid, and departed usually having spent about four minutes at the market.

This innovative retailing operation, the brainchild of a computer consultant to the Jewel Food Stores in Chicago (one of the leading users of information systems among supermarket chains) and an entrepreneur who founded the Malibu Grand Prix amusement center, was to expand over the next two years by opening 16 additional markets, mostly in the West. Prime targets were upscale suburbs and Snow Belt cities. At these new outlets, customers with push-button phones would be able to key in their orders automatically. Eventually, of course, the chain planned to accommodate shoppers with home computers. Unfortunately, these plans were never to be realized. Like the imaginative failures described elsewhere—Imnet (see Chapter 1), ZapMail (see above), and Gemco (see Chapter 9)—Phone In–Drive Thru folded after only a brief period of operation, as the market for its innovation failed to materialize.

Service Processing

In the home-buying market, the traditional process of financing the sale is undergoing a radical change. High interest rates, the secondary market for mortgages, and deregulation in the financial services industry account for some but not all of it. Technological advances in information processing and telecommunications need to be factored in as well.

Until the early 80s, the purchase of a home had been largely a local affair involving buyer, broker, and banker. The broker, familiar with the available properties, would show them to the prospective buyer. To finance the sale, the buyer would arrange a mortgage with the neighborhood savings and loan or bank, which financed it from the deposits of local customers.

First Boston, an entrepreneurial investment banking house, detected an opportunity to disrupt this long-standing triad. It invested about $10 million in the development of a nationwide, computer-based mortgage network to put buyers and lenders together directly, in many cases bypassing the local banker. Called Shelternet, the system allows a prospective home buyer to apply for a mortgage through a real estate broker and receive a conditional commitment for a loan in less than an hour.

The service links borrowers with lenders by matching the financial qualifications of the former with the mortgage terms of the latter. According to a First Boston representative, "You can take an application, do an appraisal, do the follow-up work, and clear the loan inside of three weeks, whereas in California right now, it is taking anywhere from 60 to 90 days for a bank to process a mortgage."[31]

First Boston wrote the software for Shelternet in-house. It is offered to brokers as part of a package that includes an IBM personal computer, installation, and the cost of establishing a separate mortgage service company, which is considered a necessity if currently unlicensed brokers hope to be certified as mortgage originators. First Boston receives a fee of $200 for each loan closed through Shelternet.

Most prospective Shelternet clients are large, metropolitan realtors with no mortgage banking experience. First Boston also offers Shelternet to banks that cannot (because of interstate banking laws prohibiting such moves) open branches across the country but that can offer mortgage loans anywhere. In addition, such national realty chains as Century 21 and Coldwell Banker use Shelternet under their own labels. After nine months of operation, the system generated $14 billion worth of mortgages.

As expected, some mortgage bankers have not looked too kindly at this innovation. According to the president of the Mortgage Bankers Association of America, "At least a segment of the mortgage banking community thinks that we're not yet ready for a nationwide mortgage information system. They view it as a substitute for the close, interpersonal relationships so crucial between lenders and home buyers."[32]

In the energy management business, Honeywell and Johnson Control share at least 70 percent of the market. Both offer systems to cut fuel and electrical costs in large buildings. Devices that monitor and control air-conditioning, lighting, and heating systems are tied together by information systems for managing the entire building. Since the early 70s, demand for this service has attracted other suppliers; so Honeywell and Johnson, to maintain their leading positions, have had to devise new strategies.

Honeywell's approach represents a strategic innovation thrust for reducing customer costs through the use of a new information processing capability. For the manager of a building as small as 50,000 square feet who is neither willing nor able to acquire a computer, Honeywell offers DeltaNet, a service designed to eliminate the need for an on-site system. Honeywell places sensors and controls in the building, ties them together in a local network, and transmits readings to 1 of 51 Honeywell processing centers in 26 cities. A center computer with a profile of the customer's building stored in its memory analyzes the transmitted data, determines what needs to be done, and sends commmands back to the building automatically for action. This system (which took more than four years to develop), together with Honeywell's reputation for being a reliable supplier that provides installation and maintenance support, gives the firm a competitive edge in this newly formed segment. To enter it, the competition must match Honeywell's investment in time and information system resources.

Process innovations may occur at more than one point on a product network (see Chapter 4) and thereby make the whole process innovative. Benetton, Italy's largest sportswear manufacturer, exemplifies this kind of innovative multiplicity. In 1979, it opened its first U.S. store. Seven years later, it had over 400 outlets nationwide, with a goal of becoming the McDonald's of midpriced apparel stores. Worldwide, there are over 3,200 outlets in 53 countries, the majority franchised, with a new one opening somewhere almost every day. From a single factory in 1964, Benetton has become the largest commercial consumer of wool in the world, manufacturing in many plants outside Italy. In 1986, with only 1,750 employees, it produced close to 50 million garments, most of which were farmed out to over 300 small companies. As a consequence of this production policy, the firm carries virtually no inventory. The keys to Benetton's success lie in its entrepreneurial management, its imaginative designs, and its innovative use of information technology at three points on its product net:

1.   Producing only for orders in hand, its inventory control system matches purchasing and production requirements. This cuts inventory-carrying costs and costs associated with demand misjudgments.

2.   Using its computer-aided design and manufacturing systems to lay out patterns and cut fabric waste to about 15 percent gives Benetton an advantage over rivals lacking such systems. Up to 40 percent of a manufacturer's cost goes to the purchase of raw materials such as fabric.

3.   Monitoring consumer preferences through on-line computer links to its principal agents and via point-of-sale terminals in its stores, Benetton predicts demand with a high degree of confidence. These monitoring systems allow it to respond ahead of the competition when changes in demand arise. The firm can, for example, dye goods to order and ship quickly so that within 10 days, sweaters, slacks, and the like are on the shelf of the store that placed the order.

Benetton's innovative thrusts at these points on its product net set it apart from its rivals. Its strategic use of information technology has transformed the way business is conducted in the sportswear industry. With its systems expertise, it is in a position to respond rapidly to the fashions of the time.

Just as Benetton, Banc One (see Chapter 1), and McKesson (Chapter 1) have become leaders in their industries—women's sports apparel, banking, and distribution, respectively— through innovative applications of information technology and the inspired leadership of senior executives possessed with SIS vision, Giant Food Inc., a Washington, D.C.–based regional supermarket chain, has climbed to the top of its business.

In 1987, Giant ranked as the most profitable of the 12 publicly held regional chains. But it wasn't in that position in the early 70s. Its rise to the top depended on a number of factors, not the least of which was its innovative use of information technology for both process and product applications. As Banc One was the first bank to install automatic teller machines in its territory, Giant was the first supermarket chain to install check out scanning systems company wide. The data obtained from these systems enabled Giant to analyze current sales, warehouse space requirements, promotion schedules, and inventory position. And electronic purchasing triggers, linking Giant to its largest suppliers, allowed the chain to keep its inventory carrying costs low. Giant was also the first supermarket company to use a fleet management system for the scheduling and maintenance of its 170 tractors and 1,100 trailers. These cost avoidance/reduction efforts made it difficult for rivals like Safeway, A&P, Pantry Pride, Lucky Stores, and Grand Union to compete. Giant is in a position "to wage nasty price wars,"[33] and it has the will to do it.

In 1985, Giant entered the banking business, forming a joint venture with the Suburban Bank of Baltimore to install automatic teller machines (ATMs) in its stores. Unlike most supermarkets venturing into this new electronic world, Giant rather than the bank operated the cash-dispensing machines. It therefore earned money on each transaction and saved maintenance dollars that would normally go to an ATM service firm such as TRW.

Giant's technological innovations complement other innovative moves it has made over the years. For example, it pioneered with specialty sections and new offerings like delicatessens, single-portion foods, homemade pasta, and in-store baking of bread and croissants.

A FINANCIAL SIS

Let us close this chapter with a more esoteric example of a SIS. The use of information technology to support competitive strategies of leading financial institutions in the international swapping game—the large commercial banks, brokers, and others—has been for most a well-kept secret. But as we shall soon see, the phenomenal spread of this innovative product depends essentially on information technology. To appreciate the critical part played by computers and global electronic networks, we need first to understand the rudiments of the swap technique and how it has developed over the past few years.

Interest-rate swapping, an innovative financing technique pioneered by major New York City banks, has evolved rapidly and grown globally since its inception in the early 80s. While the total volume of the relatively unregulated international swap market escapes precise documentation, estimates in the mid-80s ranged from $175 billion to $350 billion. In Euromarkets, roughly 60 percent of the $130 million of capital raised involved swap transactions. Citibank, considered the market leader, booked about $25 billion worth in 1985. In 1987, with swap specialists in New York, Tokyo, London, Hong Kong, and Toronto, Bankers Trust claimed it completed "an average of five deals every day." Senior swappers are considered valuable corporate assets, commanding salaries of between $500,000 and $700,000 a year.

In basic form, an interest-rate swap involves three players: two counterparties—Borrower A and Borrower B—and an Intermediary M, the financial institution arranging the deal. Imagine the following scenario. A has cheaper access to fixed-rate financing than B but would prefer to fund its debt with floating-rate interest payments, at lower than the public market rates. And B would prefer to fund its debt with fixed-rate payments also at lower than the market rate. Can the counterparties be brought together so that each would get what it wanted at costs less than the available alternatives open to them on the public debt markets? Enter now M to arrange a swap, a deal enabling the counterparties to swap their interest payments and thereby achieve their objectives. For this matchmaking effort, Intermediary M generates a handsome arbitrage fee.

To illustrate the swap idea, consider a $40 million deal with a maturity of 10 years in which M makes $200,000 a year on a swap with the following features:

1. B, a U.S. company, pays M interest payments on $40 million borrowed at a fixed rate of 9.50 percent.
2. M makes dollar payments at a fixed rate of 9 percent to A, a Japanese firm; M retains as its fee $200,000 (i.e., 50 basis points or 9.50 percent minus 9 percent, times $40 million).
3. A pays M dollar-denominated interest payments on $40 million at a rate determined by the floating-rate market (i.e., the London international rate).
4. M passes A's interest payments on to B.
5. A issues a $40 million public bond (via M) at a fixed rate of 9.50 percent.

Transactions 1–4 are scheduled to occur annually on the same day. Each of the counterparties has achieved its objective: A gets floating-rate payments, B gets fixed-rate payments, and both are satisfied that the deal is better than the separate arrangements each would have had to make without the swap arranged by M.

This example illustrates a rather straightforward swap, with only one kind of debt security (a bond), one currency (dollars), and only two counterparties (A and B). Over the years, more complex swaps have evolved involving multiple counterparties, different kinds of debt instruments, and several kinds of currency. In addition, a swapper may act not only as the broker but also as a principal of the deal, swapping debt terms with the counterparties and then trading its exposure to another firm.

Part of the risk faced by a swap deal maker lies in the contractual commitments it makes with the counterparties. If, for example, one of the counterparties defaults, the financial intermediary that arranged the swap is still obligated to the other counterparty for certain annual payments.

Initially, information technology played a minor role in the international swap market. Hand calculators and personal computers were used only for calculating the terms and risks of fairly simple deals like the one described above. But as the market for swaps grew in volume and complexity and competition intensified, the use of information technology assumed a far more strategic importance. Gone were the halcyon days for firms such as Citibank or Manufacturers Hanover that had learned to exploit the inefficiencies of the floating- and fixed-rate debt markets and pocket the 40- to 50-basis-point fees on multimillion-dollar swap deals.

In addition, the intermediaries realized that they needn't have both counterparties in place before they could cut a swap deal. One was enough if the intermediary could warehouse the swap position, hedge it, and then search for the other counterparty or counterparties to close out the deal. To perform these tasks, computers and global electronic networks are critical: managing inventory in swap warehouses and hedging the risk of open positions would be unthinkable without them.

An intermediary now keeps its inventory of swap positions stored on a personal computer. Its swap marketers have immediate access to the latest swap quotes. The speed and distribution of this information often give an edge, albeit not sustainable for any length of time, to the marketers. The availability of a swap printout also helps marketers search for new corporate finance applications. Perhaps more important, the computerized inventory focuses the bank's attention on strategic risk and pricing issues that can only be addressed by analyzing the entire set of swap positions with elaborate, proprietary, computer-driven models. It is these models, experts believe, that can lead the intermediary to a dominant position in this hotly contested arena.

NOTES

1. Brian Twiss, *Managing Technological Innovation*, 2d ed. (London: Longman Group, 1980). See also C. J. Sutton, *Economics and Corporate Strategy* (Cambridge, Eng.: Cambridge University Press, 1980); Arnoldo Hax and Nicolas Maljuf, *Strategic Management: An Integrative Perspective* (Englewood Cliffs, N.J.: Prentice-Hall, 1984).

2. Theodore Levitt, *Marketing for Business Growth* (New York: McGraw-Hill, 1974).

3. Michael Karnow, "Federal Express Wins Award for Its Excellence in Technology," *InformationWeek*, June 16, 1986.

4. Stephanie Walter, "High Tech at Federal Express: How Jim Barksdale Runs His Marvelous Machine," *Management Technology*, May 1985.

5. Ibid.

6. Ibid.

7. Ibid.

8. Ibid.

9. Ibid.

10. Stanley Gibson, "Federal Express Cancels ZapMail Service," *Computerworld*, October 6, 1986.

11. Ian MacMillan, "Preemptive Strategies," *Journal of Business Strategy*, Fall 1983.

12. William Martorelli, "Cowboy DP Scouting Avoids Personnel Fumbles," *Information Systems News*, November 16, 1981.

13. Ibid.

14. Randall Smith, "Money Manager Wins by Letting Computer Carry Out Strategies," *The Wall Street Journal*, May 8, 1984.

15. Ibid.

16. David Burnham, "Have Computer, Will Travel the Campaign Trail," *New York Times*, September 22, 1983.

17. Ibid.

18. "The Powerful New Machine on the Political Scene," *Business Week*, November 5, 1984.

19. Steven Roberts, "Politicking Goes High-Tech," *New York Times Magazine*, November 2, 1986.

20. Steven Roberts, "Behind '86 Races, Battle of Computers," *New York Times*, October 21, 1986.

21. Aaron Bernstein and Jonathan Tasini, "Chavez Tries a Computerized Grape Boycott," *Business Week*, September 9, 1985.

22. Hal Lancaster, "American Hospital's Marketing Program Places Company atop a Troubled Industry," *The Wall Street Journal,* August 24, 1984.

23. Ibid.

24. Ibid.

25. Ibid.

26. Ford Worthy, "A Health Care Merger that Pains Hospital," *Fortune,* June 24, 1985.

27. Michael McCarthy, "Baxter Travenol to Buy Compucare for $73 Million," *The Wall Street Journal,* March 4, 1985.

28. Ibid.

29. Pauline Yoshihashi, "Travenol, in Stock Deal, Will Acquire Caremark," *New York Times,* May 12, 1987.

30. Russell Mitchell, "Comp–U–Card Hooks Home Shoppers," *Business Week,* May 18, 1987.

31. Ed Scannell, "Banker-Realtor Net Cuts Mortgage Processing Time," *Computerworld,* September 5, 1983.

32. Eric Berg, "Rise of National Mortgage Market," *New York Times,* January 22, 1984.

33. Bill Saporito, "The Giant of the Regional Food Chains," *Fortune,* November 25, 1985.

CASE REFERENCES

INNOVATION: PRODUCT

Merrill Lynch

Richard Mattern, Jr. "IBM 3800: Individualization and the New Technology." *Direct Marketing*, February 1980.

Tim Carrington. "Cash Management Accounts Proliferating as Bankers, Brokers Vie for People's Money." *The Wall Street Journal*, November 16, 1982.

Jon Friedman. "Wall Street's Cash Management Battle Heats Up." *New York Times*, November 21, 1982.

Tim Carrington. "Merrill Lynch Agrees to Buy New Jersey S&L." *The Wall Street Journal*, April 25, 1983.

Harvey Schapiro. "Putting All Your Assets in One Basket." *New York Times*, November 20, 1983.

"Merrill Lynch Wins Cash Account Row with Dean Witter." *The Wall Street Journal*, December 28, 1983.

"Merrill Lynch's Big Dilemma." *Business Week*, January 16, 1984.

Scott McMurray. "Merrill Lynch Tests Asset Management for Small Investors." *The Wall Street Journal*, March 12, 1984.

"Merrill's New Bank Challenge." *New York Times*, April 11, 1984.

Richard Layne. "Merrill Lynch Is Bullish on CMA." *InformationWeek*, May 26, 1986.

National Decision Systems

Andrew Hacker. "Census Figures for Corporate Use." *New York Times Book Review*, August 21, 1983.

Federal Express

Federal Express, annual reports, 1982–83.

"Federal Express Wants to Deliver in Space." *Business Week*, July 4, 1983.

Katherine Hafner. "Federal Express Puts Dollars—$24 Million behind Demand for Unerring Communications." *Computerworld*, August 8, 1983.

Dean Rotbart. "Federal Express Sinks near Its 52-Week Low, and 'Buy' Recommendations Are Appearing." *The Wall Street Journal*, March 20, 1984.

Katherine Hafner. "Fred Smith: The Entrepreneur Redux." *Inc.*, June 1984.

Federal Express advertisement for ZapMail, *The Wall Street Journal*, August 29, 1984.

John Andrew. "Outlook for Federal Express Hinges Largely on Firm's ZapMail Venture, Analysts Say." *The Wall Street Journal*, January 24, 1985.

Stephanie Walter. "High Tech at Federal Express: How Jim Barksdale Runs His Marvelous Machine." *Management Technology*, May 1985.

John Merwin. "Anticipating the Evolution." *Forbes*, November 4, 1985.

Diana ben-Aaron. "DP Helps Fedex Get It There Overnight." *InformationWeek*, May 26, 1986.

Michael Karnow. "Federal Express Wins Award for Its Excellence in Technology." *InformationWeek*, June 16, 1986.

Brian Dumaine. "Turbulence Hits the Air Carriers." *Fortune*, July 21, 1986.

Timothy Smith. "Federal Express Will Scuttle ZapMail, Take

$190 Million Write-Off; Stock Soars." *The Wall Street Journal*, September 30, 1986.

Stanley Gibson. "Federal Express Cancels ZapMail Service." *Computerworld*, October 6, 1986.

Bob Wallace. "Stung Federal Express Scraps ZapMail Service." *Network World*, October 6, 1986.

Charmaine Harris. "Information Systems Deliver for Overnight Carrier." *InformationWeek*, October 6, 1986.

INNOVATION: PROCESS

Dallas Cowboys

William Martorelli. "Cowboy DP Scouting Avoids Personnel Fumbles." *Information Systems News*, November 16, 1981.

"The Computer Scores Big on the Gridiron." *Business Week*, October 24, 1983.

Allen Zullo. "The NFL Goes Digital." *Popular Computing*, November 1982.

Batterymarch

Randall Smith. "Money Manager Wins by Letting Computer Carry Out Strategies." *The Wall Street Journal*, May 8, 1984.

Randall Smith. "Batterymarch Changes Investing Strategy and Looks to Troubled Banks and Utilities." *The Wall Street Journal*, November 9, 1984.

Paul Schindler. "Investment Firm's Computers Pay Off." *InformationWeek*, January 27, 1986.

Democrats and Republicans

William Martorelli. "Democrats, GOP Jump on Computer Bandwagon." *Information Systems News*, November 1, 1982.

David Burnham. "Have Computer, Will Travel the Campaign Trail." *New York Times*, September 22, 1983.

David Burnham. "Mondale Campaign ahead of All Others in Use of Computers." *New York Times*, January 28, 1984.

Dudley Clendinen. "Small Computers Open Politics to Citizens with Little Money." *New York Times*, February 15, 1984.

David Burnham. "Reagan's Campaign Adds Strategy Role to Use of Computer." *New York Times*, April 23, 1984.

Rodney Smith. "The New Political Machine." *Computerworld*, July 16, 1984.

"The Powerful New Machine on the Political Scene." *Business Week*, November 5, 1984.

"Plugging In Pols." *Harvard Magazine*, January–February 1986.

David Burnham. "Democrats Chase Dollars with Computer Aid." *New York Times*, March 5, 1986.

Alice LaPlante. "Micros Finding New Uses in the World of Politics." *InfoWorld*, June 30, 1986.

Steven Roberts. "Behind '86 Races, Battle of Computers." *New York Times*, October 21, 1986.

Steven Roberts. "Politicking Goes High-Tech." *New York Times Magazine*, November 2, 1986.

Kurt Eichenwald. "What's New in Election Software." *New York Times*, November 2, 1986.

United Farm Workers

Aaron Bernstein and Jonathan Tasini. "Chavez Tries a Computerized Grape Boycott." *Business Week*, September 9, 1985.

American Hospital Supply and Baxter Travenol

American Hospital Supply, annual reports, 1981–83.

William Martorelli. "Hospital Supplier Opts for Mixed Vendor Shop." *Information Systems News*, August 9, 1982.

Burt Schorr. "Hospitals Scramble to Track Costs as Insurers Limit Reimbursements." *The Wall Street Journal*, December 2, 1983.

"Mail Shipping System Speeds Customer Service." *Office*, December 1983.

Hal Lancaster. "American Hospital's Marketing Program Places Company atop a Troubled Industry." *The Wall Street Journal*, August 24, 1984.

Anne Fisher. "The New Game in Health Care: Who Will Profit." *Fortune*, March 4, 1985.

Michael McCarthy. "Baxter Travenol to Buy Compucare for $73 Million." *The Wall Street Journal*, March 4, 1985.

Ford Worthy. "A Health Care Merger that Pains Hospital." *Fortune*, June 24, 1985.

Wendy Wall. "Baxter Bid for American Hospital Called a Better Fit than Prior Merger Accord." *The Wall Street Journal*, June 25, 1985.

John Helyar and Carolyn Phillips. "Baxter Eases into Its Big Acquisition." *The Wall Street Journal*, July 19, 1985.

"Baxter Plans Layoffs; Merger Is Completed." *The Wall Street Journal*, November 26, 1985.

Robert Buday. "AHSC On-Line System Ships Supplies ASAP." *InformationWeek*, May 26, 1986.

Pauline Yoshihashi. "Travenol, in Stock Deal, Will Acquire Caremark." *New York Times*, May 12, 1987.

Marion Underhill and Pauline Yoshihashi. "The Head of Caremark Is a Pioneer in His Field." *New York Times*, May 12, 1987.

Comp–U–Card

"Members Find Comp–U–Card Means Convenient Shopping." *Direct Marketing*, April 1981.

John Gallant. "Comp–U–Card Plys High-Tech Merchandising." *Computerworld*, January 23, 1984.

John Gallant. "Comp–U–Mall Marks Next Step in Electronic Shopping." *Computerworld*, January 23, 1984.

"New Video Game: Shopping." *New York Times*, April 26, 1984.

Jeanne Saddler. "Computer Users Shop at Home over the Phone." *The Wall Street Journal*, February 20, 1985.

"Comp–U–Card to Buy Marketer of Services in Stock Transaction." *The Wall Street Journal*, October 8, 1985.

"Comp–U–Card Joins with Financial News in TV Shopping Plan." *The Wall Street Journal*, July 2, 1986.

"Comp–U–Card to Buy Certified Collateral for $98 Million Stock." *The Wall Street Journal*, October 3, 1986.

Russell Mitchell. "Comp–U–Card Hooks Home Shoppers." *Business Week*, May 18, 1987.

Phone In–Drive Thru

Bernie Whalen. "Computer 'Shops' for Customers at Phone In–Drive Thru Market." *Marketing News*, November 25, 1983.

First Boston Shelternet

Ed Scannell. "Banker-Realtor Net Cuts Mortgage Processing Time." *Computerworld*, September 5, 1983.

Eric Berg. "Rise of National Mortgage Market." *New York Times*, January 22, 1984.

Joanne Lipman. "Home-Buying Process Is Changing Rapidly because of Technology." *The Wall Street Journal*, January 25, 1984.

Jennifer Beaver. "Micro Modems Let You Reach Out to the World." *Computer Decisions*, June 1984.

Honeywell and Johnson Controls

"The Race to Sell Energy-Saving Systems." *Business Week*, May 23, 1983.

Honeywell advertisement. *The Wall Street Journal*, April 26, 1984.

Benetton

"Benetton: Bringing European Chic to Middle America." *Business Week*, June 11, 1984.

Lisa Belkin. "Benetton's Cluster Strategy." *New York Times*, January 16, 1986.

John Winn Miller. "Benetton: Rags to Riches in the Rag Trade." *The Wall Street Journal*, June 25, 1986.

Giant Stores

Janet Fix. "My Dad Was Active until He Was 90." *Forbes*, November 4, 1985.

Bill Saporito. "The Giant of the Regional Food Chains." *Fortune*, November 25, 1985.

Swaps

James Sterngold. "Raiding the Rate Swappers." *New York Times*, January 14, 1986.

Robert Juelis. Research paper on swaps prepared for a course on the strategic use of information technology, Columbia University Graduate School of Business, 1986.

8

Growth

DIMENSIONS OF GROWTH

The growth of firms may be plotted along two dimensions: *product* and *function*. Product growth involves the firm's offerings—its various lines, sublines, and individual products. As such, it may entail the expansion of markets, satisfaction of additional customer needs, and adoption of alternative technologies associated with the product. Functional growth, on the other hand, involves the various functions (e.g., R&D, manufacturing, distribution, retailing) performed by the firm's product network. *Global growth* and *spinoffs* combine features of both dimensions.

The examples that follow illustrate the range of strategic growth opportunities open to firms with the vision to support or shape them through the use of information technology. Like its close relatives—differentiation, cost, and innovation—growth has bonds with other thrusts. A firm may execute a growth thrust, for example, that simultaneously reduces cost, differentiates its product, and innovates in the processing of customer orders.

GROWTH: PRODUCT

IBM offers its customers a wide assortment of product lines: computers, peripherals, typewriters, supplies, telephone switches, and so on. Each line consists of groups of related products. In its 1984 computer line, for example, the mainframe group comprised 3033s, 3081s, and 4300s; the minicomputer group, 8100s and System/1s; the microcomputer group, PCs and PC Jrs.

For any product in an IBM line, three questions may be asked: (1) At whom is it aimed? (2) What needs does it satisfy? (3) How does it satisfy these needs?[1] Answers to Question 1 determine the *customer groups* or *market segments* targeted. For consumer products, these may be specified by the values of a number of variables: geographic (region, country, city, climate), demographic (age, sex, family size/life cycle, income, occupation, education, religion, race, nationality), psychographic (social class, lifestyle, personality), and behavioral (frequency of use, benefit sought, loyalty, readiness to buy, attitude toward product). For industrial products, markets may be segmented by industry, geography, size, and so forth.

Answers to Question 2 determine the *customer needs* met by the firm's product. An automatic teller machine, for example, may satisfy needs to receive cash, make deposits, and transfer funds from one account to another at any time.

Answers to Question 3 determine the *technologies* associated with the product. If the customer need is land transportation, alternative technologies include those associated with automobiles, trucks, tanks, bicycles, and so on. Answers to Question 3 also include the various channels through which the firm delivers its product to the customer.

The firm's products fall into various lines, depending on whether they satisfy sameness or similarity relations defined by customer groups, customer needs, technologies, distribution channels, prices, and so on. The IBM PC and PC Jr. fell into the microcomputer line, being targeted at the same or similar customers, meeting roughly the same or similar needs, and selling through many of the same channels, within a price range that separated them from IBM's minicomputer line and from each other.

To *lengthen* its line, the firm can add new products. IBM entered the microcomputer market in 1981 with the PC. In 1983, it lengthened its microcomputer line by adding the PC Jr. model.

To *deepen* its line, the firm can add product variants. Building on the success of its PC, IBM deepened this line by introducing in 1983 the PC/XT, a second version of the personal computer intended primarily for business use and distinguished from the firstborn by its extended data storage capacity.

To *widen* its line, the firm can add other lines, complementary or unrelated. Widening its PC computer line, IBM introduced a line of color monitors, items previously unavailable from IBM (although sold by others) to purchasers of the PC.

Growth along the product dimension (i.e., *product growth*) may occur with the addition of customer groups targeted, customer needs met, or technologies employed. It may result from the firm's decision to lengthen, deepen, or widen its lines. Such moves may be motivated by a desire to:

- Exploit underutilized resources, human or material, released in the course of the firm's normal business.
- Improve performance by reducing risk and uncertainty through product line diversification.
- Meet competitive thrusts posed by full-line rivals.
- Fill gaps between desired and projected sales.
- Prevent competitors, by denying them shelf space, from encroaching on the firm's territory.

The firm may also pursue a growth strategy along the product dimension by increasing the *intensity* of its involvement or penetration relative to customer groups, customer needs, or technologies. Here, no new groups are targeted, no new needs satisfied, and no new technologies introduced. What changes is the intensity of involvement or penetration. The firm may pursue a product growth strategy in a particular segment, for example, by hiring 25 more sales reps to sell its line.

Toys "Я" Us, the nationwide discount chain, opened 25 new toy stores in 1983, bringing its total to 169. By far the largest chain in the United States, Toys "Я" Us commanded an 11 percent share of the highly fragmented toy market. The company's winning game plan combined ample parking lots, good management, large, well-organized stores with thousands of items ranging from yo-yos to electronic games, and information systems. Among other things, the systems kept track of what was selling in all stores so that Toys could take quick markdowns to rid itself of slow movers. In the toy business, this application counted as an innovative strategic thrust transforming the traditional inventory control process.

But it also played another strategic role for the company. In

1984, Toys announced the formation of Kids "Я " Us, a chain of children's apparel stores modeled after its toy supermarkets. This strategic move represented a product growth diversification thrust, widening the firm's existing line from toys to children's apparel. Just as information systems supported the company's strategy in the toy business, it fulfilled a similar function in this new undertaking. More significant, the system itself shaped the firm's diversification move, its expansion into a new industry.

What led to advantage in one game might not apply in another. At least that's the conventional wisdom on these matters. But Toys' move seems to have evoked considerable fear among at least 285 small specialty and department store owners across the United States. This may be inferred from the remarks of the president of a buying office in New York City that represents them. "This new chain has upset everyone in the market. You come up against a giant like this, with every major line discounted, and where do you go? If you're the average kiddy shop next door, do you take gas or cut your throat?"[2]

On the other hand, being in a new league, Toys faced some formidable competition: Sears, J. C. Penney, and Federated Stores (a 102-store chain), to name a few. But this new competition didn't daunt Toys, which seems to be on a roll in the games it plays. At the close of 1984, it became the world's largest toy specialty retail chain, operating about 200 toy stores in the United States, four in Canada, and one in Singapore. By the start of 1986, the number had reached 246 worldwide, with 50 new stores envisioned. In addition, it ran four department stores and 23 children's clothing stores. Plans called for the opening of 20 more Kids "Я" Us stores. (See below for more on Toys' global growth moves.)

While Toys executed a strategic growth thrust by diversifying into a new industry, Wetterau, the fourth largest U.S. food wholesaler, followed a different recipe. Up to 1982, it prospered by concentrating on small, independent supermarkets.

According to Ted Wetterau, the chairman, "the cornerstone of our whole business was that we would not service the chains."

But the slack economy in 1982 and a costly battle to defeat an unexpected takeover attempt in fall 1981 stalled the company's efforts to gain new business. Moreover, with the total number of independent grocers declining by 35 percent in 10 years (from 174,000 units in 1970 to 113,000 in 1980), Wetterau had to revise its strategy. For the first time, the St. Louis-based concern decided to offer its wide array of services and volume discounts to chains of 10 to 20 units, thus expanding its traditional customer groups.

Wetterau's knowhow in computerized inventory control and electronic checkout (point-of-sale) systems backboned this product growth strategic thrust. With more than 100 scanner-equipped stores tied to its host computer, Wetterau updated prices, tracked reordering data, generated shelf labels, and performed other functions that supermarket executives hesitate to reveal, because a competitive edge may be lost.

From St. Louis, we move now to Bentonville, a small town in the northwest corner of Arkansas, where Sam Walton plots the future of the company he founded over 25 years ago—Wal-Mart, one of the fastest growing retailers in the United States, with average annual sales growth of 39 percent between 1980 and 1984. Occupying key locations in rural communities of 5,000 to 15,000 people, spread over Arkansas, Missouri, Louisiana, Oklahoma, and Texas, Wal-Mart expects to continue its uninterrupted march across the United States. Current plans call for a doubling of sales every two or three years and geographical expansion of Alexandrian proportions—the opening of as many as 125 new stores annually. Second to K mart in the discount business, Wal-Mart (with sales of about $16 billion in 1987) has passed both Woolworth and Montgomery Ward in the general retail marketplace.

Wal-Mart's past conquests and future prospects combine "an aggressive expansion with a state-of-the-art computerized merchandise information system, a strong distribution network, and a progressive employee relations program."[3] By offering low prices and name brands, the chain dominates the market wherever it has stores. Using the information generated by its system strategically, Wal-Mart pressures suppliers to lower their prices and thereby help it operate as a low-cost discounter.

Wal-Mart aggressively pursues the policy of ordering directly from manufacturers via computer hookups rather than through intermediaries. This puts considerable pressure on independent sales reps and other middlemen who live by the commissions (usually between 2 percent and 6 percent) they receive for selling a manufacturer's line. Some have complained that mass merchandisers like Wal-Mart "are trying to put us out of business."[4] They charge that such actions constitute "a violation of the Robinson-Patman Act, which makes it illegal to pay or receive a discount in lieu of a broker's fee."[5]

Like Toys "Я" Us and Wetterau, Wal-Mart successfully pursues a product growth strategic thrust backed by information systems that deliver. Computer technology at Toys supported a diversification move into another industry, at Wetterau a thrust into a new market segment, and at Wal-Mart a territorial expansion drive.

While Toys, Wetterau, and Wal-Mart pursue internally driven growth thrusts backed by information technology, Dillard Department Stores Inc. moves along a different growth trajectory. This Little Rock, Arkansas, chain owned over 117 stores in 11 southern and midwestern states in 1987. About 70 were obtained via acquisition; most were foundering when bought. Dillard depends heavily on information systems to transform such dying businesses into healthy, growing enterprises.

In 1986, for $130 million it bought 10 poorly performing stores in Kansas run by R. H. Macy & Company. The resurrection strategy followed here mirrors the one used when Dillard acquired the 12-store Stix Baer & Fuller chain of St. Louis in 1984: renovation of fading interiors; addition of new lines; doubling of advertising; hiring of sales personnel, and installation of point-of-sale inventory control systems.

The systems register all transactions and report them to headquarters; corporate knows what sells and where. Dillard avoids merchandise buildups and shortages, and it does it with fewer midlevel managers. This explains in part why Dillard's average gross margins top 35 percent when many less computerized department stores barely reach 30 percent. In 1987, seizing another strategic information system (SIS) opportunity, Dillard acquired 31 underperforming department stores in Texas, Arizona, and Tennessee from Campeau Corp. for $255 million.

Similar stories can be told in other industries about firms that undergo wrenching contraction while others experience dramatic expansion. To talk, for example, of growth in the trucking industry, with its landscape littered with the wrecks of the worst shakeout since the Depression in the 30s, one might be accused of gross insensitivity or worse. Yet deregulation here, as in the airline and financial service sectors, has produced winners as well as losers. Among the former is Yellow Freight, one of the nation's largest trucking companies, based in Shawnee Mission, Kansas.

Yellow Freight is a focuser (see Chapter 3), specializing in the less-than-truckload (LTL) market. In the full-truckload segment of the freight-hauling industry, you need only a truck and driver. With these in tow, you're in business. Not so in the LTL segment. Success depends on whether you're endowed with fleets of tractors and trailors, hundreds of terminals, battalions of workers, and, not least, computer and telecommunication facilities to keep track of the thousands of shipments traveling through the system each day.

Yellow takes the hub-and-spoke distribution model seriously, as seriously as American Air (see Chapter 1) and Federal Express (Chapter 7), two other exponents of the virtues of this idea. Yellow's 57-acre terminal hub in Kansas City runs 24 hours a day, seven days a week, sorting packages from other terminals and repacking them on trucks bound for final destinations or Yellow terminals across the country.

In 1985, Yellow operated 21 hubs as part of a 500-terminal network, with 40,000 shipments flowing through the system daily. It earned $44 million on sales of $1.4 billion and employed 19,550. Compared to its position just five years before, these are impressive figures. In 1980, in the midst of a recession and at the start of deregulation in the trucking industry, Yellow owned 248 terminals, lost money on sales of $775 million, and counted 13,250 employees.

Yellow's noteworthy growth resulted from decisions taken during the five-year span to invest over $400 million in freight terminal acquisitions and information technology. As less well prepared rivals filed for bankruptcy (e.g., Gateway Transportation, which owned a large terminal in Chicago, and Gordon's Transportation, which owned a comparably sized facility in Memphis), Yellow acquired its terminals and networks at prices far below what they would have cost to build new. The technology investments created an elaborate electronic network to track the complex paths of partial shipments across the country.

The transforming effects of information technology sometimes reach beyond the firm to the town in which it resides, as the case of specialty retailer L. L. Bean from Freeport, Maine, demonstrates. In the 60s, Freeport looked like its neighbors: a sleepy New England town with a hardware store, luncheonette, pharmacy, grocery, church, and fire station. To tourists, the only thing that distinguished Freeport was L. L. Bean, the small, 50-year-old retail/mail-order store named after its founder, Leon Leonwood Bean, who still ran it, a man adamantly opposed to the wonders of modern technology.

Bean's 1965 catalog displayed over 1,000 items, none with stock numbers. If you wanted a pair of its by-then classic hunting shoes, you'd write or call in your order and reference it by page number. The stock picker who handled it could easily locate the shoes, for her training included memorizing the catalog and the location of merchandise in the stock room.

Visitors to Freeport today will no longer find a sleepy New England town. It has been transformed into a retailing mecca, inhabited by name brand outlets such as Dansk, Ralph Lauren, Hathaway, and McDonalds. And the principal reason for this unprecedented transformation is L. L. Bean.

When Bean's new president Leon Gorman (L. L.'s grandson) decided to install computers in the mid-70s, sales of the 8,000 or so items in stock hovered around $20 million, with about 350 employees on the payroll. In 1985, sales of the more than 50,000 items in stock reached $200 million, making Bean the eighth largest mail-order operation in the United States, and the number of employees stood at 1,650. During this period, data processing expenses increased ten fold.

In just a decade, Freeport and Bean underwent a transforming growth. And information technology made it possible, indeed shaped it. Today, Bean uses computers and telecommunication facilities for every aspect of its business: from identifying prospects for its catalogs to controlling inventory, filling orders, and shipping them in a timely fashion. Bean ships in 4.5 days compared to the industry average of about 2–3 weeks.

To get an idea of the extent of automation in place, consider the following tasks performed by information systems at L. L. Bean:

- In the warehouse: Tracking the location of merchandise, mapping the most efficient picking paths, determining where on the cart to place items, printing shipping labels, and deciding on the least expensive method of shipping.
- In sales and marketing: Identifying prospective customers, receiving orders, deciding on mailing lists, and analyzing customer purchases.

Without information technology, Bean's growth would be inconceivable. It employs over 500 computer terminals to handle (with an accuracy of 99.89 percent) the more than 30,000 orders received daily. And it mails about 60 million catalogs each year, with catalog customers constituting 85 percent of its business. By seizing SIS opportunities, Leon Gorman transformed his grandfather's business and the town of Freeport as well.

Lengthening the product line represents a different form of product growth. For a manufacturer, this almost invariably translates into adding another kind of physical object to be sold. Service organizations, on the other hand, tend to supplement their offerings by hiring those with the requisite new service skills, assuming current staff members are fully occupied. Alternatively, technology can be used to shape the growth thrust.

DePaola, Begg & Associates, a small Hyannis, Massachusetts, CPA office, followed this latter path. With 75 accounts in the mid-70s, the 15-year-old firm was eager to expand its services. The president, Tom DePaola, saw an opportunity to provide *online* general ledger, accounts receivable, payroll, and accounts payable processing for his clients. After installing a minicomputer, purchasing some standard programs, and developing a few of its own, DePaola, Begg expanded its client base within $2\frac{1}{2}$ years to 350, increasing revenues by 50 percent and staff by only three.

Another New England service organization, Inncorp, a manager of hotels and conference centers in the region, supported its product growth thrust in a somewhat different fashion. As the owner and operator of five hotels employing over 1,000 people, its five-year plan called for the acquisition of six more units by the end of the period.

To achieve its growth objectives and maintain profitability, Inncorp moved, through the strategic use of information systems, to centralize and integrate its activities. Prior to its growth thrust, the company permitted each hotel to operate independently, with its own accounting staff, purchasing department and so on. With the acquisition of a computer and the development of software, Inncorp reduced the number of local staff required to run a hotel, negotiated volume purchasing agreements to cover all its units, and cut its general operating expenses.

In Hicksville, New York, Cain Electric (a contractor) saw its growth prospects short-circuited because it couldn't compete in the market for jobs over $100,000. According to president Jerry Cain, "Doing estimates on smaller jobs was not a major problem. But when you step from $100,000 jobs to million-dollar jobs, there is a great more detail involved, and the chances of making errors . . . are magnified tremendously."[6]

Cain met its growth challenge—estimating the cost of larger projects and translating the estimates into winning bids—by purchasing off-the-shelf personal computer software developed especially for contractors. According to Cain, "The vertical market software has opened up many more doors for additional business. . . . Bottom line, I stand as a winning contractor on a $500,000 motel and as a final contestant on a million dollar hotel. I could not have been able to bid on these if I did not use this approach. I just wouldn't have tackled it."[7] After plugging in the system, Cain doubled its net income and revenue.

GROWTH: FUNCTION

Firms proffer many reasons for increasing their participation at critical points along the industry chain: lower cost, greater control, competitive pressure, and so on. But for our purposes here, the *direction* of functional growth interests us more than the *motive* for it.

The firm can grow via *backward expansion* if it involves itself in functions performed by its suppliers, from raw material vendors to those who provide services. Involvement is *complete* if the firm acquires a supplier; otherwise, *partial*. Partial involvement takes different forms, from performing some or all of the functions normally undertaken by a supplier to acquiring some but not all of the supplier's equity. IBM followed a partial backward growth thrust when it acquired a 15 percent share of the Rolm Corp., a leading manufacturer of telephone switching systems (devices considered by many to be essential ingredients in the office automation marketplace), for $228 million. Subsequently, IBM decided on complete involvement and acquired Rolm. Earlier, IBM bought a 12 percent stake in Intel Corporation, a leading manufacturer of semiconductors and IBM's source for the chips powering its PC.

A firm can grow via *forward expansion* if it involves itself in functions performed by its channels of distribution or ultimate customers. Involvement here, as with backward expansion, can be complete or partial. IBM followed a partial forward expansion thrust when it opened its own computer stores to perform the functions of retailers, such as Computerland and Sears, Roebuck & Co., that market many of the products sold in IBM outlets.

In the service sphere, computer-backed functional growth thrusts pose threats to the revenue streams of telephone, health insurance, and pension management organizations. These and other service businesses can be brought under complete or partial corporate control through the use of information technology.

"We want to control our own destiny."[8] This sentence, usually uttered vehemently by leaders of newly independent states, came from the mouth of a Citicorp vice president for communication services. He used it in offering a rationale for his firm's backward expansion move into voice and data transmission services. Another Citicorp vice president added, "We got rid of Ma Bell years ago, long before it became fashionable. Within New York, we have our own telephone network, with our own fiber-optic links and switches."[9] Nationally, Citicorp *owns* its own satellite network, Citisatcom, having purchased transponders on Western Union's Westar 5 satellite. With earth stations in San Mateo, Los Angeles, San Francisco, Sioux Falls, and New York connected to Westar (and others planned for the near future), Citicorp's dream of telecommunication independence has become at least a partial reality.

In the United States, for example, it uses Citisatcom to operate regional credit and collection centers. These handle its more than 5 million Visa and MasterCard accounts, 80 percent of them outside New York State. In the emerging world of electronic banking, at least as Citicorp envisions it, a versatile and powerful telecommunications network is a necessary condition for success. When Citibank markets "electronic banking," it means

> handling the request, production, and delivery of our services. We offer customers the ability to electronically obtain and control the specific Citibank services they need whenever and wherever they need them. Our primary electronic banking goal is to deliver *all* our services electronically, and secondly, over time, also integrate our services, delivery mechanisms, and access technologies.[10]

Internally, the net provides bulk data and voice communication, interactive computing, database access, facsimile transmission, and videoconferencing.

While opportunities to reduce and avoid cost certainly encouraged Citicorp's move, its strategic vision demanded it. Citicorp sees itself as a global provider of a full line of financial services to businesses and individuals. According to its vice president for communications, "We had to ensure that we have the telecommunications capacity to meet our needs. . . . In some cases, the capabilities we need are just not available today from common carriers."[11] To pursue its pioneering path in the new world of deregulated financial services, Citicorp *internalized* telecommunication services, making them an integral part of its competitive strategy.

While perhaps not integral to strategy in most organizations, telecommunication is hardly a trivial matter, constituting as it does the third largest administrative expense after payroll and property outlays. With a private network, a firm can at least control the cost of services among its own facilities. According to a recent estimate, a firm can obtain a 30–70 percent return on investment (ROI) within an 18-month payback period. Atlantic Richfield, for example, operates ARCOnet, a $20 million top-of-the-line system providing voice, data, and teleconferencing services. Electronic traffic flows through satellite pipelines linking Alaska's north slope to ARCO headquarters in Los Angeles, to its data center in Dallas, and to other locations across the country.

The Harris Corporation, a large electronics firm located in Florida, erected a satellite net to link its various plants in Texas, California, and Rhode Island. According to company officials, the net saves Harris over $1 million a year and develops valuable knowhow for use elsewhere.

Backward expansion made possible by information systems proceeds in other service areas as well. In Lincolnton, North Carolina, Cochrane Furniture processes about 400 health insurance claims each month for its approximately 725 employees and their families. Cochrane had been paying $40,000 a year in administrative service charges to a major insurance company. Instead of developing its own system to do the processing, Cochrane bought a turnkey system (see Chapter 9) that required no additional staff to operate; personnel formerly handling health benefits were trained to run it.

In the pension management field, the integration theme repeats itself. Air Canada's managers now run a $1.25 billion fund, where formerly this work was subcontracted to bank and trust companies, the organizations actually holding the securities. These financial institutions reported on the maturity dates of securities, transactions, and cash on hand. In general, however, they didn't provide daily data on current assets or earned income; nor did they develop cash forecasts.

With its pension management system, Air Canada no longer needs nor pays for these outside services. But compared to the benefits of more timely, critical investment information, this is small change. The new in-house application tracks settlement deadlines and alerts managers when payments on account are due, payments that in the past were often delayed by security brokers, banks, or trust companies. "A difference of one or two days in settlements can mean a loss of hundreds of thousands annually for a fund as large as ours," said the carrier's senior vice president for corporate finance and planning.[12]

GROWTH: GLOBAL

When a firm grows by introducing foreign elements—either new products or functions—into its product network, it executes a *global growth* thrust. The manufacturer that expands its domestic market as a result of acquiring overseas suppliers engages in global growth just as much as the U.S.-based retailer that enlarges its international presence by opening outlets in France, Germany, and Japan. A global growth thrust is simply a growth thrust involving foreign points on the firm's product net (see Chapter 4).

Organizations may pursue global growth opportunities in conjunction with other strategic thrusts (see, e.g., Reuters and Jamaica Agro in Chapter 9). And some may launch global differentiation, cost, innovation, or alliance thrusts that don't involve growth. For example, Hewlett-Packard, the electronics firm, operates 53 manufacturing plants worldwide. These facilities link to HP's global telecommunications network. To process each plant's orders, HP developed a centralized, electronic procurement system. From this SIS, it reaps economy-of-scale benefits, obtaining more favorable pricing and delivery terms from its vendors. HP uses information technology here to support a global cost thrust targeted at the supplier arena.

Consider the maneuver of Rupert Murdoch, the Australian-American-British press baron who transferred from New York to his London publishing operation the information technology knowhow for automating the printing process and reducing production costs, knowhow gained at the *New York Post*, one of the daily newspapers in his chain. Global growth did not figure in this move. Rather, it sought to reduce the bargaining power of British printers. Members of the printer's union, while knowing about printing automation in the United States, were caught sleeping by Murdoch's computerization move. Awake, they found that many of their jobs had vanished.

American firms such as Mead Data Central (see Chapter 6), which produces and distributes computerized databases for lawyers (Lexis) and researchers (Nexis), subcontract an undisclosed amount of their data-entry work overseas in search of lower costs. China, for example, can participate in this new electronic business by offering its customers rates of $6 a day compared to $6 to $12 an hour in the United States. The mail plane from the United States now includes packages of financial statements, mailing lists, and the like from American companies. Chinese data-entry typists, with no knowledge of English, transform this raw, written material into digital form. Since timing is not critical, the Chinese mail the finished goods back to the United States. The work doesn't require the use of an electronic network, and its primary intent is not global growth.

But rather than introduce at this time a sixth strategic thrust, the *global*—which from a theoretical standpoint might be justified at some later date to cover the growing number of moves in the international sphere—I shall describe only those cases in which information technology is used to support or shape international expansion efforts.

Due to increased competition from firms following global strategies, production cost pressures, and a myriad of other factors, SIS global growth thrusts are emerging as important competitive options. In some instances, they may take the form of an *information technology transfer*, similar to a move involving manufacturing technology that transfers domestic hardware and knowhow to another country via direct foreign investment, joint venture, or licensing agreement.

In other cases, SIS global growth thrusts take a different form, more directly related to the *electronic linkage* of foreign points on the firm's product net so that it can achieve some growth objective, either domestically or internationally. The following examples illustrate both forms.

Southland Corp., which owns a chain of retail outlets across the United States—7–Eleven convenience stores, Citgo gas stations, and Chief Auto Parts stores, to name the largest—expanded its operations in 1974 by opening the first 7–Eleven outlet in Japan under a joint venture pact with Ito Yokado Co., which owns 51 percent of the publicly traded 7–Eleven Japan. By 1987, 3,000 7–Eleven Japan stores had sprouted along Japan's rural roads and urban neighborhoods. Like its American progenitor, 7–Eleven Japan relies on information technology to nourish its growth.

"In 1983, 7–Eleven Japan became the first Japanese retail chain to introduce point of sale terminals in all its stores. It also pioneered a vendor system in which suppliers pooled their deliveries to outlets."[13] Previously, the thought of putting the goods of one vendor on the same truck with those of another was unthinkable. Triggering a revolution in Japanese distribution, it threatened mom-and-pop stores and the small wholesalers that serve them.

The information technology applications used by 7–Eleven Japan were *cloned* from its U.S. parent, which operates five regional processing centers that backbone its automated distribution system. At 7–Eleven's Dallas headquarters, the staff tracks store requests for merchandise daily. By the next morning at 7 A.M., after the incoming data has been processed and rerouted to 7–Eleven warehouses, delivery trucks are rolling to the stores.

Toys "Я" Us, as discussed above, has enjoyed considerable success in the United States, winning by 1986 about 15 percent of the $12 billion toy market after a decade of steady, relatively unimpeded expansion. But the firm is under no illusion that its domestic growth will continue at the same pace forever. Also, the global marketplace, which industry watchers estimate to be at least twice as large as its U.S. playing field, appears to be wide open.

Since 1984, Toys has established beachheads in England and Hong Kong. In 1987, its first store in West Germany opened, with stores in France, Italy, and Japan to follow. Over the next 10 years, it expects to open at least 200 stores outside the United States. If the response achieved by its first Hong Kong outlet is indicative, Toys looks like a very successful global player: During the 1986 Christmas season, the Hong Kong store attracted 40,000 shoppers each weekend day, with managers forced to tie up the shopping carts to prevent them from further blocking already packed aisles.

Toys adheres globally to the same formula for success that has played so well in the United States. "Overseas stores are virtual *clones* of their U.S. counterparts: warehouse-like buildings crammed to the rafters with some 18,000 items ranging from puzzles to strollers to home computers. As in the U.S., they are mostly freestanding buildings. . . . Some 80 percent of the merchandise is the same as in the U.S. stores, although the chain makes concessions to local taste."[14][Italics added.] But on one item, Toys makes no concessions at all. According to a spokesperson for the company, "Generally speaking, the data processing systems are the same as in the U.S. stores."[15]

Citibank, a firm that doesn't need to be persuaded about the strategic use of information technology (see Chapters 1 and 9), pursues its SIS vision around the world. In England, rather than attempting duplication of the 2,000 to 3,000 brick-and-mortar branches operated by the four leading British banks, Citi has opened 250 automatic teller machine equipped offices, each within minutes of 90 percent of the British population. It expects to attract customers by offering higher interest rates on deposits than its competitors, for it operates with lower costs due to its technological edge, an edge based on systems expertise transferred from the United States. It also expects to attract home-loan customers; it has installed systems enabling it to approve or reject applicants in about 10 days, compared to 30 or more for local banks.

In France, Citi follows the same information technology transfer script. To the French scene, it adapts systems developed in the United States to link the bank electronically with automobile dealers for the rapid processing of auto loan applications. While perhaps not clones, these applications exploit Citi's information technology knowhow to gain an edge on local competitors.

Prior to 1983, Citi had been on a restricted European growth diet, limiting its expansion to a few internal moves. But from 1983 to 1985, it went on an investment binge, acquiring banks in Spain, Belgium, and France, buying stockbrokers and insurance brokers in England, opening investment banking operations in 14 cities, and building a new branch-banking network in Great Britain and West Germany. "Bringing its U.S. experience to Europe is one of the strongest cards Citi has to play. By applying electronics and direct marketing to consumer banking, as it did in the states, the New York giant thinks it can steal a lead on its slower-moving European rivals."[16] Citi's commercial division, for example, sights over 40,000 potential customers among the middle-sized companies of Europe. Its vice chairman says that such companies "want the services the bank pioneered in the U.S. such as electronic cash management."[17]

But Citi hasn't confined itself to information technology transfer applications. Its global telecommunications net is used for a multiplicity of SIS applications, from corporate cash management to compiling "target lists for clients seeking specific industry acquisitions."[18] For the latter, account officers around the world can assemble detailed data on possible candidates and reply electronically to the acquisition group in New York within three days, which is considered excellent response time for such applications. Measured by the number of deals consummated, Citi ranked third in mergers and acquisitions in 1985. While currently not capable of arranging the largest acquisitions, Citi is nonetheless proud of its rise to the number three position, which it attributes in large part to its use of information technology.

Global growth via joint-marketing SIS alliances (see Chapter 9) represents another form of international expansion undertaken by Citi. To help penetrate foreign markets, Citi offers as bait, access to its U.S. ATM network. The Tokyo newspaper *Yomiuri Shimbun* reported that Japan's largest bank, Dai-Ichi Kangyo Ltd. and Citi agreed to let each bank's customers use ATMs in the other bank's country. In addition, Dai-Ichi agreed to support Citi's MasterCard in Japan. The Japanese bank will issue Citi's MasterCard (using Citi's name) and process the transactions for Citi. From Citi's point of view, the move helps it overcome barriers the Japanese have erected to prevent foreigners from establishing full-service consumer banks on their islands.

American and United Air Lines also confront national barriers to entry as they pursue their global objectives. With dim domestic expansion prospects among travel agents for their computerized reservation systems (see Chapter 1), the two carriers launched growth thrusts to capture the European market. The ability of the two systems to perform mathematical calculations, create customer files registering flight preferences, print schedules, keep the books for travel agents, and offer word processing seems to have a universal appeal. A Belgian agent, for example, who opted for United's Apollo over the locally developed Sabena Air system, said that "in Apollo, you can do everything—invoices, accounting, ticketing. You can order a limousine in New York, book a package tour, order flowers in Hawaii, orchids or roses. You can get British Railway tickets. You can go into KLM's computer and book a seat. . . . Sabena's system, which emphasizes Sabena flights, but is linked to other airlines' reservation data, *just can't compete*. I book Sabena reservations in Apollo."[19][Italics added.]

The threat posed by Sabre and Apollo mobilized 20 leading European carriers. Fearing loss of control over their data, operations, and much more, they contracted in 1986 with a U.S.-based airline consulting firm for a $500,000 study to explore options. By 1987, the advance of the American carriers had been repulsed. Both were forced to lower their sights and accept smaller pieces of the pie than they perhaps had envisioned when mounting their penetration drives for Europe's 30,000, predominantly uncomputerized travel agents.

Three carriers—British Air, KLM Royal Dutch Air, and Swissair—persuaded United to join them in building a $120 million European model of Apollo; the new system will, of course, be tied to Apollo in the United States. Each line will take an equity stake in the joint venture and share in the profits. To counter this alliance, Air France, Lufthansa (West Germany), Iberia (Spain), and Scandanavian Air have joined to form the Amadeus group, which also plans to build a European reservation system. Amadeus is being wooed by both American and Texas Air, with American's Sabre the clear favorite—except for one sticking point: American, unlike United (which doesn't fly to Europe and says it has no intention to), is increasing the number of its European flights. The battle for Europe is far from over.

Limited Inc., a nationwide collection of over 2,800 women's specialty apparel stores selling a variety of lines from lingerie (Victoria's Secret) to clothes for trendy 18- to 35-year-olds (The Limited) to high-fashion items (Henri Bendel), exemplifies another form of global growth. Between 1976 and 1986, it expanded rapidly through acquisition and internal development, with sales and stockholder equity rising 46 percent a year (compounded) from 1981 to 1986. Housed in Columbus, Ohio, its founder, president, and chief executive officer Lesley Wexner sits on the board of Banc One (see Chapter 1), the information processing pioneer headquartered in the same town; John McCoy, the head of Banc One, is a member of Limited's board.

Standardization and vertical integration, both supported by information technology, govern the growth of Limited's businesses. Entering the Limited store in Columbus, for example, you'll find to the left or to the right of the entrance precisely the same thing you'd find in those positions at any of the other Limited stores across the United States. This policy also guides merchandise display in its other chains (e.g., Lane Bryant stores, Lerner shops).

The Limited ships over 200 million garments a year from its automated warehouse complex in Columbus, which spans the equivalent of 30 football fields. On average, it takes about 48 hours for an item to pass through the system. Stores expect at least two shipments a week.

In Limited's businesses, the ability to respond to the ever-changing fashions of the day spells success. "You can't patent anything in the clothing business," Wexner says, "so you've got to get the stuff to the consumer first if you want to be successful."[20] Limited's retailing innovations have revolutionized the industry. Instead of seasonal changes, merchandise flows continuously, with stores featuring new items every two weeks.

The acquisition of Mast Industries, a clothing manufacturer and distributor with interests in Far Eastern factories and relations with close to 200 other producers worldwide, enables Limited to eliminate delay problems caused by intermediaries. Vertical integration even extends to distribution, where shipments are carried on a fleet of trucks owned by the company and operated by Walsh Trucking.

Limited has automated the major elements on its product net (production, warehousing, distribution, marketing, retailing) and linked them to a global telecommunications system so that it can do a number of things rivals can't match. With point-of-sale terminals in every store, for example, Limited can test-market new fashion ideas precisely. With Mast's long-term relations with suppliers, Limited can speed delivery to its stores and possibly preempt other retailers. It can coordinate shipments from anywhere in the world so that within four or five days, if needed, sweaters manufactured in the Far East can be flown to the main warehouse, sorted, and shipped to any point in the country. There is no way this could be achieved without the sophisticated use of information technology that, among other things, makes possible a merchandising system that tracks inventory and sales at each store daily. It is the backbone of the business, comparable to the SIS used by Banc One, Federal Express, and other leaders in their fields.

Limited's expertise in systems also pays off in the acquisition arena. When it acquired the 800-store Lerner chain in 1985, Lerner's was near bankruptcy. By 1986, it had an operating profit of $19 million, due in part to the processing of Lerner's inventory data on Limited's systems. Other applications running on Limited's computers provided detailed financial information and operating data vital to running a profitable business. In much the same way that the specialty bank, Banc One, transfers the data processing operations of its newly acquired banks to its computers, Limited does it in the specialty apparel business.

In the financial information business, Dow Jones & Company follows a variety of growth thrusts supported or shaped by information technology. On January 31, 1984, it approved a $155 million plan to expand plant and press capacity for *The Wall Street Journal*. In 1982–83, Dow Jones authorized $55 million for similar expansion. A press announcement at the time noted that "the expansion will accommodate circulation increases and meet news and advertising space needs in the latter part of this decade." The chairman of Dow Jones reported that most of its publications and services operated at record levels in 1983, with advertising at the *Journal* increasing by 8.2 percent and circulation by more than 60,000 to over 2.1 million.[21]

The *Journal*'s product growth strategy depends on satellite technology and information systems associated with it. Dow Jones pioneered in this area, being the first private company in the United States licensed to own and operate its own earth stations. These stations transmit full pages of the *Journal* from five originating plants to a satellite that beams them to a dozen *Journal* printing facilities across the United States.

When *The Wall Street Journal*'s Asian Edition adopted the satellite/printing plant production methods of the U.S. Edition, it was a case of global growth via information technology transfer. When its European Edition was printed after satellite transmission of the pages from the United States, it was a case of global growth via an electronic network. (The same is true for the North American edition of England's *Financial Times*, a daily financial newspaper, and for the *Economist*, a weekly news and business magazine. The *Economist* started printing in the United States in 1981. By 1986, it had doubled its circulation.)

But Dow Jones has not limited itself to internally driven expansion moves, appreciating as it does that necessity is one of the most potent strategic drivers. The globalization of financial services and increased competition in the electronic financial information services industry, where Dow Jones is a major competitor with its news ticker and stock and news retrieval systems, led the firm to make its biggest acquisition in 1985. It executed a product expansion strategic thrust by purchasing for $460 million (with its partner, Oklahoma Publishing Company) 52 percent of Telerate, a firm that provides computerized price quotations and other data on such financial instruments as government securities, foreign currencies, and commercial paper. Telerate transmits its information to over 24,000 networked terminals located in banks, brokerage houses, corporations, and governmental agencies around the world. Traders enter data directly, which makes it possible for each to see the latest transactions and bids of others on the system.

While this SIS alliance broadens the Dow Jones product line, it more importantly positions the company to face the new global competition posed by firms such as Reuters (see Chapter 9), which combines in some services information and the capability to act on that information, and Citibank, with its recently acquired Quotron Systems, the leader in stock market quotation services. Dow Jones already markets Telerate services outside North America in a joint venture called AP–Dow Jones/Telerate (where AP–Dow Jones is an international business news service owned jointly by the Associated Press and Dow Jones).

Other kinds of financial service firms also play in the global growth game. Fidelity investments, based in Boston and founded by Edward Johnson II in 1946, has become the largest private U.S. mutual fund company, managing over $75 billion in assets. In the last decade, it diversified into discount brokerage, real estate development, venture capital, and institutional money management. Fidelity International, formed in 1969, expanded the company's scope of activities into the global arena. It created a family of offshore funds, sold them overseas, and invested in stock markets around the world. With offices in London, Bermuda, Hong Kong, Sydney, and Tokyo, it manages over $3 billion in assets. Edward (Ned) Johnson III became chairman and CEO of Fidelity when his father retired in 1974; at that time, total assets under management stood at just under $2 billion.

Ned Johnson, unlike his father, invested heavily in information technology. This investment explains, in part, the extraordinary growth of Fidelity since 1974. In 1981, he created the Fidelity Systems Company and recruited as its president Mike Simmons, a top banking executive from Indiana, who reported directly to him. FSC's noteworthy achievements include the following applications.

Customer service and marketing system.   Fidelity agents in Boston, Dallas, and Salt Lake City, with terminal access to multiple databases, receive an average of over 100,000 calls daily. They answer customer questions about the company's 100 mutual funds or place orders to buy, sell, transfer, or redeem accounts. This 24-hour-a-day service still remains unmatched by any of Fidelity's rivals. Prospective customers also use the service for information purposes. After they call, their names are added to Fidelity's marketing database as targets for direct mail campaigns.

Hourly pricing system.   Introduced in late 1986, this unique system prices 35 of Fidelity's sector mutual funds (e.g., broadcasting and media, regional banks, paper and forest products) hourly instead of at the end of the day. In effect, the system creates a miniature stock market or, as the marketing manager for the Select Portfolios puts it, "a proxy for the stock market."[22] Fidelity charges Select's over 300,000 customers $10 each time they switch their investments from one fund to another.

Fidelity USA account.   Fidelity's answer to Merrill Lynch's cash management account (CMA), the USA asset management account offers more than the CMA and requires a smaller investment. Its benefits include up to 75 percent saving on commissions through the use of Fidelity's discount brokerage services, margin borrowing, option trading, Gold Master-Card or Visa, unlimited check-writing with checks returned monthly, access to a nationwide ATM network, direct deposit, bill payment services, access to Fidelity's mutual funds, and a comprehensive monthly statement.

FAST (Fidelity automated service telephones).   This voice response system provides information on fund prices and yields. It can also be used to open accounts and transfer money between accounts. FAST now handles over 60 percent of Fidelity's calls and 15 percent of its fund transactions.

FIX (Fidelity investors express).   This system links Fidelity's discount brokerage customers to the Dow Jones/News Retrieval Network where they get exclusive on-line access to *The Wall Street Journal* and software tools to analyze, represent graphically, and filter investment information from the *Journal* and other sources. With a FIX account, you can cogitate on the Dow Jones data and then place a buy or sell order for listed securities on any of the major exchanges, 22 hours a day, seven days a week. In addition, customers can access their own account information and pay their bills while signed on to FIX.

Discount brokerage wholesaling.   This system enables Fidelity to wholesale its discount brokerage service to regional banks so that they can offer it to their clients. Terminals in the banks are connected to Fidelity computers so that client transactions can be executed automatically.

Fidelity contends that these and other applications give it an edge in the highly competitive U.S. financial services arenas. "It's a strategic advantage," in the words of Mike Simmons, "to have our customers call in and do anything that needs to be done while they're on the phone."[23] Fidelity also believes that its technological superiority can be transferred to the global arena, with appropriate modifications to suit local requirements.

In England, for example, Fidelity International offers bro-

kers and other investment advisors (who are its most important customers in the United Kingdom) "an online service
which gives information on all their clients' holdings in all
funds (not just Fidelity's) and stocks."[24] In addition, Fidelity
International has "established communication links between
all offices that integrate telex, electronic mail, word processing,
account information, research, etc."[25]

The international systems group, while independent from
the domestic one, meets with it periodically so that both can be
apprised of current and future applications. It is the professed
goal of the international group "to learn from the domestic
company's experience and then try and 'leapfrog' them to produce a more sophisticated system."[26] In a number of cases, this
goal has already been reached:

> For instance, the domestic company originally had its customer
> accounts on a so-called product-based system. This meant that
> originally it was not possible to discover what other accounts a
> particular customer had with Fidelity, and consequently it
> caused all sorts of problems when talking to customers on the
> telephone and when products like the USA account, linking
> holdings in several different funds together, were being devel
> oped. The international operation, on the other hand, was able
> to learn from these experiences and therefore had enough fore
> sight to install a customer lead database system from the very
> start.[27]

Granted, the market for financial services is quite different
abroad from what it has become in the United States. Local
customs, cultures, government regulations, and competitors
display great diversity. And information technology sophistication and resources are, in general, less than what they are in
the United States. Nevertheless, Fidelity knows the strategic
importance of information technology firsthand and, as indicated above, is already putting this knowhow to use in support of its global growth thrusts. Whether it be a local variant of
the FAST, FIX, or Fidelity USA system or the development of a
discount brokerage operation, an alliance with another finan-

cial or information services firm, or a videotext service, one can be sure that Fidelity will seize the opportunity if it arises.

GROWTH: SIS SPINOFFS

The firm can grow via *projective expansion*, or *vertical disintegration* as some have dubbed it, if it projects resources dedicated to a functional activity into a new, independent business unit dedicated to selling the goods or services associated with the function. In such cases, the line between product and functional growth vanishes. A manufacturer with a large fleet of trucks engaged in transporting its products may decide to create a new business unit to provide freight-hauling services for shippers located along its principal routes. Similarly, a firm may create a business unit with resources drawn from its information management function. I call such strategic growth thrusts *strategic information systems spinoffs*.

Two objectives motivate SIS spinoffs: (1) to exploit economies of scope (see Chapter 6) arising from the firm's investment in information technology or (2) to create a new line of business with information technology at its core. While these do not exclude one another—indeed, the second usually develops from the first—an important distinction should be drawn. An enterprise forming an SIS spinoff to exploit economies of scope ties its product line and strategy to those information systems directly related to the parent's business. An enterprise creating an SIS spinoff to start a new line of business, on the other hand, suffers no such restriction, for it seeks to sell those technology-based products and services best suited to meet its customers' needs, no matter what the source of the product or service. The latter spinoffs represent major diversification moves, while the former reflect only the preliminary steps.

To illustrate this distinction, consider Weyerhaeuser, the forest products company. In 1986, it transformed its 400-person information systems group into a profit center called Weyerhaeuser Information Systems. WIS sells software developed originally for its corporate users: systems for manufacturing maintenance, workers' compensation claims, and managing data on truck and rail rates. WIS also offers the typical services provided by any large user organization to its internal users: systems planning and development, telecommunications consulting, and educational programs. WIS expects to generate at least 50 percent of its revenue from outside sources within five years.

J. C. Penney, the retailing giant with sales of close to $14 billion in 1985, set up three subsidiaries to exploit computer and telecommunication systems developed internally. J. C. Penney Systems Services markets access to its nationwide credit authorization network, which checks the ratings of its 60-million credit cardholders. When Shell Oil decided to use Penney's network for its 4,000 stations, Systems Services linked each station to the nearest Penney store via leased telephone lines. The store transmits the credit authorization request to Penney's processing center, where the Shell customer database resides on a Penney computer. Shell maintains the database, updating it from Penney-supplied terminals.

The success of Systems Services led Penney to form another SIS spinoff: J. C. Penney Credit Systems. Credit Systems "provides a full range of credit-card related services, from issuing a private-label card to collecting and processing receipts."[28] Credit Services also processes Visa and MasterCard receipts through the J. C. Penney Bank. When asked about the revenues generated from these spinoffs, a Penney spokesman grinned and said: "It's a good business. I don't want to tell people how good because I don't want to encourage competition."[29]

In 1986, another SIS spinoff, J. C. Penney Travel Services, began operation. Travel Services exploits Penney's expertise in computerized telemarketing, which it developed in building the catalog sales business, an enterprise employing 5,000 operators at 14 telemarketing centers across the country. Penney promotes its travel service in its monthly statements sent to customers, believing that "people can shop travel the same way they shop catalogs—completely by phone."[30]

But you don't have to be a giant to enter the packaged software business via the internal route. Small- and medium-sized firms can also participate. For instance, a small food distributor in Philadelphia, Rotelli Inc., created Data Tech Services, an SIS spinoff dedicated to marketing a distribution management package the company built for its own use. Rotelli, like any other enterprise following this path, hopes to exploit economies of scope and offset its overall data processing expenses.

Spinoffs such as the above represent limited growth thrusts. Others prefer to make a more grand entry by diversifying into the information services industry with a far larger line of products. This is the course taken by a number of today's industry leaders (e.g., Boeing Computer Services, Grumman Data Services, and Martin Marietta Data Systems). Each started with substantial hardware, software, and human resources dedicated to internal users, but all were determined to build strong, independent units to serve the external marketplace.

Intermountain Health Care, a holding company with a non-profit subsidiary and a growing list of profit-oriented units, illustrates the SIS spinoff idea in support of a major diversification initiative. Faced with rising costs, patient declines, and competition from profit-making hospitals and newly formed groups of specialized physicians, the Intermountain chain of 23 hospitals in Utah, Wyoming, and Idaho reorganized in 1982 to form IHC. The chain itself became the nonprofit subsidiary.

Among the units dedicated to profit, IHC created an SIS spinoff, a purchasing arm that buys over $500 million worth of supplies and equipment for 125 other hospitals, an operation to provide hospitals with insurance, and a variety of specialized clinics and occupational health care centers. Shortly after its launch, the spinoff signed contracts for processing services, with 24 of the 125 hospitals already benefiting from IHC's volume purchase deals.

While IHC's SIS spinoff evolved from its infancy, others

(such as those spawned by McDonnell Douglas, the aerospace company, and General Electric) have been growing for over two decades. In the early 60s, McDonnell created McAuto (McDonnell Douglas Automation Company) and GE formed Geisco (General Electric Information Services Company) to leverage their internal investments in computer technology. The paths pursued by these two companies should be of interest to those with infants or with thoughts of SIS spinoff thrusts.

McDonnell originally chartered McAuto to provide consulting, systems analysis and design, programming, and remote processing services for its divisions and for anyone else willing to pay. GE established Geisco to exploit the concept of time-sharing, which it had developed internally. In 1970, 85 percent of Geisco's revenue came from this segment of its business; a similar percentage of McAuto's revenues were derived at the time from its processing operations.

Since 1970, however, both organizations have diversified to reduce their dependence on the increasingly competitive commoditylike processing business. Today, the magic word is *value-added.*

Consider, for example, McAuto's position in the health care industry. In the early 70s, it acquired a group dedicated to providing data processing services and applications to hospitals. From a customer base of 21 at its inception, McAuto's Health Services Division has installed systems in over 1,500 hospitals across the country.

In 1979, McAuto acquired Microdata, a manufacturer of minicomputer systems. This led to the development of a new product line, turnkey systems for hospitals that run on Microdata computers and use software (for patient registration, control, and accounting and for payroll, general ledger, accounts payable, and other conventional applications) created by analysts and programmers from the Health Services Division.

During the 70s, through internal development and alliances, McAuto expanded its offerings to include online financial control systems for hospitals and systems for nurses, physicians, and clinical laboratories. Indeed, the Health Services

Division presents itself to hospitals as "the single source for all your data processing needs."[31]

In the early 80s, after determining that its aerospace operations would probably level off in the 90s, McDonnell formulated a new growth strategy. It decided to become a major player in the fast-growing information services industry. Using its successful experience in health care as a model, McDonnell created a major new division, the Information Services Group (ISG), which it organized by industry. The health services unit, for example, comprises the Health Services Division of McAuto, portions of Microdata, and Vitek, a manufacturer of automated laboratory testing equipment acquired by McAuto in the 70s. Other units target the telecommunication, manufacturing, financial service, and travel industries.

To implement this new SIS vision, ISG executed the following thrusts:

1. Acquisition in 1984 of Tymshare, an information services company that operates Tymnet, the largest nationwide, public, value-added data communications network. Tymnet provides a mechanism for users of incompatible devices, such as terminals and computers, to communicate with each other. "We're going to sell Tymnet as a public network that anybody can use—and develop businesses around it," says an ISG official.[32] As the initial venture, the health services unit built a nationwide health claims clearinghouse for insurance companies to make use of the net. In the electronic funds transfer sector, Tymshare plays an important role as one of the largest credit card processors in the world and, through its acquisition of Telecheck, as a provider of point-of-sale services to merchants (e.g., check guarantees, credit verification).

2. Acquisition of Computer Sharing Services, a supplier of computer services to Bell operating companies, AT&T, and others. CSS fits into ISG's new $100 million telecommunications unit.

3. Agreement with IBM to sell CAD/CAM software developed by ISG's manufacturing unit that will run on IBM minicomputers. Estimates put the cost of a typical system, consisting of an IBM minicomputer, software, and four workstations, at about $600,000.

4.   Acquisition of Science Dynamics Corp., a supplier of information systems for physicians. SDC fits into ISG's health services unit.

With its evolving SIS vision of industry-by-industry penetration, McDonnell's SIS spinoff shapes its destiny through the execution of strategic thrusts like the ones just mentioned. How effective these thrusts will be depends on a number of factors, not the least of which are the strategies and moves of ISG's rivals. Among them, ISG counts GE. "They've said point-blank that they want to be in the factory of the future," a top ISG executive said. "So they're going to be competing with us."[33] But if its strategic intelligence system identifies just GE's factory automation efforts as threatening, ISG is in for a surprise. For the SIS vision of GE's Geisco calls for thrusts in many of the industries staked by ISG as areas of opportunity.

Consider, for example, Geisco's Easy-Claim system, a computerized claims-processing and office automation package for physicians. First installed at Blue Shield of Illinois, it allows physicians to file claims automatically through a computer in their offices, eliminating errors and payment delays. This innovative application signals Geisco's intention of developing a position in the health care industry. Behind it lies one of the most powerful and extensive infrastructures in the information services industry, comprising such facilities as:

- Mark III, the world's largest commercial teleprocessing network. Customers may connect to the net by placing a local telephone call in more than 750 cities, in 24 countries, in 23 time zones, 24 hours a day, 365 days a year. Worldwide, Geisco counts over 6,000 users of Mark III.
- MarkNet, a value-added network like ISG's Tymnet or GTE's Telenet, which reaches over 600 cities in the United States. Designed to handle data, text, and graphics, with

plans to support image and voice processing, MarkNet allows users of terminals from over 36 vendors to communicate with personal computers from IBM, Wang, Apple, Tandy, and others.

- Quick-Comm, an electronic mail system, which is part of Geisco's plan for providing end-to-end document distribution services.
- A range of software packages and systems.
- A worldwide staff of consultants, system designers, and the like to support Geisco's products.

Today, less than 30 percent of Geisco's revenues come from its processing operations; this percentage is expected to shrink to about 10 percent as it expands its line with more proprietary products. Being part of GE, a corporation that takes pride in its ability to manage strategically, Geisco finds itself encouraged to transform its identity from a commodity operation to a full-service, value-added colossus. For GE sees itself as "in the business of creating businesses," businesses expected to be number one or two in their industries. At the GE board of directors meeting in April 1981, Jack Welch, GE's new chairman and CEO, expressed his strategic vision as follows:

> A decade from now we would like General Electric to be perceived as a unique, high spirited, entrepreneurial enterprise . . . a company known around the world for its unmatched level of excellence. We want GE to be the most profitable highly diversified company on earth, with world quality leadership in every one of its product lines.[34]

Welch's tone and imprint are already having their effect. As one GE executive put it, "He wants GE to make money, to develop an 'unfair advantage' over the competition, to reflect top quality, and to put bright people in to run the businesses."[35]

In August 1981, Welch announced the formation of three sectors to manage GE's multiplicity of businesses, ranging from aircraft engines to light bulbs. Two of GE's fastest growing businesses found their new home in the services and materials sector: the General Electric Credit Corp. (GECC) and Geisco. The strategic slogan for this sector is "growth and integration," which means (among other things) closer ties between GECC and Geisco. In 1983, GE made acquisitions and other investments totaling about $650 million in this sector.

Supported by GE's new strategic imperatives, Geisco's management formulated programs to implement its SIS vision. According to Geisco's senior vice president for programs and management operations:

> The only way we're going to get big in packaged software is through acquisition. We want to keep growing in that area. . . . My long-term competition is AT&T and IBM. Those are the people I worry about and the people I think about when I'm deciding what strategy to use and what kind of capabilities we need. . . . We've seen IBM move into insurance. . . . They've built a position in insurance. . . . Maybe we've done the same in banking, and AT&T will pull it off in something else. Have I targeted the industries where we should be going? Yes, but I'd rather not say what they are. That would give those two more information than I want to give them.[36]

To enhance its position in the packaged software and microcomputer distribution markets, Geisco executed the following thrusts:

- Acquisition of Software International, a leading producer of accounting, financial, and manufacturing software.
- Acquisition of Energy Enterprises, a software house specializing in on-line monitoring and evaluation systems for over 250 gas and oil industry customers.
- Acquisition of Banking Systems, a software company supplying banks with automatic teller, bill payment, and data-entry systems.
- Acquisition of LTI (formerly Lambda) Consulting, a software consulting firm focusing on large mainframe and minicomputer systems.

- Agreements with IBM and Apple to resell PCs and Macintoshes with value-added Geisco software and optional installation and maintenance services.

These thrusts signal Geisco's intention of establishing information systems positions in the manufacturing, energy, and banking industries. If McDonnell's ISG group failed to identify this giant as a rival in the past, it has ample evidence to draw the inference now.

It is interesting to note a recent change in Geisco's strategic direction, away from single-client software packages and consulting assignments that fail to exploit its global network and toward such growing specialized services as electronic data interchange, a necessary ingredient of interorganizational systems linking the firm with its suppliers, channels, customers, and, in some instances, rivals.

"Corporate executives are making more sophisticated demands on MIS departments, so we've become a partner to the MIS manager, rather than the competitor of the past,"[37] says Geisco's president. The strategy, according to one analyst, "is to get wired into an industry, via electronic data interchange or something similar, and then add additional layers of service on top of that. . . . Their strengths are in building intelligent applications, like a cash management system, an order entry system, or a dealer network."[38]

Consistent with this change in strategic direction, Geisco sold Network Consultants, the Chicago-based subsidiary specializing in wire-transfer software for banks, and Software International (see above). Both companies had been bought within the past five years by Geisco. According to a GE spokesman, Software was sold because "it doesn't fit the strategy that the company is currently following in information services."[39]

The evolution of McAuto and Geisco, the 60s' spinoffs of McDonnell and GE, reflect increasingly complex SIS visions. In both cases, further growth may well depend, even more than it has in the past, on their ability to forge SIS alliances, the subject we turn to next.

NOTES

1. Derek Abell, *Defining the Business* (Englewood Cliffs, N.J.: Prentice-Hall, 1980). See also Philip Kotler, *Marketing Management: Analysis, Planning, and Control,* 5th ed. (Englewood Cliffs, N.J.: Prentice-Hall, 1984); E. A. G. Robinson, *The Structure of Competitive Industry,* 2d ed. (Chicago: University of Chicago Press, 1958); R. E. Thomas, *Business Policy,* 2d ed. (Oxford, Eng.: Philip Allen, 1983).

2. Claudia Ricci, "Children's Wear Retailers Brace for Competition from Toys "Я" Us," *The Wall Street Journal,* August 25, 1983.

3. Isadore Barmash, "The Hot Ticket in Retailing," *New York Times,* July 18, 1984.

4. Karen Blumenthal, "A Few Big Retailers Rebuff Middleman," *The Wall Street Journal,* October 21, 1986.

5. Ibid.

6. Steven Burke, "Specialized Packages Help Increase Profits," *InfoWorld,* July 15, 1985.

7. Ibid.

8. Robert Violino, "Sky-High Phone Bills Cause Citicorp to Set Up Its Own Satellite Network," *Information Systems News,* October 31, 1983.

9. Eric Arnum, "Large Users Say Reliability Is Key in Choosing Datacom Vendors," *CommunicationWeek,* August 13, 1984.

10. *Electronic Banking: An Executive's Guide* (Citibank, undated).

11. Violino, "Sky-High Phone Bills."

12. "System Helps Airline Manage Assets In-House," *Computerworld,* November 28, 1983.

13. Christopher Chipello, "Small Shopkeepers Losing Grip on Japanese Consumers," *The Wall Street Journal,* March 18, 1987.

14. Mark Maremont, Doris Jones Yang, and Amy Dunkin, et al., "Toys " Я " Us Goes Overseas—And Finds that Toys " Я " Them, Too," *Business Week,* January 26, 1987.

15. Personal communication with firm.

16. Andrew Wilson, "Citicorp's Gutsy Campaign to Conquer Europe," *Business Week,* July 15, 1985.

17. Ibid.

18. Richard Schmitt, "The Technology Gamble," *The Wall Street Journal,* September 29, 1986.

19. Susan Carey, "Europe Bristles at U.S.–Airline Computers," *The Wall Street Journal,* November 21, 1986.

20. William Myers, "Rag-Trade Revolutionary," *New York Times Magazine,* June 8, 1986.

21. "Dow Jones Earnings Grew 37% in Quarter; Plant Expansion Is Set," *The Wall Street Journal*, January 24, 1983.

22. Jeffrey Laderman and Lois Therrien, "Fidelity's Hot Little Stock Market," *Business Week*, July 28, 1986.

23. Robert Buday, "Fidelity Invests Its Funds in Leading-Edge Systems," *Information-Week*, November 17, 1986.

24. Simon Fraser, "Fidelity Investments and Fidelity International Limited: A Case Study in the Strategic Use of Information Technology in the Financial Services Industry and the Opportunities for Transferring Domestic Experiences Internationally," Paper prepared for the Columbia University Graduate School of Business seminar on the strategic use of information technology, December 1985.

25. Ibid.

26. Ibid.

27. Ibid.

28. Richard Layne, "Penney Makes Dollars with MIS Spinoff," *InformationWeek*, November 10, 1986.

29. Ibid.

30. Ibid.

31. "The Only Data Processing Service You Will Ever Need: McAuto Health Services" (McDonnell Douglas, no date).

32. Sherie Shamon, "Turnkey Systems for Industry: McDonnell Douglas Builds an Information Business," *Management Technology*, September 1984.

33. Ibid.

34. "GE—Business Development," Case studies (Boston: Harvard Business School, 1982).

35. "GE Strategic Position in 1981," Case studies (Boston: Harvard Business School, 1981).

36. Willie Schatz, "Geisco Goes for the Gusto," *Datamation*, February 1983.

37. Mitch Betts, "Geisco Changes Tack, Angles toward Network Applications," *Computerworld*, May 5, 1986.

38. Ibid.

39. "Computer Associates Plans to Buy GE Unit to Expand Division," *The Wall Street Journal*, November 12, 1986.

CASE REFERENCES

GROWTH: PRODUCT

Toys "Я" Us

Claudia Ricci. "Children's Wear Retailers Brace for Competition from Toys "Я" Us." *The Wall Street Journal*, August 25, 1983.

"Toys "Я" Us Net Rose 68% for Third Quarter as Sales Advanced 46%." *The Wall Street Journal*, November 21, 1984.

"Toys "Я" Us Reports 28% Jump in Earnings for Fiscal 3rd Quarter." *The Wall Street Journal*, November 23, 1983.

"Toys "Я" Us Sales Data Hurt Stock." *New York Times*, December 28, 1984.

Anthony Ramirez. "Can Anyone Compete with Toys "Я" Us?" *Fortune*, October 10, 1985.

Hank Gilman. "Founder Lazarus Is a Reason Toys "Я" Us Dominates Its Industry." *The Wall Street Journal*, November 21, 1985

"Toys "Я" Us: King of the Hill." *Dun's Business Month*, December 1985.

"Toys "Я" Us Inc. Sales Increased a Slim 2.8%." *The Wall Street Journal*, January 3, 1986.

Wetterau

"A Food Supplier's Bigger Bite." *Business Week*, February 22, 1982.

Wal-Mart

Isadore Barmash. "The Hot Ticket in Retailing." *New York Times*, July 1, 1984.

Hank Gilman. "Rural Retailing Chains Prosper by Combining Service, Sophistication." *The Wall Street Journal*, July 2, 1984.

Todd Mason and Marc Frons. "Sam Walton of Wal-Mart: Just Your Basic Homespun Billionaire." *Business Week*, October 14, 1985.

Karen Blumenthal. "A Few Big Retailers Rebuff Middleman." *The Wall Street Journal*, October 21, 1986.

Karen Blumenthal. "Arrival of Discounter Tears the Civic Fabric of Small-Town Life." *The Wall Street Journal*, April 14, 1987.

Isadore Barmash. "New Moves from Two Grand Old Men of Retailing." *New York Times,* January 24, 1988.

Dillard Stores

Jim Hurlock and Amy Dunkin. "Why William Dillard Loves a Lost Cause." *Business Week*, May 5, 1986.

Paul Duke, Jr., and Ann Hagedorn. "Dillard to Buy Campeau Units for $255 Million." *The Wall Street Journal*, April 14, 1987.

Yellow Freight

Agis Salpukas. "Trucking's Great Shakeout." *New York Times*, December 13, 1983.

Agis Salpukas. "What's Fueling Yellow Freight." *New York Times*, December 22, 1985.

L. L. Bean

Stephanie Walter. "Full Function Folksiness: How Computers Led L. L. Bean Out of the Maine Woods." *Management Technology*, February 1985.

Steven Prokesch. "Bean Meshes Man, Machine." *New York Times*, December 23, 1985.

DePaola, Begg & Associates

"Minicomputer Helps CPA Firm Support More Clients." *Information Systems*, September 1981.

Inncorp

"Hotel Firm Finds Room to Grow with Mini." *Computerworld*, November 30, 1981.

Cain Electric

Steven Burke. "Specialized Packages Help Increase Profits." *InfoWorld*, July 15, 1985.

GROWTH: FUNCTION

Citicorp

Julie Salamon. "Bank of America, Continental Illinois, Chase Join Others in Teller Network." *The Wall Street Journal*, April 8, 1982.

Robert Bennett. "Inside Citicorp: The Changing World of Banking." *New York Times Magazine*, May 29, 1983.

"A Productivity Revolution in the Service Sector." *Business Week*, September 5, 1983.

Robert Violino. "Sky-High Phone Bills Cause Citicorp to Set Up Its Own Satellite Network." *Information Systems News*, October 31, 1983.

Daniel Hertzberg. "Interstate Banking Spreads Rapidly despite Laws Restricting Practice." *The Wall Street Journal*, December 19, 1983.

Tim Carrington. "Citicorp Wins Fed Approval to Buy 2 S&L's." *The Wall Street Journal*, January 23, 1984.

Daniel Hertzberg. "Citibank Unveils New Marketing Strategy in Bid to Become National Consumer Bank." *The Wall Street Journal*, March 29, 1984.

Daniel Hertzberg. "Citibank Leads Field in Its Size and Power—And in Its Arrogance." *The Wall Street Journal*, May 11, 1984.

Leslie Wayne. "Citi's Soaring Ambition." *New York Times*, June 24, 1984.

Eric Arnum. "Large Users Say Reliability Is Key in Choosing Datacom Vendors." *CommunicationWeek*, August 13, 1984.

Electronic Banking: An Executive's Guide. Citibank, no date.

Charmaine Harris. "Citi's Interest in ATMs Pays Off." *InformationWeek*, May 26, 1986.

Atlantic Richfield (ARCO)

J. H. McCormick. "ARCO Finds Private Network Invaluable." *Information Systems News*, October 31, 1983.

Charles Bolger, Jr. "Using Teleconferencing as a Management Information Tool." *Office*, November 1983.

Harris

David Hemings. "Private Networks Can Control Soaring Communications Costs." *Office*, November 1982.

Cochrane Furniture

"Furniture Firm Carves Out In-House Insurance Plan with Turnkey Installation." *Computerworld*, November 14, 1983.

Air Canada

"System Helps Airline Manage Assets In-House." *Computerworld*, November 28, 1983.

GROWTH: GLOBAL

Hewlett-Packard

Brian Cook. "The Tie that Binds: How to Cope with Company Growth." *Electronic Business*, April 15, 1985.

Rupert Murdoch

Joseph Lelyveld. "Murdoch Savors His British Coup." *New York Times*, March 2, 1986.

Herb Greer. "Murdoch Strikes for Press Freedom." *The Wall Street Journal*, (European Edition), April 24, 1986.

Mead Data Central

Kenneth Noble. "America's Service Economy Begins to Blossom—Overseas." *New York Times*, December 14, 1986.

Southland

Jean Bozman. "Southland's MIS Department Gets Things Revvin' at 7–11." *InformationWeek*, June 23, 1986.

Christopher Chipello. "Small Shopkeepers Losing Grip on Japanese Consumers." *The Wall Street Journal*, March 18, 1987.

Toys "Я" Us

Mark Maremont, Doris Jones Yang, and Amy Dunkin. "Toys "Я" Us Goes Overseas—And Finds that Toys "Я" Them, Too." *Business Week,* January 26, 1987.

Citibank

Andrew Wilson. "Citicorp's Gutsy Campaign to Conquer Europe." *Business Week,* July 15, 1985.

Charmaine Harris. "Citi's Interest in ATMs Pays Off." *InformationWeek,* May 26, 1986.

Richard Schmitt. "The Technology Gamble." *The Wall Street Journal,* September 29, 1986.

"Citicorp, Dai-Ichi Seen Close to Alliance." *New York Times,* January 5, 1987.

American Air and United Air (Allegis)

Susan Carey. "Europe Bristles at U.S.–Airline Computers." *The Wall Street Journal,* November 21, 1986.

Susan Carey. "Europe Airlines Discuss Joining Forces." *The Wall Street Journal,* June 10, 1987.

Agis Salpukas. "United Air in Venture in Europe." *New York Times,* July 10, 1987.

Agis Salpukas. "American Air Venture Is Reported." *New York Times,* July 13, 1987.

Robert Rose. "Allegis Aims for More Profit, Passengers with European Reservations Venture." *The Wall Street Journal,* July 13, 1987.

David Ludlum. "Airlines in Dogfight over Reservation System." *Computerworld,* July 20, 1987.

Limited

Brian O'Reilly. "Leslie Wexner Knows What Women Want." *Fortune,* August 19, 1985.

Jolie Solomon. "Limited Is a Clothing Retailer on the Move." *The Wall Street Journal*, October 31, 1985.

William Myers. "Rag-Trade Revolutionary." *New York Times Magazine*, June 8, 1986.

Carol Hymowitz. "Limited's Morosky, Wexner's 'Partner,' Resigns Unexpectedly as No. 2 Executive." *The Wall Street Journal*, June 16, 1987.

Dow Jones

"Dow Jones Earnings Grew 37% in Quarter; Plant Expansion Is Set." *The Wall Street Journal*, January 24, 1983.

Dow Jones advertisement. *The Wall Street Journal*, January 31, 1984.

"Dow Jones Plans to Buy Stake in Telerate Inc." *The Wall Street Journal*, July 9, 1985.

David Sanger. "Publishers Plan Stake in Telerate." *New York Times*, July 9, 1985.

"Dow Jones's New Voltage." *Financial Times*, August 5, 1985.

"Dow Jones Purchases Telerate Inc. Shares from Publishing Firm." *The Wall Street Journal*, January 23, 1987.

Financial Times and *Economist*

Mark Vamos and Ann Borrus. "*Financial Times* Beams into the U.S." *Business Week*, June 24, 1985.

Fidelity

"The Rationale for Investing Internationally." Fidelity International, 1981.

"Fidelity Fights Off the Money-Fund Blues." *Business Week*, March 28, 1983.

"Can Fidelity Keep Up?" *Boston Globe*, July 19, 1983.

"The Rewards of Fidelity." *New York Magazine,* 1983.

"Fidelity Earns a Reputation as Innovative." *Dallas Times Herald,* October 30, 1983.

Fidelity Investments, annual reports, 1984 and 1985.

"Financial Services in the United Kingdom—A New Framework for Investor Protection." *Her Majesty's Stationary Office,* January 1985.

Johnnie Roberts. "Fidelity Group Strives to Grow and Compete with Financial Giants." *The Wall Street Journal,* March 8, 1985.

"Computers in Banking and Finance." *Financial Times Survey,* October 21, 1985.

Fidelity advertisement. *The Wall Street Journal,* January 30, 1986.

Michael VerMeulen. "The Son Also Rises." *Institutional Investor,* February 1986.

Thomas Lueck. "Can Fidelity Maintain Its Frenzied Growth?" *New York Times,* March 16, 1986.

Jan Wong. "Fidelity Unveils 8 More Specialty Fund Portfolios." *The Wall Street Journal,* July 3, 1986.

Jeffrey Laderman and Lois Therrien. "Fidelity's Hot Little Stock Market." *Business Week,* July 28, 1986.

Pamela Sebastian and Jan Wong. "Fidelity Is Scrambling to Keep Flying High as Magellan Slows Up." *The Wall Street Journal,* August 15, 1986.

Robert Buday. "Fidelity Invests Its Funds in Leading-Edge Systems." *InformationWeek,* November 17, 1986.

Simon Fraser. "Fidelity Investments and Fidelity International Limited: A Case Study in the Strategic Use of Information Technology in the Financial Services Industry and the Opportunities for Transferring Domestic Experiences Internationally." Paper prepared for the seminar on the strategic use of information technology, Columbia University Graduate School of Business, December 1985.

GROWTH: SPINOFFS

Weyerhaeuser

David Ludlum. "Weyerhaeuser Branches Out." *Computerworld*, June 16, 1986.

Rick Cook. "In Pursuit of MIS/DP Profits." *Computer Decisions*, June 30, 1986.

Philip Gill. "Weyerhaeuser MIS Branches Out." *InformationWeek*, October 13, 1986.

J. C. Penney

Charles Babcock. "J. C. Penney's Subnetworks Reduce Downtime Danger." *Computerworld*, May 13, 1985.

Richard Layne. "Penney Makes Dollars with MIS Spinoff." *InformationWeek*, November 10, 1986.

Rotelli

Rick Cook. "In Pursuit of MIS/DP Profits." *Computer Decisions*, June 30, 1986.

Intermountain Health Care

"Intermountain Health Care: Financing Hospital Treatment for the Poor." *Business Week*, May 16, 1983.

McDonnell (McAuto)

Ulric Weil. *Information Systems in the 80s: Products, Markets, and Vendors.* Englewood Cliffs, N.J.: Prentice-Hall, 1982.

"McDonnell Douglas' Rationale for Taking on a Money-Loser." *Business Week*, December 5, 1983.

Robert Johnson. "McDonnell Says Negotiations to Acquire Tymshare for $372 Million Have Ended." *The Wall Street Journal*, December 20, 1983.

"McDonnell to Create an Information Group Including Tymshare." *The Wall Street Journal*, March 7, 1984.

William Martorelli. "McDonnell Douglas Seals Tymshare Buyout." *Information Systems News*, March 12, 1984.

"MasterCard, Tymshare Pact." *The Wall Street Journal*, March 13, 1984.

John Curley. "McDonnell Is Taking a Risk on Tymshare." *The Wall Street Journal*, March 20, 1984.

"McDonnell Douglas Completes $306M Takeover of Ailing Tymshare Inc." *Computerworld*, April 9, 1984.

Sherie Shamon. "Turnkey Systems for Industry: McDonnell Douglas Builds an Information Business." *Management Technology*, September 1984.

"McDonnell Douglas Buys Information-Systems Firm." *The Wall Street Journal*, November 16, 1984.

"McDonnell Douglas to Sell Systems Using IBM Minicomputers." *The Wall Street Journal*, December 6, 1984.

Robert Crutchfield. "A New McAuto Appears." *Datamation*, March 1, 1985.

"The Only Data Processing Service You Will Ever Need: McAuto Health Services." McDonnell Douglas, no date.

Geisco (General Electric Information Services Company)

"GE Strategic Position in 1981." Case studies. Harvard Business School, 1981

"GE—Business Development." Case studies. Harvard Business School, 1982.

GE, Annual Report, 1983.

Willie Schatz. "Geisco Goes for the Gusto." *Datamation*, February 1983.

Paul Gillin. "T/S Vendors Must Integrate Micros, Survey Warns." *Computerworld*, September 12, 1983.

Randall Smith and Dennis Kneale. "GE Net Rose 14% in First Quarter . . . Plans New Data Network." *The Wall Street Journal*, April 11, 1984.

Johanna Ambrosio. "Geisco Aims to Move into Telecom Fore." *Information Systems News*, April 16, 1984.

Mitch Betts. "Geisco Changes Tack, Angles toward Network Applications." *Computerworld*, May 5, 1986.

"Computer Associates Plans to Buy GE Unit to Expand Division." *The Wall Street Journal*, November 12, 1986.

9

Alliance

FORMS OF ALLIANCE

As I use the term, *alliance* means any combination of two or more groups or individuals joined together for the purpose of achieving a common objective. By this definition, mergers are alliances. Some might find this unacceptable, arguing that combinations failing to preserve the separate identities of the partners should not be counted as alliances. Granted, a case could be made for narrowing the sense of the term in this fashion. But for our purposes, it pays to adopt a more catholic position, admitting mergers and acquisitions (whether partial or complete) as legitimate alliance forms. This broader conception opens, as we shall soon see, a rich vein of strategic initiative opportunities in which information technology may play a critical part.

Strategic alliances are intra- or interfirm combinations designed to support or shape the competitive strategy of one or more of the allies. Such alliances take a variety of forms. For example, Japan's Suzuki Motor Company manufactures Chevrolet's minicars and ships them to GM dealers; GM owns 34.2 percent of Suzuki. GM and Toyota, the world's two largest automobile companies, together roll Chevrolet subcompacts off the line at their Freemont, California, plant. Partial acquisition (GM/Suzuki) and a 50–50 joint venture (GM/Toyota) represent two forms of strategic alliance. With both GM/Suzuki and GM/Toyota, GM hopes, among other things, to exploit the automotive production capabilities of these Japanese firms and thereby support its worldwide cost reduction strategy.

There are three forms of strategic alliance: acquisition, joint venture, and agreement. To count as a *strategic acquisition alliance* in which X acquires (partially or completely) Y, the alliance X/Y must be such that Y performs some function on X's product net or produces a product related to X's product line. With these stipulations, I exclude those mergers and acquisitions often called "unrelated." For it hardly makes sense to talk of the competitive strategy of a conglomerate with unrelated business units or divisions in its portfolio.

In a *strategic joint venture alliance,* X and Y may participate in varying degrees, from a 50–50 partnership like the GM/Toyota deal to myriad other proportional arrangements. Unpopular for many years in the United States, joint ventures have undergone a government-sponsored renaissance.

In the 1980s at least, the Justice Department no longer looks suspiciously at these combinations. Indeed, the department's attitude seems to encourage them. In 1984, the head of its Antitrust Division indicated the agency would not oppose ventures, even between rivals in concentrated markets, if efficiencies could be expected as a result of the deal. He told the New England Antitrust Conference that "an awareness of the role these valuable business arrangements play in creating efficiencies and bringing forth new products and technologies is replacing an attitude of suspicion born of ignorance."[1] Further, he claimed that joint ventures "will play a vital role in promoting the growth and international competitiveness of the American economy."[2]

Under a *strategic agreement alliance,* X and Y negotiate an agreement whereby X licenses Y to use its product or process, or X produces a product and Y uses, distributes, markets, or otherwise augments it to form some new offering that Y sells. In each of the strategic alliance forms just sketched (acquisition, joint venture, and agreement), the defining conditions can be extended easily to cases involving more than two organizations.

When X and Y forge an alliance, X may exploit the resources of Y that it lacks, Y might exploit the resources of X that it lacks, or both may exploit the resources of another party in addition to their own. In GM/Suzuki, GM exploits the production capabilities of Suzuki, and Suzuki exploits GM's dealer network.

The source of the resource to be exploited depends on your point of view. When brainstorming for alliance opportunities, three questions related to the required resource should be addressed:

1. Do we possess it?
2. Does another organization possess it?
3. Does it need to be created?

In other words, is the key resource yours, theirs, or other—
something that must be created by you, your ally, both of you
working together, or by another party?

Combining alliance forms with resource sources opens up
nine possible strategic alliance moves (see Figure 9–1). If we
possess the key resource (Opportunities 1–3), can we find an
ally via acquisition, joint venture, or agreement that possesses
resources we need to exploit the key resource? If we lack the
key resource (Opportunities 4–6), do we possess resources that
we could exploit by forging an alliance via acquisition, joint
venture, or agreement with an organization possessing the key
resource? Finally, if we lack the key resource because it doesn't
exist but we possess another exploitable resource, can we find
an ally via acquisition, joint venture, or agreement that will
develop the key resource or, using its resources and ours, find
another organization that can create the key resource (Opportunities 7–9)?

Figure 9–1   SIS Alliance Opportunities

		Acquisition	Joint venture	Agreement
		Form of Alliance		
Source of Resource	Yours	1	2	3
	Theirs	4	5	6
	Other	7	8	9

If an organization has developed information technology assets, then the examples cited below should stimulate its thoughts on how to identify and design strategic initiatives that will leverage these resources. But if its cache of information system assets to parlay is skimpy, it need not lose hope. It may be able to exploit the information systems developed by others.

Such considerations lead naturally to the question: Why do firms make alliances? As the reader may have surmised, the motives for strategic alliances are found among the strategic thrusts of differentiation, cost, innovation, and growth. Alliances are forged to enable the organization to:

Further differentiate its product.

Reduce the differentiation advantages of its strategic targets.

Reduce its costs.

Raise the costs of its competitors.

Develop innovative products or processes.

Imitate those who have developed such products or processes.

Grow by expanding customer groups, customer needs satisfied, technologies used, or functions controlled.

All of these, and others, may serve as ground(s) for alliance formation.

Being tied so intimately to such moves, should strategic alliances be considered as independent thrusts—different in kind, not just in form, from the others? On theoretical grounds, perhaps not. But there are two practical reasons for treating them separately as thrusts in their own right. First, they are commonly understood in the popular press as strategic moves. Second, such alliances may serve other objectives, purposes not met by the strategic thrusts of differentiation, cost, innovation, and growth.

Information technology may be used to support or shape strategic alliance thrusts. I call such thrusts, not unexpectedly, *strategic information systems (SIS) alliances.* The class of SIS alliances that can be used in conjunction with the firm's other strategic thrusts may take the form of an acquisition, joint venture, or agreement and may exploit its key information technology assets, those of an ally, or those that will be developed as a result of the alliance. The examples below illustrate the range of opportunities open to firms with the vision to use information technology assets to gain or maintain competitive advantage or reduce the edge of a rival by forging strategic alliances.

I have classified these opportunities into four groups: product integration, product development, product extension, and product distribution. Each case, however, may also be seen from the vantage point of the thrust it exemplifies. The fourfold scheme introduced here encourages, I believe, the identification of SIS alliance opportunities.

ALLIANCE: PRODUCT INTEGRATION

Product integration alliances create new offerings by bringing together parts or all of products that can be sold separately. The amount of value added in this process shows great variation. In some cases, the offering merely places in one box what normally would be packaged in two. In others, it weaves the products of the partners into an organic whole whose parts are inseparable.

The cases that follow illustrate this variety. I have divided them into four classes, depending on the number and kind of ingredients involved. In *simple turnkey alliances*, the offering comprises a single information system and a single hardware system on which it runs; in *complex turnkey alliances*, more than one information or hardware system is involved. In *simple software alliances*, the offering comprises the combination of two information systems or modules of information systems. In *complex software alliances*, more than two systems or modules are involved. In general, product integration alliances enable some partners to expand their product lines.

Simple Turnkey Alliances

Computervision Corp., the 1984 revenue leader in computer-aided design/computer-aided manufacture (CAD/CAM) software, formed a simple turnkey alliance with IBM whereby it became a value-added remarketer of certain IBM computer models. While it was Computervision's closest competitor in this marketplace, IBM realized that it couldn't satisfy the needs of customers in every niche.

Comshare, Inc., a leading time-sharing company and developer of a decision support system software tool called System W, also signed a complementary marketing agreement with IBM. Under the terms of this pact, IBM markets System W through its sales force, while Comshare provides leads to IBM for its mainframe series of computers and retains the rights to the package. IBM sells computers and Comshare sells System Ws. The IBM connection enabled Comshare to develop a good position with users of the mainframe series. As a result of this simple turnkey SIS alliance, Comshare gained an edge over its numerous rivals. A minor player prior to its agreement with IBM, it became one of the leading decision support package vendors. The pact also helped the company diversify from time-sharing, its principal but declining line of business, into the fast-growing sphere of packaged software.

Geisco, General Electric's information services company (also in the time-sharing business) forged a simple turnkey agreement with IBM in which it became a value-added remarketer of the IBM PC. Geisco saw this as an SIS alliance opportunity to leverage some of the information systems it offered on its network by repackaging/modifying them for the PC.

IBM and other computer vendors have signed similar pacts with firms possessing valuable databases and related information systems. Mead Data's complementary marketing agreement with IBM permits users to access the firm's Lexis and Nexis databases via the IBM PC, the Displaywriter, and other IBM terminal devices. Originally, Mead made Lexis and Nexis available only to those who had leased Mead's terminal.

Complex Turnkey Alliances

The John Hancock Mutual Life Insurance Company solved the problem of providing its agents with computing power by forming a complex turnkey alliance. Unlike Fireman's Fund (see below), which acquired a software producer to attend to its agents' needs, John Hancock assembled an offering composed of such items as a PC from IBM, a spreadsheet from Lotus, a word-processing package from Softword, and a system for developing policy proposals from its own (in-house) microcomputer programming staff. When an agent orders the turnkey system, John Hancock's data processing department handles the entire transaction, from putting the pieces together to delivery, training, and so on.

Blue Cross and Blue Shield (BC/BS) of Greater New York, which serves over 25,000 physicians in a 17-county region, offers a complex turnkey system to speed the submission of claims from doctors and perform a variety of office functions. The system, Amicus I, cuts six or more days off reimbursement time, produces reminder letters for delinquent accounts, lists patients according to diagnostic category, and "streamlines office operations, communications, and financial transactions among physicians, patients, and private and public health insurers."[3]

BC/BS developed this system by forming alliances with IBM (IBM PC), Okidata (Microline 93 printer), Hayes Microcomputer Products (Smartmodem 1200), and Davong Systems (tape backup unit). Along with software, installation, and support, BC/BS offered Amicus I in 1984 for $16,200 to the estimated 85 percent of physicians in the area lacking computer support.

Simple Software Alliances

Applied Data Research, a leading developer of database, data communications and other system software packages, inked agreements in 1984 with two archrivals in the application software business, Management Science America and McCormack & Dodge, the Dun & Bradstreet subsidiary. These pacts were defensive alliances struck in response to Cullinet Software's full-line strategy of offering integral system and application packages. Under the terms of these alliances, the partners cooperated in both developing and marketing their integrated wares.

Along somewhat similar lines, Software AG, another system software house, signed at least 10 joint marketing agreements with application development firms. Software AG offers its "software engine," consisting of modules from its database management system (Adabas) and its fourth-generation query language (Natural), to replace whatever routines the applications use to handle data management and retrieval functions. Here, the application vendor gets the added value of a popular database system, and the system's house penetrates accounts it might not otherwise reach.

Information Sciences, a software vendor specializing in human resources and payroll applications, made a different kind of arrangement with Artificial Intelligence, Inc. when it signed a marketing pact with them. AI, the developer of an easy-to-use query package called "Intellect," provides copies of its code to InfoSci's customers. This gives them access to personnel and payroll databases when unexpected calls for information arise.

Do simple software alliances lead inevitably to a pot of gold? Management Science America (MSA), a large mainframe software producer, evidently believed that they did when it purchased Peachtree, a leading microcomputer software house. Unfortunately for MSA, however, its alliance with Peachtree foundered. "We diversified into something that we aren't expert in," lamented MSA's chairman in December 1984, when announcing that Peachtree was for sale.[4] But he maintained that the alliance, while a financial disaster, had some benefits: MSA acquired Peachtree in 1981 in part to learn how mainframe and microcomputer might be linked. In this regard at least, according to its head, MSA gained valuable know-how.

While the acquisition route failed for MSA and Peachtree, a

more natural combination promises a far better outcome. SPSS Inc., the developer of a mainframe package of statistical routines (called SPSS, which originally meant statistical package for the social sciences), teamed with the microcomputer software vendor Microsoft to offer a microcomputer version of SPSS, called SPSS/PC, closely coupled with Microsoft Chart, a graphical presentation package. The offering provides users with a "seamless interface between SPSS/PC and Chart. Data can be transferred between the programs as if between tables in the same application."[5]

Complex Software Alliances

In 1984, Extendicare Ltd., a Toronto conglomerate that owns Crown Life Insurance Company (one of Canada's largest) and Crowntek (a high-technology subsidiary), acquired Computer Corporation of America (CCA), a Cambridge-based software house. Crowntek folded CCA into a group that included Kaptron (a developer of fiber-optic communications devices), Polaris Technology (a software and consulting company that was the Canadian distributor of CCA's product line), and Waterloo Micro Systems (a microcomputer software developer).

Extendicare believed the acquisition of CCA would yield synergistic products, due to the close bonds expected to form among Crowntek's stable of entrepreneurs. Just six months after the deal was cut, the first fruits of the alliance ripened. CCA announced an office automation product that included a microcomputer operating system developed by Waterloo and a file transfer package from Polaris.

The Inter-Financial Software joint venture represents another kind of complex software alliance. Three software companies, Hogan Systems, Monchik-Weber, and Continuum, decided to work together on satisfying the converging needs of their customers for new information systems–based products and services. Each firm provided systems and services to segments of the financial market. Hogan built systems for com-

mercial banks; Monchik-Weber served securities and investment management firms; Continuum provided systems to
individual life, health, and annuity companies in the insurance
industry. The new organization, Inter-Financial, produced *integrated* information systems for customers in need of applications that crossed the banking, brokerage, and insurance
fields.

ALLIANCE: PRODUCT DEVELOPMENT

Firms desiring to create new products based on information
technology form *product development alliances.* In 1982, Kroger Company—a supermarket chain with 1,200 food stores,
500 pharmacies, and 32 food-processing plants in 21 states—
announced that it had begun selling insurance, money market
funds, and IRAs in one of its stores. Behind the announcement, believed to be the first notice of a financial services operation in a supermarket (but not quite a financial services supermarket), was an SIS product development alliance with Capital
Holding, an insurance company with assets of $3.8 billion.

The joint venture projected costs of about $2 million, a
substantial chunk of which was used to develop an information
system that would immediately compare a customer's current
automobile and home insurance with the offerings at the supermarket. For Capital, the alliance represented an opportunity to move into another channel of distribution, different
from the traditional agency route. For Kroger, the aim was the
same as it is for any new specialty service offered by the chain.
"It is a service the customers want, and we are in the business
of serving customers," the president of Kroger said at the time
the SIS alliance was formalized.[6]

Elsewhere the impetus is entrepreneurial. Liberty National
Bank & Trust Company, Oklahoma's second largest bank,
joined with an independent retailer to found a chain of automated gasoline stations called "Sav–A–Dollar." Having operated a network of automated teller machines, Liberty had the

information system experience to develop software to link automated fuel pumps to the bank's computers. Customers with Liberty bank cards can use them at any station in the chain to pay for their purchases. Unlike credit card transactions, sales at Sav–A–Dollar are deducted immediately from the customer's account.

Property and casualty insurance companies like Fireman's Fund are locked in an intense battle to save their networks of independent insurance agents. Large insurers have made clear their intention of luring the top agencies by helping them to automate. Industry observers see a radical realignment of the whole distribution system, with consolidations driven by the need to cut increasing information-handling costs. Some believe that as many as 20,000 of the nation's 65,000 independent agencies will either merge, sell out, or leave the business over the next 10 years.

Fireman's Fund, along with other major insurers, spends heavily on agent automation programs. In 1982, for example, it bought over $100 million worth of minicomputers destined for agency offices. To further support this critical automation program, Fireman's acquired the ARC Automation Group, a software company that produces information system applications for agents. It had, in effect, identified a need for an SIS product development alliance.

While this move may have helped Fireman's gain an edge over other insurers with independent agents, so-called direct-writing insurers who sell insurance through the mail or through exclusive agents or sales representatives still have often decisive cost advantages. But strategic agency automation programs such as the one initiated by Fireman's may slow or stem the market share erosion experienced in the past few years.

A product development alliance based on information technology carries no special guarantee of success. In 1984, for example, Citicorp and McGraw-Hill Inc. formed a joint venture, Global Electronic Markets Company (Gemco), to supply traders with data on commodities (e.g., oil, chemicals, metals) and allow them to buy, sell, and finance their goods by using terminals in their offices. At the time, Citi's chairman John Reed said: "We're creating the first global commodities market-place fulfilling all of the customer's needs."[7]

The system allowed buyers to view the latest prices and industry news from over 70 sources. This done, a buyer could enter a bid for a commodity from the terminal. Once a seller was identified, the two parties could electronically negotiate terms; issue instructions to banks for letters of credit, payment or receipt of funds, and the like; and arrange for shipping and insurance.

The partners took their electronic market to be more efficient than the traditional modes of doing business—that is, by telephone or through established commodity exchanges. For Citi, the venture supported its drive to diversify into the information services business (identified as a key growth area by the bank), a component of its "Five I Strategy," representing the division of the firm into the individual bank, the institutional bank, and the investment, insurance, and information banks. For McGraw-Hill, it represented an opportunity to make its vast store of information more directly useful to traders.

To traders, however, it meant something else: a threat to their livelihoods. Commodity traders, it seems, aren't too keen on electronic transactions. They prefer the old ways of plying their trade. As a board member of the Mercantile Exchange put it, with reference to the area of initial focus for Gemco, "The oil industry likes the personal contact. It's a fraternity and there's a lot of negotiation that takes place—time, price, quality, shipping details."[8]

In operation just over a year, Gemco closed its doors at the end of 1985 for lack of industry response, another honorable SIS fatality buried beside such illustrious relatives as ZapMail, Sharetech (see below), and Imnet. "The problem wasn't in the joint venture," said a Citi vice president for global electronic markets, "The problem was with the market. We basically concluded that there wasn't a critical mass."[9]

Unlike Gemco, a vendor-sponsored alliance that failed to

find customers, the joint venture between the Presbyterian Hospital of New York and AT&T avoided this fatal condition from the start. In this case, the customer was a participant. The hospital acted as an investment banker for the development of "a unique 'bedside terminal' that would let hospital staff view historical information and enter data about a patient as he or she is treated."[10]

As stated by the head of Advanced Systems Development (ASD), the Presbyterian's information technology venture group:

> Not only are we a living laboratory, we're also jointly funding some of the development. When some of the things that we help develop ultimately will be sold, we would expect a return. . . . While we struck a good business deal, the true focal point is the development of the system we need. . . . With each joint venture that I develop, I do better in a lot of ways. I don't want to say what the specifics are. I don't want one of my competitors to come along and work out a better deal.[11]

This effort represents an interesting prescription for joint ventures between vendors and their customers. It is also noteworthy because the head of Presbyterian's ASD group views it competitively, as a contest between (presumably) hospitals like Presbyterian. It will be fought, however, not in the customer arena over patients but in the vendor arena over investment opportunities.

The last example of an SIS development alliance concerns a joint venture involving 25 Japanese firms. "Only in Japan could a consortium like this work," said the president of the Pacific Telecommunications Council when the creation of a second Japanese telephone company, Dai-Ni Den-Den Kikaku Co. Ltd. (DDK), was announced.[12] DDK is the only Japanese competitor of Nippon Telegraph and Telephone, the government-owned monopoly that became a privately held corporation in 1985. Among the participants in the DDK venture are leading Japanese businesses in such disparate fields as banking, electronics, printing, and international trade (e.g., Sumitomo

Bank, Sony, Dai Nippon Printing, and Mitsui). DDK sells data transmission products and services, many dependent on information technology, in Japanese and international markets.

ALLIANCE: PRODUCT EXTENSION

Product extension alliances create new uses, markets, or applications for products based on information technology.

Under the leadership of Prime Minister Edward Seaga, Jamaica in the early 80s adopted a policy of encouraging technological ventures designed to reduce the island's dependence on low-profit crops like sugar and introduce products with high market value. When an Israeli entrepreneur saw a news report detailing President Reagan's support for Seaga's policies, he also noticed the lush foliage on the island. Within a month, the entrepreneur had sent someone to Jamaica to collect soil and water samples for testing.

The entrepreneur, Eli Tisona, identified an opportunity to develop an SIS product extension alliance with the Jamaican government. If the soil and water tests proved positive, Tisona could leverage Israeli-developed information system applications in the agricultural field. When the tests confirmed his hunch, Tisona negotiated an agreement with the government to lease 4,500 acres and formed a partnership, Jamaica Agro Products, to grow winter vegetables, bananas, ornamental flowers, and nursery shrubs.

Perforated plastic hoses run through 125 acres of melons to deliver exact amounts of water and fertilizer, individually, to each plant. An Israeli-developed minicomputer system makes this possible by controlling the opening and closing of valves connecting over 250 sources of water and nutrients, as well as an intricate series of underground sensors that send data to the mini. Just 15 months after the start of the venture, the partners declared the project a success.

As margins on traditional lending activities erode due to the increasing intensity of competition in the financial services industry and to fluctuating rates, banks seek new sources of profit. Some offer fee-generating services, such as training or health programs developed for their own employees, to other institutions. According to the senior vice president for planning at Chemical Bank, "The banks, if they want to remain at the center of the payment system, are going to have to develop innovative services. If the banks don't do it themselves, somebody else is going to do it. We want to provide that service, and we think we can make money off it."[13]

Licensing information systems and services, some large money center banks have discovered, presents a promising alliance opportunity for new revenue. Chemical's Trust and Investment Division, for example, franchises Trust Link, a new program that delivers trust services to smaller banking institutions in the United States. Trust Link makes use of ChemLink, another computerized system providing cash management services (under license) to both domestic and international banks. For an investment of about $200,000, Chemical offers Pronto, its innovative home computer banking system, to banks that can't afford a $10 million development effort. Even before introducing Pronto to its New York customers, Chemical had signed six licensees.

For another product extension variant, consider the joint venture Sharetech, created by AT&T's shared tenant services subsidiary Intelliserve and United Technologies' building systems group. The partners contributed personnel, products, and capital to a new business aimed at office building developers and others who provide tenant services. Sharetech offered leaseholders a variety of products and services: data and voice communications, information processing, security systems, and so forth. It also offered building owners automated systems to control elevators, heat, air-conditioning, and other building operations. In effect, this SIS alliance attempted to create the intelligent building. A number of other joint ventures in this area have been announced, some between suppliers and others between suppliers and owners.

The market for intelligent buildings, however, has not materialized. By the start of 1987, Sharetech and Intelliserve had failed. When 55 real estate developers were asked where they felt tenants would rank shared services, 90 percent said at the bottom of the list, behind price, location, parking, and the like. Developers evidently consider shared tenant services as only an amenity, not a source of advantage. Similar results were obtained from surveys of tenants and real estate brokers. Indeed, just before Sharetech pulled its cables in 1986, a spokesman for the venture lamented: "I've heard it said that there has yet to emerge a tenant that will move into a building just because of shared services."[14]

ALLIANCE: PRODUCT DISTRIBUTION

Product distribution alliances create new channels of distribution for a product. In the cases to follow, information technology plays a role integral to the product itself or to its channel of distribution.

American Express's acquisition of Investors Diversified Services (IDS) from the Alleghany Corporation reflects this kind of SIS alliance. While legally unlike the Israeli-Jamaican partnership described above, the $773 million deal between American Express and Alleghany is similar in objective: to leverage existing information system assets.

American Express saw in IDS a vehicle for distributing, either electronically or through the IDS sales force, the myriad of its information systems–based financial products and services, including those developed by its various units: Shearson in the brokerage area, Fireman's Fund in the insurance realm, and so on. The acquisition permitted the financial giant to tap into IDS's massive market of over 1.1 million customers, located primarily in small and medium-sized cities. Previously, American Express's only penetration point had been through the direct mail route. Now it uses IDS's 4,500 salespeople, who already peddle mutual funds, tax shelters, and other investments to their clients.

Electronic Data Systems (EDS), the large, Dallas-based information system company acquired by General Motors, provides facilities management and remote data processing services worldwide. Under alliances forged with Hogan Systems and Cullinet Software, EDS enlarged the range of systems it offers to customers and enabled these software companies to penetrate market segments previously inaccessible to them.

Hogan and Cullinet sell expensive systems that only the largest organizations can afford to purchase. By making their wares available to EDS customers via the latter's regional processing centers, both vendors gain access to new groups of users from smaller firms. In the case of Hogan, for example, its software—originally designed for banks with more than $1 billion in assets—is now available to over 700 EDS banking customers, the majority with under $1 billion in assets. According to Hogan's president, "This agreement opens up a new market for our software. With EDS, our software will now serve institutions of all sizes."[15] By making its powerful database management system available to small users via the EDS network, Cullinet also expands its customer base.

SIS alliances can be arranged with rivals as well as with suppliers and customers. In the demilitarized zone of financial services, rivals or potential rivals (one is never quite sure here) often find it profitable to trade with each other. This is particularly true when your potential partner is a player in a financial services sector encroaching on your territory. For example, Dreyfus Corp., the large mutual fund outfit, arranged with Chase Manhattan Bank to manage funds for its clients. Bank of America agreed with a large insurance company to provide space in its branches for agents to sell insurance products. It takes the skills of a diplomat and the cunning of a guerrilla to strike deals that will serve your strategic ends and satisfy your partner's interests as well.

Paine Webber, for instance, seized an alliance opportunity in 1984 that no other brokerage house had previously been able to capture. It negotiated a pact with the State Street Bank and Trust Company of Boston enabling it to participate in Master-Teller, the nationwide automated teller network run for banks by MasterCard International, a credit card and traveler's check organization owned by 24,000 banks and other institutions. The MasterTeller network lets cardholders withdraw cash from the over 1,500 automated teller machines scattered throughout the United States. Up to this time, banks had been very careful to exclude rivals offering competitive financial services from entry to their networks. (Indeed, two of the largest bank-owned nationwide nets, the Plus and Cirrus systems, rejected requests from Merrill Lynch and Fidelity (see Chapter 8), a Boston-based mutual fund company, to establish similar arrangements.)

As a result of this agreement, Paine Webber customers use cards issued by State Street to get the same 24-hour access to cash that bank cardholders enjoy. A cardholder with a Paine Webber account can withdraw money at automatic teller machines (ATMs) across the country. The final chapter on how Paine Webber will use this new alliance in packaging its products has yet to unfold. In any case, the deal illustrates how, to serve its own strategic ends, the broker capitalized on information systems assets *developed by others.*

An interesting variant of this move involves the joint sharing of assets developed by others. In March 1985, a group of eight New York–area banks (excluding Citibank, the largest bank in the United States) formed the New York Credit Exchange, a for-profit network of over 800 ATMs at 650 locations around the city. Known as NYCE (pronounced "nice"), it provides cash withdrawal, inquiry, and other services to any customer of a member bank holding the bank's ATM card, or a Master or Visa credit card issued by one of the group. As the *New Yorker* magazine so eloquently put it: "In the lines, therefore, you see displayed a range of colors and allegiances—the navy and silver of Chase, the gray and sky blue of Chemical, the aqua and white of Barclays—as varied and distinctive as racing silks."[16] For each network transaction involving a cardholder from its bank, the bank pays a fee to NYCE and to the member bank whose machine was used for the transaction.

Membership in NYCE is open to all banks in the region

paying a one-time fee of up to $20,000. Network growth has been nothing short of spectacular. In just one year, over 60 banks joined. The number of ATMs multiplied from 800 to 1,600, cards in use jumped from 2.5 million to 6 million, and interbank transactions rose to 11 percent of the total.

In the past, the network partners, fearing the loss of customers in the fiercely competitive New York retail banking market, were reluctant to cooperate. Yet, each knew that the growth of Citi's ATM network, with over 635 units at 250 locations, was far more than any of them could hope to achieve acting alone. Moreover, each felt victimized by Citi's phenomenal growth due to its ATM dominance. (From 1978 to 1987, Citi almost tripled its share of depositors, moving from about 4.5 percent to 13 percent. In consumer loans, its share jumped from 1 percent to 21 percent.) And they knew that information technology, in the form of Citi's ATM net, led to this expansion.

But biting the cooperation bullet seems to have paid off. According to industry analysts, NYCE "has proven to be a powerful tool in *reducing* the *competitive advantage* in electronic banking long held by Citibank."[17] [Italics added.] The successful launch of NYCE suggests three points. First, the SIS of a dominant organization can be matched by a group of weaker rivals who develop an equal or better SIS alternative. Second, partners in such a cooperative effort, if it succeeds, are in a position to explore other opportunities (e.g., network applications such as point-of-sale and debit card systems) that they might not have undertaken because each was constrained, individually, by lack of development resources and (perhaps) fear of failure. Third, cooperative SIS may reduce the competitive advantage of the leader(s) for a whole group of rivals formerly disadvantaged. According to the vice president at Chemical Bank who serves as chairman of NYCE, "It's worked out well beyond our initial expectations. . . . We definitely have a much better competitive footing versus Citibank in terms of the numbers of machines and geographic spread."[18]

In the United States, cooperative efforts involving information technology have been the exception rather than the rule. But in Japan, the situation—at least among small and medium-sized enterprises, which ship 51 percent of all manufactured goods, account for 62 percent of wholesale and 79 percent of retail industry sales, and export 40 percent of all industrial goods—seems to be reversed. Cooperatives jointly purchase hardware and software and operate the systems. In some cases, the purpose is not to gain an edge but rather to reduce advantages possessed by larger rivals. The cooperative society of shoe manufacturers in Kobe, for example, developed a CAD system for designing new shoes; the cooperative society of textile manufacturers in Kyoto developed a video response system that enables members to select for viewing and processing from over 300,000 designs stored in the system. Finally, a group of 175 small, independent drugstores in the Osaka area belong to a voluntary chain called Pharma that purchases medical supplies from large wholesalers. This cooperative helps the small stores compete against their larger retail rivals. Pharma accomplishes this by reaping economy-of-scale benefits when it purchases from wholesalers and then passing these savings on to its members so that they can compete on price with the large retailers. Pharma also helps the cooperative members reduce their operating costs by providing value-added networking services such as electronic order entry, invoicing, and bill payment. In addition, members receive electronic reports on best- and worst-selling products, rival's prices, new products, and so on. Cooperative SIS is an area of active research in Japan, and there is keen interest in Italy and France, where one also finds a large percentage of small- and medium-sized firms.

As the closing case for Part II, let's look at Reuters Holding PLC, a company with SIS vision that has forged alliances and executed thrusts—innovation, differentiation, cost, and growth—to transform its strategic course. In each instance, information technology supported or shaped the strategic move. Reuters' evolution not only illustrates the strategic use of information technology but also exemplifies emerging competitive forces related to this use, forces that will inevitably occupy a large portion of the time top managers spend thinking about SIS opportunities and threats (see Chapter 11).

In 1851, Baron de Reuter had an idea. He believed that news of stock transactions on the Brussels exchange could be sold if distributed with dispatch. With the aid of carrier pigeons, he made this idea a reality and, in the process, founded the Reuters News Service. Over the years, ownership passed from the Reuter family to a primarily British consortium of press groups: the Newspaper Publishing Association, a Fleet Street trade group (41 percent share); the Press Association, a wire service owned by provincial English newspapers (41 percent share); the Australian and New Zealand press associations (16.4 percent share); and Reuters' management (1.4 percent share).

In 1984, the private consortium decided to put 28 percent of Reuters up for sale. The news agency known to millions for its stories from around the world was valued at about $370 million when its stock was publicly offered. What few realized, however, was that the bulk of Reuters' revenue derived not from general news stories but from reporting and processing of financial data in the world's financial capitals. Reuters' recent growth has been breathtaking, with revenue climbing from $125 million in 1980 to $254 million in 1981, $337 million in 1983, and over $800 million in 1986; pretax profit soared from $2.7 million in 1980 to $30 million in 1981, $43.5 million in 1983, and over $100 million in 1986. Reliable estimates put about 85 percent of revenue and between 95 and 100 percent of profit in the financial information sector of its business. To achieve these heights, Reuters needed to rely on more than the undisputed talents of its carrier pigeons.

Unlike its traditional rivals, the Associated Press and the financially troubled United Press International, Reuters was among the first to realize that information systems are the wings of the future. In 1973, it fashioned an innovative strategic thrust: a new, computerized information service called "Monitor" for foreign exchange price quotations. At the heart of the Monitor system was a video screen and keyboard giving traders immediate access to Reuters quotations and general news databases.

Unlike Gemco, the failed SIS effort initiated by Citicorp and McGraw-Hill to handle oil trading just as the petroleum market dried up in the mid-80s (see above), Monitor rode the wave formed when the world's financial powers, led by the United States, jettisoned the Bretton Woods agreement. The breakup of this treaty, which among other things fixed foreign-currency exchange rates, led to the new age of currency fluctuations. At first, Monitor merely permitted banks and other subscribing financial institutions to display their rates and see those of others. Over the next decade, Reuters expanded its offerings to include stock prices, commodity quotes, and virtually everything else that was traded. Growing steadily since the introduction of Monitor, Reuters now counts more than 86,000 terminals in 110 countries, each linked to its global telecommunications network. It has become the world's largest electronic publisher, far ahead of Mead Data Central with its Lexis and Nexis services (see Chapter 6), Quotron (now a subsidiary of Citicorp; see Chapter 8), and Telerate (now owned by Dow Jones; see Chapter 8).

With massive financial databases registering news and market events, Reuters, like many other information collectors, reaps economy-of-scope benefits by providing, for example, shipping advice on the availability and demand for oil tankers and cargo vessels; daily profiles of selected countries, designed for risk analysts at financial institutions and government agencies; historical reports, with a graphical analysis package included, for plotting past performance and future trends of financial instruments. On the horizon are unique services and products sculpted from Reuters databases to meet the information and trading needs of individual clients.

The electronic distribution of market news and the crafting of special studies tell only part of the story. In 1981, Reuters launched a service to provide traders with systems to deal—to execute and settle orders for the purchase and sale of the currencies, commodities, and equities whose prices appear on the screen. With this innovative move, Reuters further differentiated itself from rivals such as Telerate and Quotron, who only offered quotations. By 1986, its trading activities contributed about 8 percent of Reuters' revenue, a bit more than its global news service but with a higher profit margin than the latter.

In 1986, to complement its fast-growing electronic market data and trading services and to shape its global growth thrust aimed at becoming the world's electronic market in stocks, currencies, and the like, Reuters acquired Instinet, an American firm that operates an automated stock trading network by the same name. Instinet allows stock buyers to bypass the established exchanges and obtain the lowest price being offered on the net; sellers get the highest price offered. As a result of this strategic thrust, Reuters now confronts a new set of actual and potential rivals: the New York Stock Exchange, which hasn't allowed Instinet to forge direct links with it, and stock exchanges in London, Paris, Tokyo, and elsewhere.

Prior to the purchase, Reuters had sold the Instinet service in Europe to investors who wanted to trade in American stocks. With a direct link to the American Stock Exchange, Instinet gives investors access to the trading floor (for both stocks and options) through its electronic order-execution system. Also, links to several regional stock exchanges and the over-the-counter (OTC) quotation system NASDAQ enable Instinet subscribers to trade in New York Stock Exchange issues and most OTC equities. In 1987, a unit of Instinet purchased a seat on the Toronto stock exchange, adding 1,500 Canadian stocks to the over 8,000 U.S. issues already traded on the net. Reuters now makes Instinet available to all its subscribers around the world, flexing the distribution muscle that Instinet had never been able to develop.

In another alliance to support its global growth strategy, in particular to penetrate the U.S. market, Reuters bought Rich & Co. in 1984 for $2 million in cash and $55.5 million in stock. Rich, an American firm, custom-designs telecommunication systems for trading rooms. Its systems can handle data from more than 40 sources, including market news and price information (Reuters and non-Reuters) on a full range of financial instruments. At the time of sale, Rich's executive vice president noted that this strategic link "would give his company a healthy *advantage* in developing and marketing new products and services, which [he added] is what *competition* is all about."[19] [Italics added.] With its dominant position in government securities trading rooms, the Rich acquisition opens a U.S. market segment previously closed to Reuters: quotations and trades in government securities.

From the Reuters perspective, the ideal electronic marketplace (preferably unregulated) would consist of traders around the world ensconced in their Rich-tailored trading rooms, receiving relevant data from Monitor, executing orders on a Reuter's trading system like Instinet, reporting to Reuters when they want to change quotes on the items to be traded, taking home a Reuters pocket device to receive a Reuters satellite or radio transmission on the latest market news, and executing more orders. "The faster and further you move information, the more valuable it becomes," maintains Glen Renfrew, Reuter's chief executive officer.[20] Reuters, of course, would collect fees at each point on this chain. While the head currency trader at Chemical bank may, for example, win or lose on a deal with a counterpart in Tokyo, New York, or Milan, "Reuters will make money no matter what."[21]

Reuters' success in distributing market news and providing electronic trading systems to act on that news—abetted in large part by the globalization and deregulation of financial markets, coupled with a long-running, worldwide bull market in equities (1981–87)—has transformed the company from the premier foreign news service that it was for over 100 years into a global financial information systems and services giant. But like most Goliaths, it faces formidable adversaries, ranging from large enterprises such as Citicorp, Dow Jones, and the London Stock Exchange to smaller operations targeting special segments served by Reuters.

For example, to counter Reuters' challenge in the United States, Citicorp's Quotron and Dow's Telerate are expanding into the international sphere, which had been the British-based firm's almost exclusive preserve. To foil Reuters' efforts to provide a system for British stock trading, the London Stock Exchange acted forcefully to preserve its regulatory powers and its main line of business. The LSE "proposed that any market maker in listed stocks be required to furnish price-quote and last-sale information to the exchange before passing it to any vendor such as Reuters. Without such a rule, the exchange argues, it couldn't enforce trading suspensions because it couldn't stop market makers from obtaining price data independently."[22] A Reuters spokesman replied that such a rule "would put Reuters at a *disadvantage* in offering not only trading services but also simple quotation data."[23] [Italics added.] Some industry analysts believe that Reuters will file an antitrust suit against the exchange if this rule is put into practice. Finally, there are the threats posed by such companies as Lotus Development, publishers of the spreadsheet standard, Lotus 1-2-3. Lotus offers a product called "Signal" that receives real-time market data, transmitted not through expensive telephone lines, but rather via FM radio waves. Among the items received are U.S. and foreign stock quotations. The Reuters information advantage, achieved because of a keen SIS vision, timely moves, and a conducive environment, can expect to remain under siege in the foreseeable future from competitors armed with a knowledge of SIS planning and management principles, subjects to which we now turn.

NOTES

1. Robert Taylor, "Joint Ventures Likely to Be Encouraged by Friendlier Attitude of U.S. Officials," *The Wall Street Journal*, November 5, 1984. See also Charles Wiseman, "Securing Competitive Edge through Strategic Information Systems Alliances," *Strategic Management Planning*, April 1984.

2. Taylor, "Joint Ventures."

3. "NYC Blue Cross Offers Turnkey Micro System for Regional Doctors," *Computerworld*, July 2, 1984.

4. "The Software Troubles at Management Science," *New York Times*, November 15, 1984.

5. Peggy Watt, "SPSS Teams Up with Chart," *Computerworld*, March 10, 1986.

6. "Ohio Supermarket Is Selling Insurance and Mutual Funds," *New York Times*, September 28, 1982.

7. Phillip Zweig and John Marcom, Jr., "McGraw-Hill, Citicorp to Form Joint Venture," *The Wall Street Journal*, September 11, 1985.

8. Nicholas Kristof, "Oil-Trader Computer Service Set," *New York Times*, September 11, 1985.

9. Phillip Zweig, "Citicorp and McGraw-Hill Scrap Venture for Electronic Trading of Commodities," *The Wall Street Journal*, December 1, 1986.

10. R. D. R. Hoffman, "MIS I.V.," *InformationWeek*, September 15, 1986.

11. Ibid.

12. Bob Violino, "25 Japanese Firms Forming Telecom Co. to Compete vs. NTT," *CommunicationWeek*, May 21, 1984.

13. David Hilder, "Some Big Banks Begin Marketing Advanced Services to Smaller Banks," *The Wall Street Journal*, July 25, 1983.

14. John Dix, "Demand Low for Smart Buildings," *Computerworld*, June 17, 1985.

15. "EDS Users to Get Hogan Banking Package," *Computerworld*, August 20, 1984.

16. "The Talk of the Town," *New Yorker*, June 15, 1987.

17. Richard Stevenson, "Shared Cash Machines Boom," *New York Times*, March 11, 1986.

18. Ibid.

19. Jeffrey Leib, "Reuters Buys a Niche in U.S. Trading Rooms," *New York Times*, March 11, 1985.

20. Amy Borrus and Catherine Harris, "Reuters Starts to Let Its Customers Talk Back," *Business Week*, June 17, 1985.

21. Gary Putka, "Long a News Agency, Reuters Now Is Also Biggest Data Publisher," *The Wall Street Journal*, August 22, 1986.

22. Ibid.

23. Ibid.

CASE REFERENCES

ALLIANCE: PRODUCT INTEGRATION

Computervision/IBM

Ed Scannell. "IBM CAD/CAM Thrust Linked to Remarketers." *Computerworld*, August 22, 1983.

Paul Gillin. "Meet Sets Stage for Vendor 'Love-In.' " *Computerworld*, May 7, 1984.

John Gallant. "Computervision-IBM Agreement Results in CDS 5000." *Computerworld*, May 7, 1984.

Comshare/IBM

Paul Gillin. "IBM Picks Comshare DSS for Info Center." *Computerworld*, January 9, 1984.

Jacques Welter. "IBM, Comshare Jointly to Sell 4300s, DSS." *Computerworld*, 1984.

Geisco/IBM

"Geisco Joins Ranks of IBM Remarketers." *Computerworld*, February 6, 1984.

Mead Data Central/IBM

"Agreement Connects Mead Data Bases to IBM Hardware." *Information Systems News*, July 11, 1983.

"Lexis, Nexis Now Available via IBM Personal Computer." *Computerworld*, December 26, 1983.

John Hancock

James Connolly. "John Hancock Becoming Microcomputer 'Broker.' " *Computerworld*, April 30, 1984.

Blue Cross-Blue Shield

"NYC Blue Cross Offers Turnkey Micro System for Regional Doctors." *Computerworld*, July 2, 1984.

"Amicus 1." Medical Business Services, a division of Blue Cross and Blue Greater New York, no date.

ADR/McCorma

William Martorelli. "Software Firms Team Up." *Information Systems News* 1984.

"ISN Notebook Information Systems News, October 1, 1984.

"M&D, ADR Millennium Operate under ADR/Datacom/DB." *Information Systems News*, October 15, 1984.

Software AG

William Martorelli. "Software Firms Team Up." *Information Systems News*, May 14, 1984.

Information Science/Artificial Intelligence

Software News, January 1984.

MSA/Peachtree

"The Software Troubles at Management Science." *New York Times*, November 15, 1984.

SPSS/Microsoft

Peggy Watt. "SPSS Teams Up with Chart." *Computerworld*, March 10, 1986.

Extendicare/CCA

William Martorelli. "Crowntek Agrees to Acquire DBMS–Vendor CCA." *Information Systems News*, November 28, 1983.

Paul Gillin. "CCA Still a David, but Now Wields a More Powerful Slingshot." *Computerworld*, May 7, 1984.

Inter-Financial Software

"Hogan, Citicorp N.A. Sign Software License Agreement." *Computerworld*, August 22, 1983.

ALLIANCE: PRODUCT DEVELOPMENT

Kroger/Capital Holding

"Ohio Supermarket Is Selling Insurance and Mutual Funds." *New York Times*, September 28, 1982.

Steve Weiner and Hank Gilman. "Debate Grows on Retailers Bank Services." *The Wall Street Journal*, May 18, 1984.

Liberty National

"Computerized Fill Up." *Computer Decisions*,

Fireman's Fund/ARC Automation

Daniel Hertzberg. "Insurance Relying More on Automation." *The Wall Street Journal* November 9, 1982.

Citicorp/McGraw-Hill (Gemco)

Robert Bennett. "Citicorp, McGraw in a Venture." *New York Times*, September 10, 1985.

Phillip Zweig and John Marcom, Jr. "McGraw-Hill, Citicorp to Form Joint Venture." *The Wall Street Journal*, September 11, 1985.

Nicholas Kristof. "Oil-Trader Computer Service Set." *New York Times*, September 4, 1985.

Phillip Zweig. "Citicorp and McGraw-Hill Scrap Venture for Electronic Trading of Commodities." *The Wall Street Journal*, December 1, 1986.

Presbyterian Hospital/AT&T

R. D. R. Hoffman. "MIS I.V." *InformationWeek*, September 15, 1986.

DDK

Bob Violino. "25 Japanese Firms Forming Telecom Co. to Compete vs. NTT." *CommunicationWeek*, May 21, 1984.

ALLIANCE: PRODUCT EXTENSION

Jamaica Agro Products

L. Erik Calonius. "Why Are Japanese Cultivating Coffee in Jamaican Hills?" *The Wall Street Journal*, February 2, 1984.

Joseph Treater. "Making an Island Bloom: Israelis Help in Jamaica." *New York Times*, August 25, 1984.

Chemical Bank

Chemical Bank, Annual Report, 1982.

David Hilder. "Some Big Banks Begin Marketing Advanced Services to Smaller Banks." *The Wall Street Journal,* July 25, 1983.

AT&T/United Technologies (Sharetech)

"Wiring the 'Brains' into a Building." *Business Week,* September 27, 1982.

Andrew Pollack. "Business Planners Look to Telecommunications." *New York Times,* May 2, 1983.

Steven Marcus. "The 'Intelligent' Buildings." *New York Times,* December 1, 1983.

David Myers. "Landlord, United Telecomm to Build Private Net." *Computerworld,* December 5, 1983.

Stephen Solomon. "The Marriage of Smart Offices and Smart Buildings." *Management Technology,* February 1984.

"United Technologies and AT&T Units Plan to Form Joint Venture." *New York Times,* February 3, 1984.

Robert Guenther. "Office Developers Take Role of Telephone-Service Broker." *The Wall Street Journal,* February 8, 1984.

Phil Hirsch. "AT&T to Offer Shared Multitenant Services." *Computerworld,* February 27, 1984.

Frank Prial. "Wiring Buildings for Intelligence." *New York Times,* May 13, 1984.

Michael Azzara. "Opportunities Are Building in Market for Shared Tenant Services." *CommunicationWeek,* June 18, 1984.

Bruce Most. "Smart Buildings." *American Way,* October 1984.

John Dix. "Demand Low for Smart Buildings." *Computerworld,* June 17, 1985.

John Dix. "Smart Buildings Hold Little or No Interest for Tenants." *Computerworld,* June 17, 1985.

Saroja Girishankar. "AT&T Sells Off Final Vestiges of 1984 Shared-Tenant Venture." *CommunicationWeek,* January 5, 1987.

ALLIANCE: PRODUCT DISTRIBUTION

American Express/IDS

"American Express Expands Its Supermarket." *Business Week,* July 25, 1983.

Tim Carrington. "Some Officials at American Express Fear Problems if IDS Purchase Goes Through." *The Wall Street Journal,* August 12, 1983.

Tim Carrington and Tim Metz. "Alleghany to Sell IDS to American Express." *The Wall Street Journal,* September 27, 1983.

Robert Cole. "American Express to Buy IDS" *New York Times,* September 27, 1983.

David Hilder. "American Express 2nd-Period Profit Fell By 29%; Insurance, Securities Arms Cited." *The Wall Street Journal,* July 17, 1984.

EDS/Hogan, Cullinet

"EDS Users to Get Hogan Banking Package." *Computerworld,* August 20, 1984.

Paine Webber/State Street Bank & Trust

Daniel Hertzberg. "Paine Webber, despite Bank Opposition, Joins a National Teller-Machine Network." *The Wall Street Journal,* December 23, 1983.

Daniel Hertzberg. "Some Banks, Brokers Form Business Ties." *The Wall Street Journal,* February 15, 1984.

Paine Webber advertisement. *The Wall Street Journal,* April 1, 1984.

NYCE/Citibank

Richard Stevenson. "Big New York Banks Link Teller Machines." *New York Times,* March 7, 1985.

Richard Stevenson. "Shared Cash Machines Boom." *New York Times*, March 11, 1986.

Robert Norton. "Citibank Wows the Consumer." *Fortune*, June 8, 1987.

"The Talk of the Town." *New Yorker*, June 15, 1987.

Pharma

Joel Dreyfuss. "Networking: Japan's Latest Computer Craze." *Fortune*, July 7, 1986.

Shinroku Tsuji. "The Strategic Use of Information Technology in Japanese Small- and Medium-Sized Enterprises." Paper presented at the 1987 Center for Enterprise Studies Conference, Lecco, Italy, July 1987.

Reuters

"Reuters' Scoop in Financial News." *Business Week*, January 17, 1983.

"Reuters Has Good News for Fleet Street." *Business Week*, June 27, 1983.

"Reuters Tightens the Grip." *Euromoney*, October 1983.

Barnaby Feder. "Reuters Plans Sale of Stock." *New York Times*, December 15, 1983.

George Anders. "Reuters News Agency Plans to Sell Shares; Analysts Say Firm's Value near $1 Billion." *The Wall Street Journal*, December 16, 1983.

George Anders, Lawrence Ingrassia, and Lynda Schuster. "Reuters Sale May Let London Papers Junk Their Ancient Presses." *The Wall Street Journal*, January 16, 1984.

George Anders and John Marcom, Jr. "Reuters Announces Sale of 28% of Equity to British and American Investors." *The Wall Street Journal*, May 16, 1984.

Barnaby Feder. "Market Role Aids Growth of Reuters." *New York Times*, May 28, 1984.

Jeffrey Leib. "Reuters Buys a Niche in U.S. Trading Rooms." *New York Times,* March 11, 1985.

Gary Putka. "Bid by Reuters for Instinet Underlines U.K. Firm's Goal of Global Stock Trading." *The Wall Street Journal,* June 1, 1985.

Amy Borrus and Catherine Harris. "Reuters Starts to Let Its Customers Talk Back." *Business Week,* June 17, 1985.

Monci Jo Williams. "Why the Big Players Want a Piece of Instinet." *Fortune,* August 19, 1985.

Nicholas Kristof. "Computers Reshape Markets." *New York Times,* October 7, 1985.

Richard Melcher, Amy Borrus, and John Rossant. "The Electronic Threat to the World's Stock Exchanges." *Business Week,* December 2, 1985.

"Instinet and Amex to Offer Overseas Trading Hookup. *The Wall Street Journal,* December 10, 1985.

"Reuters Posts Record Profit, Plans Expanded Data Services." *The Wall Street Journal,* February 13, 1986.

Alexander Nicoll. "Electronic Bridge Boosts Global Equities Trading." *Financial Times,* April 23, 1986.

Gary Putka. "Long a News Agency, Reuters Now Is Also Biggest Data Publisher." *The Wall Street Journal,* August 22, 1986.

"The Information Business." *Business Week,* August 25, 1986.

Gary Putka. "Reuters Bids for Instinet in Attempt to Provide Off-Exchange U.S. Trading." *The Wall Street Journal,* October 27, 1986.

"Instinet Corp. Accepts Offer from Reuters after It Is Sweetened." *The Wall Street Journal,* November 11, 1986.

"Instinet Unit Bugs Seat on Toronto Exchange." *The Wall Street Journal,* February 5, 1987.

III

Implementation

10

SIS Planning and Management: I

PREPARING THE GROUND

Part I, "Through Another Lens," presented the strategic perspective on information technology and contrasted it with the conventional view that has dominated the management information systems (MIS) field since its inception. Part II, "Strategic Thrusts," described the five moves (differentiation, cost, innovation, growth, and alliance) constituting the theory of strategic thrusts and showed, through actual cases, how information technology is used to support or shape them. Part III, "Implementation," concerns itself with more mundane matters. This chapter and the next—"SIS Planning and Management: I" and "SIS Planning and Management: II"—deal with issues of immediate concern to practitioners: how to build strategic information system (SIS) vision and awareness, develop a method for discovering SIS opportunities, weave the strategic perspective on information technology into the enterprise's competitive strategy formulation process, and reorganize the enterprise's information management function to reflect the strategic viewpoint. The final chapter, "SIS Trends and Challenges," identifies some of the trends and challenges emerging as the use of information technology for strategic purposes diffuses from enterprise to enterprise, industry to industry, sector to sector, and country to country.

To prepare the ground for the growth of SIS vision and awareness (see Chapter 1), whether in the conventional organization lacking them or in the one desiring to strengthen these prerequisites for pursuing SIS opportunities and threats systematically, top management should affirm its belief in three principles. The first relates to the nature of the enterprise:

1. The general purpose of the firm is to organize the *use* of the resources at its disposal so that it can achieve its long-term profitability and growth goals.

The resources of the firm comprise its *material* (plant, equipment, land, raw materials, and other tangible things) and *human* (skilled, unskilled, clerical, technical, managerial, etc.) assets. Each resource can provide a variety of *services* to the firm, depending on how it is used. Two firms with exactly the same material and human resources may be notably different because of the services performed by these resources—that is, because of the ways top management has decided to use its resources.

The second principle covers the use of the firm's resources:

2. The range of possible *uses* of the resources at the firm's disposal is limited only by the experience, knowledge, and imagination of its employees.

As a corollary to Principle 2, it follows that even at full capacity, when all resources are employed, there exist an almost unlimited number of services these resources could perform but are not performing because management has opted for one particular resource-use configuration from the infinite set open to it. The mere magnitude of possibilities should stimulate an enterprising management group to research alternative uses of its resources; a different configuration might produce greater profit and growth than the current one.

It therefore pays to learn as much as possible about resources currently deployed and about their known alternative uses. Imaginative employees can, if properly motivated, be counted on to discover new uses for "dedicated" resources—materials, machines, or people—with which they are familiar. Some of these uses may promise greater benefits than those derived by the firm from its current deployment.

The third principle highlights the role of the firm's entrepreneurs, its agents of change:

3. Entrepreneurs are responsible for identifying new, productive *uses* of the resources at the firm's disposal.

The ideas of entrepreneurs bound the strategic-opportunity space open to the enterprising firm. Their contributions relate, in Edith Penrose's words, "to the introduction and acceptance on behalf of the firm of new ideas, particularly with respect to products, locations, and significant changes in technology, to the acquisition of new managerial personnel, to fundamental changes in the administrative organization of the firm, to the raising of capital, and to the making of plans for expansion, including the method of expansion."[1]

Entrepreneurs fall into two classes: garden variety and empire builders. The *garden variety*, according to Penrose, directs its talents

> toward the improvement of the quality of their products, the reduction of costs, the development of better technology, the extension of markets through better service to customers, and the introduction of new products in which they believe their firms have a *productive* or *distributive advantage*. They take pride in their organization, and from their point of view the "best" way to make profits is through the improvement and extension of the activities of this organization.[2] [Italics added.]

The *empire builders*, on the other hand, take delight not so much in garden-variety improvements as in radical departures from business as usual, reflected typically in the strategic thrusts of growth, alliance, and innovation. Empire builders seek opportunities to grow via vertical integration, to eliminate competitors by acquiring them, to build full-line businesses, and so on. (Nothing I have said should be construed as precluding the same person from providing entrepreneurial services, possessing strategic vision, or being part of the top management team.)

By accepting the three principles just discussed, the top management team affirms its commitment to change and to the agents of change, the firm's entrepreneurs. This commitment is a necessary condition for the development of SIS vision: it prepares the ground. SIS vision dictates *change*, envisioning as it does new *uses for information technology resources*—material or human, internal or external—as it charts the firm's strategic course.

"It is difficult to tell the short-sighted man how to get somewhere," the philosopher Wittgenstein observed, "because you can't say to him: 'Look at the church tower 10 miles away and go in that direction.' "³ But fitted with the proper glasses, even the short-sighted can discern possible paths to follow. The last six chapters, as it were, ground the strategic lenses—glasses are now available to see new uses for information technology—to exercise SIS vision.

THE SIS PLANNING PROCESS AT GTE DATA SERVICES

In 1983, members of the information systems planning function at GTE Data Services learned of the strategic perspective on information technology and of the theory of strategic thrusts. After acquiring a working knowledge of the concepts and feeling confident that top management accepted the principles just outlined, they decided to explore the new world of SIS opportunities systematically. The case study presented here (which appeared originally in *MIS Quarterly*)⁴ describes their success in developing and implementing an SIS planning process, a process aimed at introducing the strategic perspective throughout the enterprise and identifying SIS opportunities relevant to their business.

Description of GTE

GTE, a diversified, international telecommunications and electronics company with 185,000 employees and revenues over $14 billion [in 1984], provides local telephone service in 31 states, two Canadian provinces, and the Dominican Republic. . . . GTE Telenet runs a nationwide, packet-switched data communication network. In addition, GTE manufactures and markets a complete line of communication equipment, systems, and services, more than 6,000 types of Sylvania lamps and other lighting products, and precision metal, plastic, and ceramic materials used in electrical and electronic devices.

The largest business division, domestic telephone operations (TELOPS), contributes revenues of more than $9 billion and almost 90 percent of GTE's income [in 1984]. It consists of a corporate group, seven telephone companies, and a data services organization—GTE Data Services (GTEDS)—which provides information systems and services to the TELOPS units. Headquartered in Tampa, GTEDS has its own president, who is also a TELOPS corporate vice president. The methodology described below has been applied principally at TELOPS and the results discussed refer to this group. . . .

Overview of SIS Planning Process

GTEDS' information management (IM) planning staff realized the importance of the strategic perspective on information systems and took on the challenge of developing and implementing a planning process based on this point of view. They saw the task as two-fold:

1. Introduce management to this new perspective and secure its support.
2. Create a mechanism for generating and evaluating SIS proposals.

To accomplish these ends, they designed a five-phase SIS planning process (see Table 10–1) that moved from an initial dissemination of SIS ideas and identification of opportunities to a final acceptance by members of the TELOPS' senior management team. The last step in the process resulted in a portfolio of SIS applications (not described here for reasons of confidentiality) earmarked for implementation.

SIS Planning Process

In Phase A, the head of TELOPS' information management planning function introduced GTEDS' president to the SIS concept through a series of informal meetings and memoranda on the subject. The purpose here was to win top-level support for the project and approval for the next two phases.

In Phases B and C, GTEDS' information management plan-

Table 10–1   SIS Planning Process

Phase	Activity	Content	Purpose
A	Introduce IM chief executive to SIS concepts.	Overview of SIS concepts; cases of SIS applications in other companies.	Gain approval to proceed with SIS idea-generation meeting for IM group.
B	Conduct SIS idea–generation meeting for IM middle management.	Execute SIS idea-generation methodology; evaluate SIS ideas.	Test SIS idea-generation methodology; identify significant SIS ideas for executive consideration.
C	Conduct SIS idea–generation meeting for IM executives.	Execute SIS idea-generation methodology; evaluate SIS ideas.	Identify SIS ideas and evaluate these together with ideas from previous meeting.
D	Introduce top business executive to SIS concept.	Overview of SIS concept and some candidate SIS ideas for the business.	Gain approval to proceed with SIS idea-generation meeting for business planners.
E	Conduct SIS idea–generation meeting for corporate business planners.	Execute SIS idea-generation methodology; evaluate SIS ideas.	Identify SIS ideas and evaluate these together with ideas from previous meetings.

ning staff ran off-site idea-generation meetings aimed at developing the strategic perspective on information systems and identifying SIS opportunities. These sessions involved two groups of information systems professionals. In Phase B, participants were drawn from the data processing company's cadre of middle managers; in Phase C, attendees were the top information management executives within the local telephone companies and GTEDS.

The successful completion of Phases A–C led to a meeting (in Phase D) between GTEDS' president and TELOPS' top business executive. The latter was introduced to the SIS concept and told of the opportunities already discovered at the previous two brainstorming sessions. This meeting set the stage for Phase E, an SIS idea-generation meeting with TELOPS' corporate business planners, those responsible for initiating the business' strategic thrusts.

The idea-generation meetings, which occurred at Phases B, C, and E of the SIS planning process, consisted of seven explicit steps (see Table 10–2) designed to introduce the strategic perspective on information systems, stimulate the systematic search for SIS opportunities, and evaluate and select a set of projects expected to secure the greatest competitive advantage for the firm. A description of each of the steps follows.

Step 1. Present tutorial on competitive strategy and SIS. The tutorial was led by a consultant expert on the theory of strategic information systems. The tutorial emphasized the concepts of strategic targets and strategic thrusts and covered the role of information systems in supporting or shaping the competitive strategy of the firm. More importantly, it provided attendees with an analytical framework with which they could identify SIS opportunities and threats.

Step 2. Apply SIS concepts to actual cases. Following the tutorial, participants solidified their understanding of the concepts presented by analyzing a set of actual SIS microcases drawn from a variety of industries. Working through about 20 examples selected from a prepared list of 50, they learned how to identify strategic targets and thrusts.

Step 3. Review company's competitive position. This step acquainted participants with the competitive realities

Table 10–2 SIS Idea-Generation Meeting Steps

Step	Activity	Purpose
1	Present tutorial on competitive strategy and SIS.	Introduce the concepts of strategic thrusts, strategic targets, and competitive strategy.
2	Apply SIS concepts to actual cases.	Raise consciousness about SIS possibilities and their strategic thrusts and targets.
3	Review company's competitive position	Understand competitive position of the business and its strategies.
4	Brainstorm for SIS opportunities	Generate SIS ideas in small groups.
5	Discuss SIS opportunities	Eliminate duplication and condense SIS ideas.
6	Evaluate SIS opportunities	Evaluate competitive significance of SIS ideas.
7	Detail SIS blockbusters	Detail each SIS blockbuster idea, its competitive advantage, and key implementation issues.

facing the business. It was presented by the information management planning staff and covered such topics as markets, products, customers, suppliers, competitors, strengths, weaknesses, and business strategies. By understanding these elements, one is in a position to consider the question: "How can information technology be used to support or shape strategic thrusts aimed at the firm's stratetic targets?"

Step 4. Brainstorm for SIS opportunities.   In this step, the group divided into teams of 5–8 participants, and each brainstormed for different kinds of SIS opportunities. Some teams focused on leveraging existing information management assets, while others explored the possibility of creating new assets. Some concentrated on opportunities related to *suppliers* (providers of raw materials, capital, or labor) by addressing such questions as:

1. Can we use information systems to gain leverage over our suppliers? Improve our bargaining power? Reduce the supplier's bargaining power?
2. Can we use information systems to reduce buying costs? Reduce our labor costs? Reduce our supplier's costs?
3. Can we use information systems to identify alternative sources? To locate substitute products and services? To make versus to buy?
4. Can we use information systems to improve the quality of products and services we receive from our suppliers?

Other teams looked for SIS opportunities related to *customers* (those who retail, wholesale, warehouse, distribute, or use the firm's products) by responding to such questions as:

1. Can we use information systems to reduce our customers' telecommunications costs?
2. Can we use information systems to increase a customer's switching costs (make it difficult for the customer to change suppliers)?
3. Can we make our databases available to our customers?
4. Can we provide administrative support (billing, collection, inventory management, etc.) to our customers?
5. Can we use information systems to learn more about our customers and/or discover possible market niches?
6. Can we use information systems to help our customers increase their revenues?

And still other teams searched for SIS opportunities related to *competitors* by answering such questions as:

1. Can we use information systems to raise the entry cost of competitors into our markets?
2. Can we use information systems to differentiate our products and services?
3. Can we use information systems to make a preemptive strike (e.g., to offer something they can't because we have the data) against our competitors?
4. Can we use information systems to provide substitutes before the competition does?
5. Can we use information systems to improve or reduce distribution costs?
6. Can we use information systems to form joint ventures to allow entry into new markets?
7. Can we use information systems to match an existing competitor's offering?
8. Can we use a new information technology to establish a new market niche?
9. Can we use our knowledge of the information industry and markets to find new markets or better ways of doing business?

To aid in the development of an SIS idea, each team completed a short form describing the idea, the intended strategic target, the basic strategic thrust, and the specific competitive advantage. The ground rule in these SIS idea-generation sessions is that criticism or evaluation of ideas must be suppressed so that creativity is not inhibited or stifled in any way.

Step 5. Discuss SIS opportunities.   Each team reported its SIS ideas to the entire group, and a scribe posted them on a flip chart for all to see. Group discussion encouraged clarification, elimination of duplicate proposals, and identification of overlapping suggestions. But again, as in the previous step, criticism was prohibited.

Step 6. Evaluate SIS opportunities. The purpose here was to rate and rank each of the SIS proposals generated. Participants were to apply the following evaluative criteria when making their judgments:

- Degree of competitive advantage.
- Cost to develop and install.
- Feasibility (from technical and resource points of view).
- Risk (understood as the probability of reaping and sustaining the competitive advantage promised by the SIS idea).

Applying these criteria, SIS proposals were classed into four categories:

1. *Blockbuster* (potential for strategic dominance).
2. *Very high potential* (but not blockbuster).
3. *Moderate potential* (worthy of further consideration).
4. *Low potential* (not worthy of further consideration).

Step 7. Detail SIS blockbusters. Here the group concentrated on refining and recording the SIS blockbuster ideas. This refinement details the technology employed, customer benefits, competitive advantage, responsibilities, and implementation concerns that aid in the process of transforming the idea into reality.

Meeting dynamics. The SIS idea-generation meetings lasted for two full days. Each step took about two hours, with the exception of the tutorial and the exercise (Steps 1 and 2), which together needed about five hours from an outside consultant to convey the concepts. Step 4, the brainstorming session, unlike typical workshop breakouts whose effectiveness usually lasts between 45 and 90 minutes, required more time. In our meetings, the teams of 5–8 were very lively and needed a solid two hours to develop their ideas.

Results

Identification of SIS opportunities. Each of the three brainstorming meetings generated over 100 SIS ideas. At each meeting, about 10 were considered real winners. Many proposals overlapped across meetings, and there was consensus on the blockbuster suggestions. This consensus was fortunate since it validated the top ideas and built support and commitment for them from a variety of constituencies: corporate management, information management, and local telephone companies.

The SIS opportunities discovered by each group were combined after the final idea-generation meeting. Of the top 11 proposals, 6 were rated as blockbusters and 5 were classed as having very high potential. When one considers that most stories about the strategic use of information systems concern only one primary SIS idea, the process at GTE was prolific indeed. We would have scored our process a success had we uncovered 1 or 2 top ideas in this first pass, but instead we uncovered 11 worthy of implementation.

Impact on GTE.   The development of a strategic perspective on information systems and the specific ideas generated in the SIS planning process resulted in several major managerial changes at TELOPS. For the first time, members of top management focused their attention on SIS opportunities. They now believed that information systems could play a critical role in shaping business strategy. Proof of this came in management's immediate allocation of resources to implement the three best blockbuster ideas.

To ensure that their new strategic vision about the role of information systems was made part of the fabric of the organization and not just a passing fancy, top management elevated the information management function in the corporate hierarchy. They created senior information systems positions at headquarters and at the telephone operating companies. These senior positions report directly to the chief operating officer of the unit instead of to the chief financial officer as they did in the past. (The positions are very much like the chief information officer function [see Chapter 11] described by Synnott and Gruber)[5]. Information management has finally become an equal partner in setting the strategic direction of the company.

Executives at GTE's local telephone companies agreed to implement similar SIS planning processes in their operating units. These address the unique competitive environments, threats, and opportunities confronting each. The units also agreed to champion one of the original 11 SIS ideas.

To emphasize the importance TELOPS attaches to the strategic perspective on information systems, TELOPS' information management function formally added a new SIS strategy to its long-range plan, which previously focused only on operational improvements.

Impact on other GTE businesses.   TELOPS, GTE's largest division, was the first to implement the SIS planning process outlined above. Its success prompted other GTE units, in widely different competitive environments, to initiate similar projects.

The SIS planning process described above resulted in the identification of many ideas to provide GTE Telephone Operations with significant competitive advantage. Some SIS ideas require investment in new information-based assets, while others leverage existing information resources. The continued application of the SIS planning process within TELOPS will ensure that the idea pipeline is full and that quality ideas will be implemented. Beyond TELOPS, the methodology is being used by other GTE units to identify SIS opportunities. . . . It can also be used by other firms whose vision extends to using information systems as competitive weapons in their quest for advantage.

GETTING STARTED

GTE's success may be attributed, I believe, to two factors: (1) the turbulent external environment induced by the breakup of AT&T and the concomitant deregulation of the telecommunications industry by the U.S. government, and (2) GTEDS personnel who understood the strategic perspective on information technology and the theory of strategic thrusts, were in a position to support a program designed to uncover SIS opportunities, and had external as well as internal incentives to act.

A number of lessons can be derived from the GTE experience. It seems clear that members of three groups should possess SIS vision: top management, line management, and information management. Top management needs SIS vision because its task is to set the firm's strategic direction. Line management needs it because its functions are in closest contact with the firm's strategic targets. Information management needs it because it must assess the strategic significance of technologies and trends in information processing and telecommunications. Of course, the enterprise should be open to any suggestions for SIS applications. But, in general, the firm's SIS entrepreneurs will be drawn from the three groups just mentioned. They are in a position to see opportunities and to act upon them.

Suppose the firm forms a task force, with members drawn from these three groups, to investigate the possibilities of SIS systematically. What should the members of this team know? Essentially, they should be familiar with the firm's competitive strategy, its information system capabilities, and the strategic perspective on systems, which implies an awareness (conscious or unconscious) of the theory of strategic thrusts and the strategic option generator (see Chapter 4).

Knowing who should possess SIS vision and what they should be taught is relatively straightforward. But how the strategic perspective should be introduced is another matter. Should it come through the front door (top management), the side door (line management), or the back door (information management)? Should the messenger be a member of the organization, a consultant, or a vendor selling products that could be part of an SIS? Or should there be a messenger team composed of members of these groups? Clearly, there is no best path for all to follow. Everything depends on local conditions. Rather than give a set of general suggestions, I shall sketch a few actual situations that I'm familar with. These are cases in which ingredients of the strategic perspective on information technology entered the organizational bloodstream, triggering the development of SIS vision. While some examples recount programs created by vendors to aid their marketing effort—to make it, in a word, strategic—others describe efforts mounted by vendors' customers, the users of information technology.

A few, relatively large computer and telecommunication vendors have created programs to help their customers appreciate the value of using information technology for competitive purposes. These vendors sense in the emergence of SIS a good marketing opportunity to expand the range of possible applications for their products. Indeed, some have initiated marketing campaigns emphasizing the strategic use of information technology. Others have taken to merely couching their sales pitches for new hardware and software in terms of possible strategic use.

Any vendor moving in this last direction faces a number of daunting problems. First, its marketing team is usually neither equipped conceptually nor motivated by the proper incentives to grasp the competitive strategies of its current or prospective customers. Second, its customer contacts tend not to extend beyond technical personnnel in the information management group. In most instances, these are not members of the customer's strategic-movers-and-shakers clique. Third, vendors are in business to sell boxes. As many as possible. Once a firm has decided on the strategic thrust it wishes to follow, a vendor can discuss the possibility of using its technology to support or shape it. But should the vendor be offering advice on which thrust to follow or conducting strategic planning sessions for the customer? Most customers, I believe, wouldn't welcome this kind of help. Finally, if a vendor proposes a strategic solution that promises competitive advantage to Company A, what will prevent the vendor from meeting the next day with A's rivals (at separate sites, one would hope) to sell the same solution with the same promise, requiring of course the vendor's hardware, software, or knowhow? With strategically savvy customers sensitive to this problem, it certainly presents vendors with a new selling challenge, one different from the good old days when all the account rep needed to do for a sale was to point out to the head of data processing that automating payroll might be a good idea.

Despite these hurdles, some vendors realize the need to inform their own staffs about the strategic perspective on information technology and have made some preliminary moves to satisfy it. One computer manufacturer introduced the strategic perspective on information systems as a part of its three-day account manager conferences. These are held four or five times a year for 15–20 selected, high-performing sales personnel. Outsiders are invited to give presentations along with the firm's senior executives. Among recent topics covered were "The Microcomputer Perspective," "Managing End-User Computing," "A New Age in Information Systems," and "Strategic Information Systems." During the SIS session, discussion centered on possibilities for particular accounts and steps the vendor must take to encourage its clients to develop SIS vision.

In cases like this, vendors of products related to SIS (e.g., computer manufacturers, software producers, telecommunication suppliers) who understand the strategic perspective on information technology may provide the message directly to their customers. Or they may arrange for their customers to hear it, not from their mouths but from the voice of an independent presenter who has no ties to the vendor. From a vendor's point of view, this is value-added marketing, aimed at differentiating the firm's product from those of the competition. From the customer's standpoint, it is a benefit that can result in a definite advantage. Both parties are therefore ideal candidates to participate in the dissemination of SIS vision.

Other vendors conduct multiday programs for their marketing teams, dealing exclusively with the strategic use of information technology. Such programs delve into the meaning of terms such as *competitive advantage* and *competitive strategy* and initiate the process of getting the marketers up to speed on strategic issues occupying their customers.

In addition, some vendors believe they can overcome the

barriers mentioned above. They have launched programs to help their customers directly, offering them group or individual sessions developed by the vendor's internal marketing/educational/consulting staff on the subject of the strategic use of information technology. While such engagements may provoke credibility questions, there are ways to alleviate customer suspicions on this sticky point. One vendor, for example, offers mixed meetings, with external consultants complementing the vendor's experts in this area.

On the user (customer) side, enterprises follow a variety of paths. The Atlantic Richfield Company (ARCO) moved to develop its SIS vision without any vendor prompting. Under a new corporate mandate to encourage "intrapreneurship"—that is, internal entrepreneurial activities—the information management group created a unique educational program.

Initiated in 1983, it was a 10-day residential program, run about eight times a year, with an assorted staff of internal and external speakers. The program encouraged interaction, emphasized the team approach, and drew on company-developed case studies. Originally targeted for the firm's over 1,000 information processing professionals, it planned to extend its audience to the end-user community as well.

Limited to 20–25 attendees, each session attempted to satisfy the seminar's ambitious objectives, which included the following:

- Provide an opportunity for computing professionals to increase their business awareness and strategic approach to systems solutions.
- Provide technology updates from a company perspective.
- Establish a climate where appropriate technical innovation and risk is encouraged.
- Provide an opportunity for members of different operating units to learn about each other and each other's environment.

Sessions included outside experts presenting two- to four-hour modules on "Technology Directions," "Telecommunications:

Connecting People, Places, and Things," "The Changing Office," "Risk and Creativity," "Information System Accountability," "Managing the New Environment," and "Strategic Information Systems."

At the end of one SIS session, after a morning of theory and workshops, two participants rushed off before lunch to make a telephone call to the firm's executive vice president, the person who had been encouraging intrapreneurs to express their ideas across departmental boundaries or organizational levels. These two systems analysts saw an opportunity to develop an SIS that they believed could have a significant competitive impact on the firm's operations.

Unfortunately, this imaginative, innovative program terminated in 1985 when ARCO underwent a major restructuring necessitated by the precipitous fall in oil prices. Data processing expenditures dropped from $340 million in 1985 to $250 million in 1987; about 400 information systems people left the firm.[6]

Other firms, which run annual or semiannual conferences for their information management staffs, may include an SIS module among the presentations. These meetings often involve, for the first time, noninformation systems line managers who have been invited precisely so that they will be exposed to the new strategic message, usually delivered by outside specialists. As a result of such gatherings, follow-up sessions may be scheduled with business units that have caught the SIS bug.

In my experience, most enterprises have found it difficult to mobilize their troops as successfully as GTE to attack the SIS challenges before them. Whether the barriers be conceptual, political, personal, or organizational (not to mention the ever-present external forces conspiring to torpedo even the best-intentioned efforts), few firms have organized their resources to handle the opportunities and threats posed by the strategic use of information technology.

To appreciate the complexities involved, consider the case of a foreign financial services conglomerate with banking, insurance, leasing, and real estate divisions. This company has grown through acquisitions rather than internal development. After a rapid expansion, it created senior corporate vice presidencies in marketing, strategic planning, and technology, filling these with new blood drawn from outside the firm.

The major computer vendor for this company was in the process of developing an SIS program for its large users. The program manager persuaded the MIS head from the insurance division, the largest in the conglomerate, that adopting a strategic perspective on information technology was essential for his career advancement, the long-term success of his unit, and the conglomerate—in that order. The program manager then arranged a meeting, with the approval of the vendor's account representative servicing the conglomerate (a necessary condition for proceeding), to discuss details. Participants included the MIS head, the vice president for corporate technology, the MIS head from a small, newly acquired insurance company, and the vendor's program manager and account rep. Conducted by a U.S.-based consultant (under contract with the vendor) who specializes in the strategic use of information technology, the informal session covered the strategic perspective and a framework for identifying SIS opportunities. It also explored the relevance of these subjects for other units within the conglomerate.

The technology vice president decided that these subjects were indeed relevant and suggested that a meeting be held at the vendor's educational center. Participants would include those who had attended the initial session plus the newly appointed vice presidents of corporate marketing and strategic planning, together with MIS heads from other divisions.

The meeting, again conducted by the outside consultant, presented the new strategic viewpoint and ran through some cases in which competitive advantage was gained through the use of computer and telecommunication applications. To improve understanding of the ideas introduced, participants were asked to apply the concepts to a familiar application. The MIS head from one of the divisions began by describing a system currently under development. He believed it had great strategic importance. About halfway through the presentation, the vice president for strategic planning rose and said that the discussion had gone far enough. He didn't want to continue with the present people in the room.

The group sat in stunned silence. The vice president, along with other participants, had been briefed on the agenda at a dinner arranged by the vendor the evening before. He raised no objections at that time. But now he was, in effect, questioning the reason for the meeting. This, to say the least, concerned the vendor's sales rep. What had she got herself into by agreeing to serve as a test site for this new program? The program manager felt equally ill at ease, and the consultant didn't know whether to leave the room or change the subject gracefully. Eventually he asked the vice president of strategic planning for some suggestions on how to proceed. Did he want the vendor's group and the consultant to leave? "Not at all," came the instant reply. Rather, he wanted the discussion closed. Why? Because he mistrusted some of the other participants. He didn't want them to know what the division developing the SIS was up to.

Could this reaction have been anticipated? Not on the basis of the vice president's behavior the night before, so what was going on here? The objection, it was learned subsequently, was just another ploy in an ongoing political battle between the vice president for strategic planning and the vice president for corporate technology, one of the organizers of the meeting. In the months that followed, work proceeded at the local level, without the participation of corporate strategic planning.

In other situations, the success of a project may be clouded by different factors. Take the case of the packaging company that sent its general manager, chief financial officer, and head of information systems (IS) (who reports to the chief financial officer) to a two-week course on information management, which included a module on the strategic use of information technology. They left the course enthusiastic about the SIS concept, eager to explore possibilities. The head of IS was assigned the task of organizing an SIS project. On the job less than a year, he complained to an outside consultant of being understaffed, unable to plan, and deeply involved in converting from Vendor X to Vendor Y. He noted that during the last three years, "we've cut three times. We don't want to fail on this project. Large firms can win some and lose some; things will balance out. But we can't afford that luxury. We're lean and we're looking for the big bang."[7] I have found that firms like this, obsessed with the big bang, with only the blockbuster possibilities, often fail to provide environments conducive to SIS search.

Contrast this case with that of a vertically integrated European firm. For the past four years, it had been putting its information processing activities in order, replacing ancient applications with new ones and installing a new generation of computers on which to run them. Its new data processing head attended a Society for Information Management meeting with one of the company's marketing directors, heard about the strategic use of information technology, and saw a number of SIS windows of opportunity to be exploited if acted on expeditiously. With its competitors still far behind technologically and the company itself endowed with enlightened senior executives, prospects for a successful SIS planning and management effort here were certainly superior to those facing the packaging company mentioned above.

Is it difficult to introduce the strategic perspective on information technology into the mainstream of an organization? Generally speaking, yes. Nevertheless, a growing number of firms are engaging in this pursuit, prompted by the rewards emanating from the new perspective or by the fear that competitors will gain an information edge. Whatever the motive, new planning processes and management vision are required.

NOTES

1. Edith Penrose, *The Theory of the Growth of the Firm* (Oxford, Eng.: Basil Blackwell, 1959), p. 31, note.

2. Ibid., p. 39.

3. Ludwig Wittgenstein, *Culture and Value,* trans. Peter Winch (Chicago: University of Chicago, 1980).

4. Nick Rackoff, Charles Wiseman, and Al Ullrich, "Information Systems for Competitive Advantage: Implementation of a Planning Process," *MIS Quarterly,* December 1985.

5. William Synnott and William Gruber, *Information Resource Management: Opportunities and Strategies* (New York: John Wiley & Sons, 1981).

6. Juli Cortino, "Arco's MIS Gets Maximum Mileage out of Every Dollar," *InformationWeek,* June 15, 1987.

7. Personal communication.

11

SIS Planning and Management: II

DEVELOPING COMPETITIVE STRATEGY

Strategic information systems (SIS) planning and management questions arise when one thinks about how to institutionalize the new strategic perspective on information technology, to weave it into the fabric of existing organizational activities. We need to explore how the search for SIS opportunities and threats should be combined with the enterprise's process for developing competitive strategy and how the conventional management information systems (MIS) department should adapt to meet the new demands the strategic perspective places upon it.

The process of developing a competitive strategy involves three steps: (1) assessing current policies and position, (2) determining environmental factors affecting the business, and (3) formulating a strategy to meet anticipated challenges over the planning period. The systematic search for SIS should be conducted within this context. Only then can the business unit be sure that it has comprehensively explored all options for using information technology strategically. At each step in the process, SIS opportunities may be uncovered.

Step 1

The competitive strategy planning process, as Derek Abell and others suggest,[1] begins in Step 1 above by establishing a working definition of the unit's business, which captures the current scope of its activities and shows how it differentiates itself across segments and from its competitors. By analyzing the unit's products and markets, one can pin down scope in terms of customer groups targeted, customer needs satisfied, and technologies employed.

For example, a manufacturer of automatic teller machines (ATMs) may define its business as the production, distribution, and maintenance of ATMs that:

- Permit cash withdrawals, deposits, and checking/saving account transfers (customer needs).

- Serve banks in the United States and Canada (customer groups).
- Use 5-line display terminals with numerical keys linked via telecommunication channels to a mainframe computer (technologies employed).

Another manufacturer may decide on a different definition by varying the values of the three scope variables. It may, for example, provide ATMs for the international marketplace and not limit itself to banks. Second, it may supplement the services offered at the machine to include stock market quotations, weather reports, stock and money fund transactions, and the like. Or it may offer a technologically unique product with voice response and activation capabilities.

With a working definition of the business, one can specify the product network (industry, value chain) associated with it and identify the firm's strategic targets (i.e., its suppliers, channels, customers, and rivals) that its thrusts (i.e., differentiation, cost, innovation, growth, and alliance) aim at. Strategists, it should be noted, tend to follow the "ready-aim-fire" rule rather than the more immediately satisfying "ready-fire-aim" command others often issue.

Good aim presupposes an understanding of the strengths and weaknesses of strategic targets, the threats and opportunities posed, and the firm's strategies to deal with them. This can only be acquired through careful analysis performed prior to the fashioning of strategic thrusts.

Supplier analysis.   By examining the firm's product network, the analyst can derive a list of suppliers. Items purchased should then be classified according to their *profit impact* and *supply risk*. An item may be classed as having high profit impact if, for instance, it is purchased in large quantity, its cost represents a sizable fraction of the total cost of purchased items, and its presence enhances the quality and growth prospects of the firm's product. It may be classed as having high supply risk if, for example, its availability is limited, few concerns offer it, demand from competitors who need it is high, and substitutes are expensive.

Using this schema, the firm can distinguish four categories of purchased items (see Figure 11–1): *strategic* (high profit impact, high supply risk), *bottleneck* (low profit impact, high supply risk), *leverage* (high profit impact, low supply risk), and *noncritical* (low profit impact, low supply risk).

After classifying purchased items in terms such as the above, the firm can calculate its bargaining power vis-à-vis its suppliers, category by category, by weighing factors such as the following:[2]

- Capacity utilization (if supplier's capacity is underutilized, its bargaining power may be diminished).
- Break-even points (if Supplier A's break-even point is set at 60 percent of capacity and B's at 75 percent, negotiations with A may be more difficult than with B).
- Product differentiation (if supplier's product is highly differentiated, its bargaining powers may be quite high).
- Volume purchase (if the firm purchases large volumes of a

Figure 11–1   Categories of Purchased Items

	Profit Impact	
	High	Low
High (Supply Risk)	Strategic	Bottleneck
Low (Supply Risk)	Leverage	Noncritical

supplier's product, the firm's bargaining power may provide it with the leverage it needs to force a price reduction). Information impactedness (if the firm is ignorant about the supplier's activities and product, the latter may act opportunistically and therefore wield great bargaining power over the firm).

Rating its strength over against suppliers with respect to a particular item, the firm can, as Peter Kraljic suggests, "identify areas of opportunity or vulnerability, assess supply risks, and derive basic *strategic thrusts* for these items."[3] [Italics added.] At this point in the supplier analysis process, the firm should explore SIS opportunities, using the strategic option generator (see Chapter 4).

Customer (including channel) analysis.   By examining the firm's product network, the analyst can also identify buyers of its products. These buyers should be sorted into segments, each representing a well-defined set of customer characteristics. The firm's strategic marketers then need to address, for each segment, questions like the following:

Why do customers buy?

When do they buy?

How much do they purchase?

Who makes the purchasing decision?

What information do customers require before purchasing?

Do they require any technical services? Educational services? Postsale services?

How do they use the product?

What can they tell us about competitive products?

Why should they select our product rather our rival's?

What factors may change the customer's purchasing behavior?

Where do they stand on price-quality trade-offs?

How loyal are they?

Will they switch from a rival's product to ours?

Can they make the product we're offering?

How much do they know about our activities?

These questions in no way exhaust the possibilities. Customer analysis strives to establish a reliable base of information for shaping strategic initiatives. After performing a customer analysis, the firm should be in a good position to evaluate its bargaining power relative to each of its customer groups and to devise strategic thrusts beamed at them. As in the supplier analysis process, the firm should at this point explore SIS opportunities, using the strategic option generator together with the customer resource life cycle model developed by Ives and Learmonth (see Chapter 5).

Rival analysis. Rivals should be appraised comparatively—the firm versus one or more rivals pursuing similar strategies—along dimensions such as the following:

- *Function:* R&D, manufacturing, marketing, distribution, information, finance, sales, service.
- *Organization:* Flat versus hierarchical, centralized versus decentralized, independent versus business unit of a conglomerate.
- *Culture:* Beliefs and expectations about innovation, decision making, exchange of ideas, and the like.
- *Human resources:* Skills and experience of top management, technical staff, and so forth.
- *Product:* Quality versus price, wide versus narrow line, differentiated versus standardized, and so on.

After rating each factor (e.g., Is the rival in an inferior, superior, or equal position vis-à-vis the firm with respect to R&D capabilities, distribution channel strength, product quality, etc.?), the firm should ascertain the source (if any) of the advantage or disadvantage.

Strategists may, from time to time, find it illuminating to identify *empathetically* with selected rivals, to imagine what it would be like to be in their position. Supported by data drawn from a *strategic intelligence system*—which presumably represents the distillate of annual reports, Securities and Exchange Commission documents, newspaper clippings, magazine articles, product comparisons, industry journals, consultant's studies, patent files, reports from suppliers, customers, other competitors, internal staff members, informal comments, and the like—the imaginative strategist can piece together a definition of the rival's business, a statement of its policies in relation to its strategic targets, and a summary of its main strategic thrusts. This imagined world, consistent with the available empirical data, can be the starting point for a number of strategic probes on such subjects as possible responses of the rival to the firm's new offerings, to price changes, to new customer services, and to new alliances.

The strategic intelligence report should also include a new section for most enterprises: the use of information technology by strategic targets. This would involve gathering data on technological capabilities, types of systems, networks, backlogs, and so forth. This kind of strategic intelligence is important for several reasons. First, it uncovers opportunities for using information technology to serve competitive-advantage objectives. For example, if certain customers are not as well endowed with information technology resources as others, it may pay the enterprise to explore ways it can be of assistance, perhaps using the customer resource life cycle as a means of discovering what might be of value.

There are other reasons for investing in strategic intelligence systems sensitive to a target's use of information technology. Such systems can provide valuable data relevant to the creation of an SIS, data that could help the enterprise (1) design an SIS to take advantage of, in some instances, the target's weaknesses and, in others, its strengths or (2) anticipate possible responses by targets to the contemplated SIS. (See "Competitive Dynamics" in Chapter 12.)

Some strategic thrusts, for example, attempt to establish first-mover advantages. These strategic moves, known affectionately as *preemptive strikes,* often carry with them great risk and reward. Strategists need to consider (1) the "response lag" question (How long will it take rivals to respond to the strike?) and (2) the "response barrier" question (What factors are likely to slow or delay the response?). Answers to these questions bear directly on the duration, vulnerability, and value that attach to any competitive advantage derived from the thrust (see Chapter 3).

Preemptive strikes—which could take the form of strategic differentiation, cost, innovation, growth, or alliance thrusts— may occur at any point on the firm's product network. According to Ian MacMillan, "What is important is the impact of preempting the 'prime' positions [on the product net]: It is a common phenomenon that a relatively small proportion of customers, suppliers, distributors, market segments, key accounts, or geographic positions (and so on) account for a disproportionately large proportion of total revenues in a market."[4] MacMillan classes preemptive opportunities into five areas: *supply systems* (e.g., securing access to specially produced containers in limited supply, controlling the supply pipeline), *product* (e.g., creating new product lines, establishing the dominant design for a product), *production systems* (e.g., expanding capacity ahead of rivals, forming alliances with dominant suppliers), *customers* (e.g., capturing large accounts, building brand awareness), and *distribution and service systems* (e.g., occupying prime retail outlets, controlling the distribution pipeline).

In each of these five areas, preemptive strikes may be launched that take advantage of either the target's weaknesses or its strengths. For example, the enterprise may exploit a rival's weakness by moving to reshape the infrastructure (by creating a new supply system or establishing a radically new service system), occupy prime positions on the product net, or secure critical skills for the production/distribution of the firm's product. Alternatively, it may attempt to exploit a rival's strength by devising moves to force the rival to cannibalize its existing products (if it is to respond effectively); radically change its image, tradition, or strategy; or sacrifice a major investment.

"In all but the most stagnant industries," MacMillan claims, "the success of preemptive moves tends to have a limited life span, and the more dynamic the industry, the shorter the life span."[5] Since it is clearly unrealistic to expect permanent benefits from a preemptive move, the *response lag* (the time it takes competitors to overcome the first mover's advantage) becomes an "important factor to take into account when formulating a preemptive move."[6]

What then are the *response barriers* determining response lag? It depends on the strategic thrust. If the thrust directly attacks a rival's product or aims at the heart of an opponent's strategy, the barriers to response will be low and the response lag may be low. But suppose, on the other hand, that the thrust forces the rival to cannibalize an existing product or, better, to reorganize its organization in order to respond. In this case, there clearly will be high barriers, and the response lag may be substantial. Such a preemptive strategic thrust with an anticipated long response lag is every strategist's dream. A strategic intelligence system that gathers data on response barriers and possible response lags is therefore a valuable corporate asset. Its value to the firm that uses information technology to support or shape its strategic thrusts would be all the greater if it contained data on response barriers related to information technology, as well as the more familiar political, organizational, and other barriers that might inhibit the strategic target's reaction to an SIS thrust.

As more attack-counterattack scenarios unfold in competitive arenas in which information technology has been used to advantage, the necessity for collecting such data can no longer be avoided (see Chapter 12). Knowledge of the rival's organization, culture, human resources, and expected responses to strategic thrusts increases the chances of designing a thrust to exploit the rival's weaknesses and gain an edge for the firm. Just as the firm should explore SIS opportunities in supplier and customer analyses when strategic thrusts are considered, it should do the same in rival analysis, again with the aid of the strategic option generator.

Step 2

After assessing current policies and position in Step 1 of the competitive strategy development process, the strategist should in Step 2 forecast trends in environmental variables (economic, social, political, demographic, and governmental) affecting the firm's operations. This process, too, should stimulate the search for SIS openings. A trend of increased governmental regulation may prompt the design of an information system to cut through the bureaucratic morass slowing the introduction of new products.

Alternatively, an *industry analysis* may reveal SIS opportunities. By studying the $4 billion fragmented junkyard (i.e., automotive salvage) industry, for example, an analyst may uncover consolidation opportunities. The industry already uses computers to handle inventory, to aid in purchase decisions made at salvage auctions, and to prevent loss of sales because salespeople don't know whether a part is in stock.

An entrepreneurial firm may discover an opportunity to build a national service company to stock, locate, and deliver used parts to any U.S. city within 24 hours. Insurance adjusters who make 50 to 70 million requests a year for parts would certainly be eager customers for such a service, a service that could never become operational without information systems.

Step 3

After completing Steps 1 and 2, the firm constructs, in Step 3, strategic programs to exploit its strengths or the weaknesses of its rivals, to defend against expected environmental threats and anticipated moves of competitors, and so on. Again, by examining these strategic programs, the enterprising firm may find occasions to use information systems to support or shape strategic thrusts associated with them.

Several conclusions follow from the above discussion. First, the systematic search for SIS opportunities should be conducted within the context of competitive strategy development. Only then can the business unit be sure that it has canvassed all options. Second, the hunt for SIS opportunities and threats demands the active participation of *information management* professionals. Creating advantages based on information technology consumes scarce resources, so it is best to engage the professionals as early and as intensively as possible. In my experience, the rewards have invariably exceeded the costs. Third, the implementation of competitive strategies supported or shaped by any but the most primitive information systems requires close coordination between the business and technology groups. In addition, to avoid misallocations of resources, mistakes in setting priorities, and delays in systems delivery that may well jeopardize its competitive position, the business unit should synchronize its strategy with the information management group's *information systems plan*. To achieve this kind of alignment is usually not a perfunctory matter. The business unit often must take measures to reduce the noise levels that have for years inhibited communication between line and information system managers. This book, I hope, can be of some help in overcoming these communication problems, as it speaks in a language easily grasped by both groups.

MANAGING INFORMATION SYSTEMS STRATEGICALLY

The existence of SIS, a new variety of information system, should inspire the firm's *information management* (IM) function—today comprising not only computer operations but telecommunications and office automation as well—to reexamine its organizational obligations. Should IM be responsible for SIS identification and development? Should IM create a new group to handle SIS matters? Are new personnel attuned to the strategic perspective needed? If so, from where should they be recruited? Must IM change its approach to information systems planning (assuming it follows one) because of the emergence of SIS? These and similar questions should be addressed by top managers of the firm and the IM function once they have assimilated the strategic perspective on information technology. The following discussion should aid their deliberations. It covers eight areas within which questions such as the above may be tackled: redefining the IM business, reorganizing the IM function, information systems planning, linking competitive strategy with the information systems plan, market research, research and development, and the chief information officer.

Redefining the IM Business

To a large extent, the perspective one adopts on information technology predetermines not only what information systems are countenanced but also one's view of the IM function itself. In this section, I shall point out some of the organizational consequences of seeing the world through conventional glasses and show how the strategic perspective offers, at least for planning purposes, a viable alternative.

The conventional viewpoint, perhaps best represented by IBM's now classical guidelines for managing the IM function,[7] recommends that one

> analyze the management of the information resource from the enterprise or general management view. During this analysis, the guiding principle should be that data can be shared, that many demands are made of the data processing organization to produce applications, and that resources are limited.
>
> General management is concerned with *planning for and controlling* the data resource. Therefore, the IRM review should concentrate on recommending a *planning and control* function that will maximize the use of the resource, and insure that the recommended information architecture is implemented expeditiously.[8] [Italics added.]

IBM groups IM activities, when viewed as a business, under three basic processes, reflecting Robert Anthony's planning and control paradigm (see Chapter 2):

Strategic (e.g., information systems [I/S] strategic planning and control, architecture definition).

Tactical (e.g., data planning, systems planning).

Operational (e.g., project scheduling, change control).

To handle this "holy trinity," IBM recommends structuring the IM organization into four functional groups:

Data and application planning and control (e.g., I/S architecture, standards).

Data administration (e.g., logical data design, backup).

Application development (e.g., maintenance projects, information center).

Data processing and communications (e.g., networking, security).

IBM believes that its view of the IM function is "useful in analyzing the organizational and personnel skills necessary to properly manage, that is, *plan and control,* the information resource and data processing function."[9] [Italics added.]

As the above sketch suggests, the conventional perspective on information systems leads to a conventional view of the IM function. Just as the former focuses on conventional systems tied to the firm's planning and control processes, the latter (consistently enough) concentrates on IM planning and control processes intended to manage the firm's data resources efficiently.

If, as IBM claims, "general management is concerned with planning for and controlling the data resource,"[10] then shouldn't IM management also be concerned? Shouldn't it organize its activities according to technical specialties (such as those mentioned above) related directly to the resource to be planned for and controlled?

Perhaps. But it is not at all clear that general management's primary IM concern should be with the planning and control of the firm's data resources. In some enterprises, it may be; in others, perhaps not. Since it is obviously an open question, why should the IM function, a priori, organize itself and conceptualize its responsibilities in planning and control terms? Moreover, the planning and control mentality—which seems to characterize best the minds of the firm's bean counters rather than the thoughts of its entrepreneurs—reflects a passive, reactive, bookkeeping attitude. Bean counters plan and control. Entrepreneurs assume the risks associated with strategic thrusts.

To encourage the discovery and implementation of SIS opportunities, IM needs to redefine its business from the strategic perspective. It needs to emphasize its products, customer groups, and customer needs as much as, if not more than, its technology and planning and control processes. This done, IM should redefine its mission, at least for planning purposes, along customer and product line dimensions rather than along the conventional technical axis. In sum, I am proposing that IM needs to alter its management perspective to see itself as running a multidivisional, product-oriented business instead of operating a vertically integrated, technology-driven company.

Reorganizing the IM Function

To conceive of how the strategic perspective on IM might be implemented organizationally, assume that MIS, management support systems (MSS), and SIS constitute product lines. These might be folded under an IM divisional head for information systems. The directors of MIS, MSS, and SIS would then be responsible for defining their "IM business units" in terms of customer groups served, customer needs satisfied, technologies employed, and so on. Each unit would organize itself into functional departments suitable to its product line and would develop strategies and programs to deal with its various constituencies. It would be no more surprising to find different cultures, organizational patterns, or kinds of personnel in each of these units than it would to discover such differences in any three businesses with products meeting different customer needs or supplying different market segments, yet, in some cases, sharing technology. (See "Chief Information Officer" section below.)

Information Systems Planning

Narrowly defined, the term *information systems planning* signifies the planning required to develop a single computer application. This might involve such activities as defining the requirements of the application, designing the program, and allocating the proper resources for development. But the term has a wider sense in which it means the planning undertaken by an organization when it seeks to determine its information systems requirements *globally* and *systematically* so that it can prepare to meet its short- and long-term needs. I use the term here in the latter sense.

An information systems planning *methodology* is a valuable tool that an organization can use when conducting its study. A *general-purpose planning methodology* attempts to identify all the information system application opportunities that would satisfy the firm's needs; a *special-purpose methodology* focuses on particular kinds of information systems.

The two best-known conventional information systems planning methodologies developed over the past 20 years are IBM's *business systems planning* (BSP) and MIT's *critical success factors* (CSF). BSP purports to be a general-purpose approach, emphasizing MIS. But it explicitly excludes the systematic search for SIS opportunities. (See the Appendix to Chapter 2 for more details on this topic.) CSF dedicates itself to the discovery of MSS—that is, decision support and executive information systems.

Extending now the proposal advanced in the last section, I suggest that the IM business units responsible for information systems adopt methodologies suited to their missions. The MIS group might use BSP, while the MSS group employs CSF.

Planning for SIS, on the other hand, requires a joint effort on the part of line or top management and the staff of the SIS unit, as it did in the GTE case presented in Chapter 10. It should be an integral part of the firm's competitive strategy development process as sketched in the first section of this chapter. If no formal process exists, the joint team should gather enough data on the firm's suppliers, customers, rivals, products, and the like, so that it can understand the current strategic directions and what to expect in the future. SIS staff members could, among other things, contribute assessments of the information system capabilities of the firm's strategic targets and forecasts of trends in the information processing industry.

Linking Competitive Strategy with the Information Systems Plan

Following the line just proposed leads to a solution of the perennially vexing problem confronting most enterprises: how to link the firm's competitive strategy with the IM group's information systems plan.[11] Linking, aligning, or fitting the strategy with the plan, I suggest, depends primarily on identifying current SIS and future SIS opportunities and threats. The SIS concept provides the key to unlocking the linkage mystery (see Figure 11–2).

Figure 11–2   Linking Competitive Strategy (CS) with the Information Systems Plan (ISP) via SIS

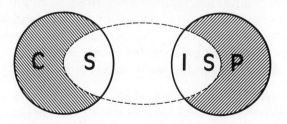

This is an operational solution to the linkage problem. It doesn't require an abstract mapping, as suggested by some, of the firm's mission, objectives, and strategies onto the information management group's counterpart mission, objectives, and strategies (see Chapter 2). Rather, it proposes a specific, concrete procedure for forging the link: conduct a systematic study to discover the set of current SIS and future SIS possibilities. If this set is empty, there is no need for linkage. If not, whatever alignment is required should be determined by the enterprise's current and proposed strategic uses of information technology. By definition, these support or shape the enterprise's competitive strategy. If the information systems plan is not aligned with the competitive strategy, the latter would be at risk, an untenable position. Hence the linkage imperative.

Market Research

For most MIS and MSS applications, conventional methods for ascertaining system requirements from the user population—the customers, in the language of marketing—should be followed. But for the design of an SIS affecting competitive advantage relations among the firm's strategic targets, stricter standards of user acceptance should be observed, especially if the SIS is intended to support a developer's differentiation thrust by providing a new value-added service to the customer.

Consider, for example, the high-technology firm with a prototype electronic service designed to help its customers gain competitive advantage through the use of the vendor's technology. Conventional requirements analysis might ask about usage patterns, baud rates, design of screens, and so on. But answers to such questions, while important for the system development effort, are patently irrelevant from a strategic point of view. What the vendor really needs is a process to:

- Determine customer reaction to the new service concept.
- Assess customer need for and use of the service.
- Select appropriate targeting strategies.

- Obtain customer reaction to proposed pricing for the service.
- Evaluate customer awareness of competing services (if any).

The tools of independent market research offer a promising approach to resolving these issues. Once a sample representing the target universe is selected, professional interviewers could meet individually with key decision makers from the sample population to explore their views on the contemplated service. The interviews would be semistructured—that is, based on a detailed topic guide covering the main areas of interest but open enough so that the interviewer could depart from the script when appropriate. In addition, a number of focus group sessions might be conducted to provide a better understanding of the issues of concern to customers and to develop a frame of reference for their perceptions of the new service.

Research and Development (R&D)

Most large information management groups have specialists to track, forecast, and assess new and emerging technologies that might be of relevance to the enterprise. In practice, these technological soothsayers usually confine their work to reviewing new hardware and software emerging from the firm's primary computer and telecommunication vendors or reading the reports of outside specialists on specific technological developments.

While such activities are not wasted effort, more needs to be done if the firm desires to be an SIS leader. Just as a company with competitive advantages achieved through the development of innovative products and manufacturing processes might have a research and development center dedicated to discovering such products and processes, the SIS advanced guard must also invest in SIS R&D. This involves not only scouting for new information technologies but also building and testing prototype SIS applications, working closely with

technology vendors to get first crack at emerging new products, and establishing close ties with strategic targets that
might contribute to the development or use of an SIS.

While few firms have had the foresight to invest in SIS
R&D, some, such as Fidelity Investors Corporation (see Chapter 8), have actually incorporated subsidiaries dedicated to implementing new SIS, either from existing or new technologies.
When a promising project requiring new technology is investigated, Fidelity's R&D unit follows a standard procedure. It
establishes a game plan for talking to vendors offering the technology, invites vendors and key line managers from Fidelity's
business units to a series of question and answer sessions, and,
as a result of data gleaned from these meetings, draws up a
preliminary list of vendors, solicits proposals, selects a vendor,
brings the technology into the lab for testing, and decides to
either implement or reject the application.[12]

The Chief Information Officer

In the early 80s, just as the consumer price index peaked in
the United States, a new acronym, CIO, entered the management lexicon. Short for chief information officer, a title that to
jaded observers reflected perfectly the inflationary age in
which we lived, the term *CIO* referred to the top executive
responsible for managing the firm's information resources,
taken to comprise everything from computer systems and telecommunication networks to mailroom and reproduction facilities.

Since its introduction, more and more heads of the information management function (directors or vice presidents of data
processing, MIS, or information systems and services) started
calling themselves CIOs. Should we understand this trend as
signifying something more than merely a name change? Or
should we take it as analogous to the movements that transformed janitors into building superintendents and garbagemen
into sanitation workers?

The emergence of the CIO position represents an important

development in the evolution of the information management function. But not everyone who claims the title deserves to be called a CIO. To separate the CIOs from the would-be CIOs, one should administer the following test:

1. Is the purported CIO a member of the firm's senior management (chief financial officer, chief operating officer, et al.) group reporting to the chief executive officer?
2. Did senior management create the CIO position because of its growing awareness of the strategic use of information technology, its realization that this technology can help the firm gain or maintain its competitive advantage or reduce a rival's edge?

When the answer to both questions is yes, count the person as a CIO; if not, label the title holder a potential CIO. To become CIOs, potential CIOs need to be elevated into the enterprise's senior management group or to raise awareness among group members of the strategic use of information technology so that it can be used (if appropriate) to support or shape the firm's strategic thrusts.

Of the two barriers to CIO-hood, the first can often be hurdled once the second is overcome. This indeed is the ideal sequence, as it puts in motion the process of institutionalizing the CIO position with special emphasis on its most critical dimension: the strategic.

At GTE's telephone operations division (TELOPS), the CIO institutionalization process is well on its way. In 1984, the data services group (GTEDS) conducted a series of brainstorming sessions to identify SIS possibilities (see Chapter 10). As a result of the project, GTE's local telephone units established a new CIO position and changed the reporting relation of the former MIS head from the chief financial officer to the chief executive officer. In 1987, to underline the strategic dimension of a CIO's responsibility, the telcos formed special SIS groups (following a model established at GTEDS in 1985) to identify, design, develop, implement, and maintain information technology applications that support or shape competitive strategy.

Cases like this illustrate the substance of the CIO concept. For GTE's TELOPS division, the CIO position represents more than a name change. It is a job woven tightly into the strategic fabric of the organization. This is the position every potential CIO should strive to attain. For if the two CIO conditions stated above are not satisfied, the potential CIO is at risk.

If you're part of a senior management group unaware of the strategic use of information technology, you're not perceived as contributing to the firm's strategic evolution. You're not seen as being involved in activities that serve to support or shape the enterprise's competitive strategies. And, therefore, you're probably vulnerable to the next shift in managerial wind that could downplay the role of the firm's information resources, seeing no strategic value in them.

On the other hand, if you're not part of a senior management group aware of the strategic use of information technology, you need to ask yourself why not. Unless you can elevate your position, the handwriting is on the wall. Senior management will eventually find someone whom they feel comfortable with to head the CIO function. In either case, the message is the same for those who call themselves CIOs but who are in reality only potential CIOs: either raise awareness among your firm's senior management group, have your position elevated, or both.

NOTES

1. Derek Abell, *Defining the Business* (Englewood Cliffs, N.J.: Prentice-Hall, 1980); Derek Abell and John Hammond, *Strategic Market Planning* (Englewood Cliffs, N.J.: Prentice-Hall, 1979); William Brand, Robert Christian, and James Hulbert, "The Planning Process," 1980; Arnoldo Hax and Nicolas Maljuf, *Strategic Management: An Integrative Perspective* (Englewood Cliffs, N.J.: Prentice-Hall, 1984); Charles Hofer and Dan Schendel, *Strategic Formulation: Analytical Concepts* (St. Paul, Minn.: West Publishing, 1978).

2. Oliver Williamson, *Markets and Hierarchies: Analysis and Antitrust Implications* (New York: Free Press, 1975).

3. Peter Kraljic, "Purchasing Must Become Supply Management," *Harvard Business Review*, September–October 1983, p. 113.

4. Ian MacMillan, "Preemptive Strategies," *Journal of Business Strategy* Fall 1983, p. 17. See also Ian MacMillan, "Seizing Competitive Initiative," *Journal of Business Strategy*, Spring 1982; Ian MacMillan and Patricia Jones, "Designing Organizations to Compete," *Journal of Business Strategy*, Spring 1984; David Montgomery and Charles Weinberg, "Toward Strategic Intelligence Systems," *Journal of Marketing*, Fall 1979.

5. MacMillan, "Preemptive Strategies," p. 17.

6. Ibid.

7. Instead of "IM," IBM prefers the term *information resource management* (*IRM*).

8. IBM, *Information Systems Planning Guide: Business Systems Planning*, 3d ed. (IBM, 1981).

9. Ibid.

10. Ibid.

11. Ephraim McLean and John Soden, *Strategic Planning for MIS* (New York: John Wiley & Sons, 1977).

12. Richard Layne, "Advanced Technology Groups: Can You Afford (Not) to Have One?" *InformationWeek*, January 19, 1987.

12

SIS Trends and Challenges

As the new perspective on organizational uses of information technology diffuses—from enterprise to enterprise, industry to industry, sector to sector, and country to country—the focus of practitioners and researchers shifts from conventional to strategic issues. This is not to say that conventional questions lose their importance, require no further attention, or resolve themselves more readily than they did before. Rather, they tend to recede in significance relative to those posed by the strategic use of information technology.

The rise of the strategic perspective marks a fundamental break with the past, a discontinuity in the formerly smooth conceptual evolution of the information management field. Over the next decade, specialists in the new multidisciplinary area of strategic use will occupy themselves with an agenda of topics radically different from those dissected during the past three decades. But the new will not replace the old as much as complement it, adding complexity, density, and scope to a subject ruled far too long by an almost exclusively technical, planning and control point of view.

In this closing chapter, I shall point out a few of the trends emerging from the strategic use of information technology and characterize the challenges posed by these trends for those who wish to explore the new terrain.

TRENDS

Competitive Dynamics

Successful strategic information systems (SIS) spur strategic responses. This attack-counterattack pattern arises in arenas in which information technology has been used to gain advantage. Just a few years ago, the bulk of SIS stories depicted pathbreaking uses of information technology. Today, a growing number of SIS cases delineate applications motivated in response to the pathbreakers: matching, leapfrogging, or circumventing them. Recall, for example, that (1) New York City banks disadvantaged by Citibank's superior automatic teller machine network dulled Citi's edge by banding together to create NYCE (see Chapter 9); (2) rivals of Pacific Intermountain Express in the trucking industry now offer similar information-based services (Chapter 5); (3) Baxter Travenol, inspired in large part by the desire to gain control of American Hospital Supply's pacesetting order-entry system, swallowed AHS, a rival twice its size (Chapter 7); (4) European airlines allied to defend their sovereignty against the expected blitzkrieg invasion of American carriers spearheaded by Sabre and Apollo (Chapter 8); (5) cosmetics firms struggle for electronic control of beauty counters (Chapter 5); (6) Democrats and Republicans, wielding sophisticated new SIS, joust for political advantage (Chapter 7); labor improves its bargaining power vis-à-vis management through the use of SIS (Chapter 7). In these and other competitive arenas, a new *competitive dynamic* is at work, a relentless attack-counterattack struggle for SIS survival and dominance.

Globalization

Recall from Chapter 8 the cases of Southland (the multiplication of 7–Eleven stores electronically networked in Japan as in the United States), Toys "Я" Us (Toys' clones around the world exploiting SIS developed at home by the parent), Citibank (ATMs in England, SIS in France), The Limited, Dow Jones, and Fidelity. As international competition continues unabated, the number of global thrusts supported or shaped by information technology grows. For the moment, windows of opportunity for SIS global pioneers remain open. But as in domestic arenas, we can expect competitive responses once the initially disadvantaged wake up to the new threats confronting them, assuming they survive the technological onslaught.

Other Sectors

The growing use of information technology to support or shape strategies of enterprises in other than profit-making sectors reflects another noteworthy trend. Outfitted with the proper SIS lens, an observer can discern the increased use of systems for strategic purposes in such sectors as politics (see Chapter 7, "Democrats and Republicans"), government (as the cases from New York, California, and Massachusetts cited at the end of Chapter 6 demonstrate), legal and medical professions (see Chapter 6's discussion of malpractice systems for lawyers and physicians), military (think of the attacks launched by Israeli and U.S. planes against Syrian and Libyan antiaircraft positions, respectively; these moves enabled the two countries to execute "surgical strategic thrusts" integrally dependent on computer and telecommunications technology), and the like.

Particularly in the governmental sector, where an SIS may be defined as any use of information technology to support or shape local, state, or national initiatives (see the appendix to Chapter 2 for a generalized version of the SIS concept), the diffusion of the strategic perspective promises to galvanize agencies at all levels to use their technological resources for other than routine operations. In 1987, for example, New York became the first state to use a computerized system that could have a revolutionary impact on the nation's welfare system. Designed "to collect child support from absent parents of children on welfare,"[1] the system matches the names of parents delinquent in their payments with the names and addresses of their employers within New York State. When a hit occurs, the State Office of Child Support Enforcement mails form letters requesting payment to the parent and the employer. If the delinquent still refuses to pay, the state orders the employer to deduct the amount owed plus whatever is necessary to maintain regular payments. The system saves the state an estimated $14 million a year in child support assistance. Senator Daniel Patrick Moynihan, chair of the Senate subcommittee on Social Security and Family Policy, said that the New York system could serve as a national model. "Such collection," he has argued, "is crucial to welfare reform."[2]

On another front, William Norris, chairman emeritus of Control Data Corporation, proposed that states and the federal government sponsor a new initiative to "improve American competitiveness in global markets . . . and arrest the dangerous decline in . . . manufacturing."[3] Designed for small and medium-sized companies unable to afford the investment, the thrust would "establish a nationwide network of regional computer-aided design and computer-integrated manufacturing centers. These facilities would perform manufacturing on a service basis,"[4] in much the same way that service bureaus did in the 60s and 70s for firms lacking funds to invest in the new computer technology.

Such SIS applications and proposals represent but the first wave of strategic uses of information technology in the governmental sector. Once the strategic perspective takes root in the minds of those responsible for policy and strategy, we can expect explosive SIS growth here and in other sectors as well.

Legal Risk

As SIS proliferate they provoke a rising tide of legal challenges. The increasing number of court cases brought by purported victims of SIS attacks reflect this movement: airlines disadvantaged by the Sabre and Apollo reservation systems (see Chapter 1); tenants blacklisted by landlords (Chapter 6); federal employees violated electronically by zealous cost-cutting agencies monitoring personal calls (Chapter 6); brokers and other intermediaries threatened by the practices of large discount chains to bypass their services and deal directly with manufacturers (Chapter 7). Baybanks of Boston, for example, filed recently in the U.S. District Court against five of New England's largest banks that had banded together to form a regional ATM network. The plaintiff claimed that the net would put it at a competitive disadvantage, arguing that the five banks had set network switching charges "with the intent of monopolizing the market for electronic funds transfer services in Massachusetts."[5] Note that this suit was filed even before the net began to operate.

SIS victims are not the only actors in the unfolding legal

dramas. SIS "perpetrators" may also play the plaintiff's role. Recall that Merrill Lynch obtained a patent to protect the software running its cash management account (CMA) innovation (see Chapter 7). As rivals joked about this ploy, Merrill used it to inhibit responses by imitators by pursuing them with lawsuits. In 1983, for example, it won a $1 million settlement from Dean Witter, its closest competitor at the time.

Since there is no established body of law on the production, distribution, and use of information and information systems, the legal rights and obligations of those involved with SIS as operators, users, or victims remain uncertain. According to Peter Marx, an information lawyer, "The standards to which the law will hold information and information systems users are likely to profoundly affect the use of such systems by businesses [and enterprises in other sectors]. What, for instance," Marx asks, "constitutes illegal use of an information system? When and on what basis will a user of inaccurate information be held liable?"[6]

Those contemplating the strategic use of information technology must keep in mind the following legal issues: unfair competition and antitrust; product liability and negligent use of information; negligent maintenance and use of information systems; libel standards for inaccurate information; liability for use of information generated by expert systems; privacy; protection of proprietary interests (e.g., patents, knowhow, trade secrets, and copyright).

Suppose, for example, that an electronic order-entry system becomes the primary mode of distribution in an industry. Further, assume that this application produces substantial barriers to entry. For some, this might appear to constitute the ultimate strategic coup. But now suppose that some of the victimized seek relief under an unfair-competition or antitrust statute. If the court decides that the SIS is essential for the conduct of business, "the owner could be compelled to give its competitors—other distributors or manufacturers—access to the system on fair, reasonable, and nondiscriminatory terms."[7] Whether the contemplation of issues like this will produce a chilling effect on the generation of SIS ideas remains to be seen. To decrease such legal risks, enterprises planning to launch SIS should familiarize themselves with the mounting body of statutes and cases in the area of information law.

Academic

In the academic realm, which tends to trail the world of practice by a few years, new courses on the strategic use of information technology have been developed for M.B.A. and doctoral students at the Columbia University Graduate School of Business, the Massachusetts Institute of Technology's Sloan School, and elsewhere. In 1987, the Harvard Business School made a new course on information technology and competition mandatory for all M.B.A. students. Executive programs and standard courses at Columbia, Harvard, MIT, Southern California, University of California at Los Angeles, and Wharton, to name just a few, have incorporated SIS-related material or devoted themselves exclusively to this subject. Case study factories, now retooled, manufacture the new product line of SIS stories. From the Harvard Business School, the leading producer, come tales of Frontier Airlines, American Hospital Supply, Otis Elevator, and Mass Mutual Life Insurance, each with important lessons for students to assimilate on the strategic use of information technology. And as publishers encourage authors to incorporate SIS topics into management information systems (MIS) textbooks, the new strategic view penetrates even tradition-bound MIS programs.

Researchers, drawing their raw material from the experiences of such innovators as American Air, Citibank, and McKesson, are creating a growing supply of SIS tools, concepts, and frameworks. Work by Blake Ives and Gerard Learmonth on the customer resource life cycle (see Chapter 5); Ives and Cynthia Beath on pricing models; James Cash and Benn Konsynski on interorganizational systems; Brandt Allen, F. Warren McFarlan, and James McKenney on SIS management issues; and Robert Benjamin, Thomas Malone, and JoAnne

Yates on electronic markets and hierarchies represent just some of the original research being produced in this area. Consultants and information technology vendors are also busily mapping the territory to assist customers who wish to initiate SIS programs or enhance those already in place.

CHALLENGES

The trends just sketched, together with issues linked in preceding chapters to the strategic use of information technology, pose challenges for both practitioners and researchers. Among those challenges facing practitioners, three are critical:

- Raising SIS awareness at all levels within their enterprises.
- Identifying SIS opportunities and threats.
- Taking steps to implement the opportunities, defend against the threats, and institutionalize SIS planning and management processes.

The material introduced in Chapters 10 and 11 should prove helpful in meeting these challenges.

The challenges for researchers are more diverse, requiring comprehensive, coordinated, multinational, and multidisciplinary efforts dedicated to SIS data collection, model building, curricular development, and research.

Data Collection

This activity should first and foremost be devoted to the gathering and updating of SIS case materials, successes as well as failures. The aim here should be a natural history of the strategic evolution of the SIS, taking into account all aspects of its development and deployment, including competitive responses. The activity should also include the preparation of comparative and cross-classificatory SIS databases by function (e.g., marketing, finance, logistics, manufacturing), industry, sector, country, and technology (e.g., expert systems, telecommunication applications, departmental systems).

Model Building

This activity should include the development and testing of models, tools, and other analytical devices for identifying, describing, and explaining strategic uses of information technology in a variety of contexts. The strategic thrusts presented in this book, for example, may not be appropriate for describing basic strategic moves in other sectors.

Curricular Development

To continue its growth, the SIS field needs multidisciplinary and multinational teaching materials and courses emphasizing strategic uses of information technology. New M.B.A. and executive education courses (e.g., in marketing or financial services) should be developed to reflect such uses. SIS planning and management within different sectors (e.g., nonprofit, governmental, military) represent other areas in need.

Research

While this is not the place to propose projects, the following questions indicate the range of issues that SIS research should address:

- What are the differences, if any, between the processes of information technology transfer and those used by multinational enterprises when transferring manufacturing technology in support of global strategies?
- If, as some maintain, "national competitiveness refers to a nation-state's ability to produce, distribute, and service goods in the international economy in competition with goods and services produced in other countries, and to do so in a way that earns a rising standard of living,"[8] should information technology be made part of the state's arsenal to achieve these noble purposes? And if so, how should it be included?

- In what ways, if any, can information technology affect industry structure, the political balance among nations, or structural features in other sectors?
- What barriers (economic, organizational, political, etc.) inhibit the use of information technology as competitive weapons by functions, enterprises, industries, sectors, or countries?
- What criteria, if any, are appropriate for assessing the strategic value of information technology uses in a particular context?
- What factors determine opportunities for using information technology strategically?
- Should a nation's industrial policy, a presidential candidate's platform, or the Defense Department's military strategy include sections on the strategic use of information technology? If so, what should be covered in these sections?
- What, if any, are the conditions under which one might predict with a fair degree of confidence the success or failure of an SIS effort? What steps, if any, might be taken to minimize the possibilities of failure and maximize the chances for success?

A university-based program that examines such questions would serve as a natural focal point for disparate groups of faculty members, researchers, and students who wish to explore information technology issues from a strategic perspective. Multidisciplinary projects might involve scientists and engineers at the cutting edge of developments in computer and telecommunication technologies; political scientists studying the role of information technology in supporting or shaping industrial or public policies; business school faculty members applying theories developed in innovation, marketing, or human resource studies to the SIS area; lawyers exploring issues mentioned in the first section of this chapter or questions related to the flow of data across national borders.

This research activity would also be of interest beyond the

borders of a university: to colleagues at other institutions as well as to managers, government policymakers, and others from private- and public-sector organizations both here and abroad. Indeed, such a program might attract members of these external constituencies as participants.

NOTES

1. Esther Iverem, "State Takes Fathers' Pay for Support," *New York Times,* June 1, 1987.
2. Ibid.
3. William Norris, "Become Competitive? Here's How," *New York Times,* August 28, 1987.
4. Ibid.
5. Stanley Gibson, "Bank Files Suit against Owner of Proposed ATM Network," *Computerworld,* January 19, 1987.
6. Peter Marx, "The Legal Risks of Using Information as a Competitive Weapon," *Information Management Review* 2, no. 4 (Spring 1987).
7. Ibid.
8. Bruce Scott, "U.S. Competitiveness: Concepts, Performance, and Implications," in *U.S. Competitiveness in the World Economy,* ed. Bruce Scott and George Lodge (Cambridge, Mass.: Harvard Business School Press, 1985).

Index of People and Products

Index of Cases and Organizations

* Case citations have asterisk (*).

437

Subject Index